Circling My Mother

Circling My Mother

MARY GORDON

PANTHEON BOOKS   NEW YORK

The following essays originally appeared in the following publications:
"My Mother's Body" in *The American Scholar* (2006);
"Bonnard and My Mother's Ninetieth Birthday" appeared as "Still Life" in
Harper's Magazine (1998); and "Bonnard and My Mother's Death" appeared
in different form in *Salmagundi* (2005).

Grateful acknowledgment is made to Hal Leonard Corporation for permission to
reprint an excerpt from "Where Is Your Heart (The Song From Moulin Rouge),"
words by William Engvick, music by George Auric, copyright © 1953
(Renewed 1981) by Screen Gems-EMI Music Inc. All rights reserved. International
copyright secured. Reprinted by permission of Hal Leonard Corporation.

Library of Congress Cataloging-in-Publication Data
Gordon, Mary, [date]
Circling my mother / Mary Gordon.
p. cm.
ISBN 978-0-375-42456-4
1. Gordon, Mary, 1949– —Family.   2. Authors, American—20th century—
Family relationships.   I. Title.
PS3557.O669Z46 2007
813'.54—dc22
[B]
2006102286

www.pantheonbooks.com
Printed in the United States of America
First Edition
2 4 6 8 9 7 5 3

For my daughter, Anna,
who makes sense of everything

Contents

PREFACE

Perhaps the question the writer most fears from her potential readers is: Why have you done this? With the implication: Why have you done this *to me*? But often in the course of writing this book, I have asked the question of myself: Why are you doing this? And what is the *this*?

What would a book like this be called? Memoir? Biography? Memoir suggests that the writer is the central character, and although, certainly, I am writing about my mother because she is my mother, I had hoped to step aside and give her center stage. But biography, with its hints of dates and exactitude—well, that's not what I'm doing either.

So, if one resigns oneself to taking a place at the end of the increasingly long line of people who have written about their parents, how, exactly, does one understand the place?

It is the attempt to understand this place that has moved me to call this book *Circling My Mother*. I came to realize that I couldn't see my mother properly by standing in one place, by standing still. For the last eleven years of her life, the years marked by dementia, she was much more a problem to me than a joy. I wanted to move from the spot where I thought of my mother as a problem. To do this, I had to walk around her life, to view it from many points— only one of which was her career as my mother.

I had hoped to tell not only the story of my mother's life, but a larger story, a story that had implications beyond her immediate biography. My mother's story is a story of physical affliction (polio, alcoholism, senile dementia), and of a historical moment importantly colored by the experience of immigration, world war, and the Great Depression. It is the story of a particular moment in American Catholicism, and of the American working class.

My mother was born in 1908; she died in 2002. In those years, America changed radically; the world my mother died in would have been unimaginable to the parents who gave her birth. So it is also the story of time, and the effects of time.

I start, then, on this journey of circling my mother, beginning and ending with the painter Bonnard: an acknowledgment that I know that, like him, I am involved in a job of making. Of making something of my mother. Or perhaps I invoke Bonnard simply to allow myself a companion on the journey. To have the companionship of a great painter on this writer's journey, this writer's task: trying to understand in the only way a writer can—by writing. A job that is never completed, and never anything but a failed attempt. And yet we begin, and we begin again, because it is the thing we do. Looking, in the way that is open to us for what Conrad calls "that glimpse of truth for which you have forgotten to ask."

Circling My Mother

Bonnard and

My Mother's *Ninetieth Birthday*

In the year 1908, Pierre Bonnard painted *The Bathroom* and my mother was born. The posture of the young woman in the painting is that of someone enraptured by the miracle of light. The light is filtered through the lace curtains, and its patterning is reflected in the water that fills the tub into which she is about to step. Even the floral spread on the divan from which she has just risen is an emblem of prosperity and joy. Bonnard is famous for painting bathing women; in all her life my mother has never taken a bath. At three, she was stricken with polio, and she never had the agility to get in or out of a bathtub. She told me that once, after I was born, my father tried to lift her into a bath, but it made them both too nervous.

Ninety years after the painting of *The Bathroom*, ten days before my mother's ninetieth birthday, I am looking at the works

3

of Bonnard at the Museum of Modern Art, a show I've been waiting for with the excitement of a teenager waiting for a rock concert. I was not brought to museums as a child; going to museums
wasn't, as my mother would have said, "the kind of thing we went
in for." It is very possible that my mother has never been inside a
museum in her life. As a family we were pious, talkative, and fond
of stories and the law. Our preference was for the invisible.

I can no longer remember how looking at art became such a
source of solace and refreshment for me. Art history wasn't anything I studied formally. I think I must have begun going to museums as a place to meet friends. However and wherever it
happened, a fully realized painterly vision that testifies in its full-
ness to the goodness of life has become for me a repository of faith
and hope, two of the three theological virtues I was brought up to
believe were at the center of things. It is no accident, I suppose,
though at the time I might have said it was, that I've arranged to
meet two friends at the Bonnard show at the same time that I'm
meant to phone the recreation therapist at my mother's nursing
home to plan her birthday party. Fifteen minutes after I arrive, I'll
have to leave the show. The therapist will be available only for a
specific half-hour; after that, she's leaving for vacation.

Am I purposely creating difficulties for myself, a situation of
false conflict, so that I can be tested and emerge a hero? There
is the chance that I will not be able to leave the dazzle of the
first room, to resist the intoxication of these paintings, so absorbing, so saturating, so suggestive of a world of intense color, of
prosperous involvement, of the flow of good life and good fortune.
There's the chance that I will forget to call the therapist. I do not
forget, but my experience of the first paintings is poisoned by the
fear that I will.

My mother has no idea that her ninetieth birthday is coming up.
She has no notion of the time of day, the day of the week, the season of the year, the year of the century. No notion of the approach-

ing millennium. And no idea, any longer, who I am. Her forgetting of me happened just a few months ago, after I had been traveling for more than a month and hadn't been to see her. When I came back, she asked me if I was her niece. I said no, I was her daughter. "Does that mean I had you?" she asked. I said yes. "Where was I when I had you?" she asked me. I told her she was in a hospital in Far Rockaway, New York. "So much has happened to me in my life," she said. "You can't expect me to remember everything."

My mother has erased me from the book of the living. She is denying the significance of my birth. I do not take this personally. It is impossible for me to believe any longer that anything she says refers to me. As long as I remember this, I can still, sometimes, enjoy her company.

The day before I go to the Bonnard show, I visit my mother. It is not a good visit. It is one of her fearful days. I say I'll take her out to the roof garden for some air. She says, "But what if I fall off?" I bring her flowers, which I put in a vase near her bed. She says, "But what if they steal them or yell at me for having them?" She asks me thirty or more times if I know where I'm going as we wait for the elevator. When I say we'll go to the chapel in a little while, she asks if I think she'll get in trouble for going to the chapel outside the normal hours for Mass, and on a day that's not a Sunday or a holy day. She seems to believe me each time when I tell her that she won't fall off the roof, that no one will reprimand her or steal her flowers, that I know where I'm going, that she will not get in trouble for being in church and saying her prayers.

I have brought her a piece of banana cake and some cut-up watermelon. There are only three things to which my mother now responds: prayers, songs, and sweets. Usually, I sing to her as we eat cake, and then I take her to the chapel, where we say a decade of the rosary. But today she is too cast down to sing, or pray, or even eat. There is no question of going out onto the roof. She just wants to go back to her room. She complains of being cold, though it is ninety-five degrees outside and the air conditioning is off. It is not a long visit. I bring her back to her floor after twenty minutes.

On my mother's floor in the nursing home, many people in wheelchairs spend most of their days in the hall. There is a man who is still attractive, though his face is sullen and his eyes are dull. Well, of course, I think, why wouldn't they be? He looks at me, and his dull eyes focus on my breasts in a way that is still predatory, despite his immobility. I take this as a sign of life. It's another thing I don't take personally. In fact, I want to encourage this sign of life. So I walk down the hall in an obviously sexual way. *"Putana!"* he screams out behind me. I believe that I deserve this; even though what I did was an error, a misreading, it was still, I understand now, wrong.

In front of the dayroom door sits a legless woman. Her hair is shoulder-length, dyed a reddish color; her lips are painted red. The light-blue-and-white nylon skirts of her dressing gown billow around her seat, and she looks like a doll sitting on a child's dresser, or a child's crude drawing of a doll.

My mother was once a beautiful woman, but all her teeth are gone now. Toothless, no woman can be considered beautiful. Whenever I arrive, she is sitting at the table in the common dining room, her head in her hands, rocking. Medication has eased her anxiety, but nothing moves her from her stupor except occasional moments of fear, too deep for medication. This is a room that has no windows, that lets in no light, in which an overlarge TV is constantly blaring, sending images that no one looks at, where the floors are beige tiles, the walls cream-colored at the bottom, papered halfway up with a pattern of nearly invisible grayish leaves. Many of the residents sit staring, slack-jawed, open-mouthed. I find it impossible to imagine what they might be looking at.

It is difficult to meet the eyes of these people; it is difficult to look at their faces. I wonder if Bonnard could do anything with this lightless room. If he could enter it, see in these suffering people, including my mother, especially my mother, only a series of shapes and forms, concentrate on the colors of their clothing (a red sweater here, a blue shirt there), transform the blaring images on the TV screen to a series of vivid rectangles, and, failing to differentiate, insisting on the falseness of distinctions, of an overly rigid individuality, saying that we must get over the idea that the features of the face are the important part—would he be able to create a scene of beauty from this scene, which is, to me, nearly unbearable? He once told friends that he had spent much of his life trying to understand the secret of white. How I envy him such a pure preoccupation, so removed from the inevitable degradations of human character and fate. So he could paint wilting flowers, overripe fruit, and make of them a richer kind of beauty, like the nearly deliquescing purple grapes, the visibly softening bananas of *Bowl of Fruit,* 1933. "He let the flowers wilt and then he started painting; he said that way they would have more presence," his housekeeper once said.

The people in the dining room are wilting, they are decomposing, but I cannot perceive it as simply another form, simply another subject or observation. I cannot say there are no differences between them and young, healthy people, no greater or lesser beauty, as one could say of buds or wilting flowers, unripe fruit or fruit on the verge of rotting. It is impossible for me to say that what has happened to these people is not a slow disaster.

And how important is it that when we read or look at a painting we do not use our sense of smell? The smells of age and misery hang over the common room. Overcooked food, aging flesh. My mother is kept clean, but when I bend over to kiss her hair, it smells like an old woman's. And there is the residual smell of her incontinence. My mother wears diapers. A residual smell that is unpleasant even in children but in the old is not only a bad smell but a sign of shame, of punishment: a curse. I cannot experience it any other way. My mother's body is inexorably failing, but not fast enough. She is still more among the living than the dying, and I wonder, often, what might be the good of that.

It is the day of my mother's birthday. Two of my friends, Gary and Nola, have agreed to be with me for this day. They are both very good-looking people. They are both, in fact, beauties. Gary is a priest; in another age, he might be called my confessor, not that he has heard my confession in the sacramental sense but because he is someone to whom I could tell anything, with no shame. Nola was my prize student; then she worked as my assistant for four years. We are proud that we have transformed ourselves from teacher/student, employer/employee, into, simply, friends.

When I thank him for agreeing to come to my mother's party, Gary says, "This will be fun." "No, it won't," I say, "it won't be fun at all." "Well, it will be something to be got through. Which is, in some ways, not so different from fun." "It is," I say, "it is." "No, not really. It isn't really," he says, and we both laugh.

Gary's mother is also in a nursing home, in St. Louis, Missouri, a city I have never visited. She accuses his father, who is devoted to her, who has been devoted for years, of the most flagrant infidelities. All he says in response is "I didn't do that, I would never do that." When we speak about our mothers, of our mothers' fears and sadnesses, particularly about the shape his mother's rage has taken, Gary and I agree that if we could understand the mystery of sex and the mystery of our mothers' fates we would have penetrated to the heart of something quite essential. We very well know that we will not. This is very different from Bonnard's secret of white.

Gary's father visits his mother in the nursing home every day. The end of Marthe Bonnard's life was marked by a withdrawal into a depressed and increasingly phobic isolation, so that the shape of a large part of her husband's life was determined by her illness, finding places for her to take cures, and staying away from people whom she feared, who she thought were staring at her, laughing at her. In 1931, Bonnard wrote, "For quite some time now I have been living a very secluded life as Marthe has become completely antisocial [*Marthe étant devenue d'une sauvagerie complète*] and I am obliged to avoid all contact with other people. I have hopes though that this state of affairs will change for the better but it is rather painful."

Did this forced isolation, in fact, suit Bonnard very well; was it the excuse he could present to a sympathetic world so that he could have the solitude he needed for his work? What is the nature of the pain of which he spoke? What was the nature of her "*sauvagerie complète*"? In the painting in which he suggests Marthe's isolation, *The Vigil*, although she sits uncomfortably in her chair, in a room empty of people, alienated even from the furniture, unable to take comfort even from her dog, she appears still young, still attractive, still someone we want to look at. In fact, she was fifty-two, and someone whose misery, if we encountered it in person, might have caused us to avert our eyes.

I do not shape my life around my mother's needs or her condition. I try to visit her once a week, but sometimes I don't make it, sometimes it is two weeks, even three. If life is pressing on me, it is easy for me to put the visit off, because I don't know how much it means to her, and I know that she forgets I was there minutes after I have left, that she doesn't feel a difference between three hours and three weeks. If I believed that visiting my mother every day would give something important to my work, as the isolation required by Marthe Bonnard's illness gave something to her husband's, perhaps I would do it. But when I leave my mother, work is impossible for me; the rest of the afternoon is a struggle not to give in to a hopelessness that makes the creation of something made of words seem ridiculous, grotesque, a joke.

Two weeks before my mother's birthday, Gary celebrated the twenty-fifth anniversary of his ordination. His father couldn't be there; he wouldn't leave Gary's mother, even for a day. That was a grief for Gary, but most of the day was full of joy, a swelling of love, a church full of all the representatives of Gary's life—musicians, artists, dancers, writers, the bodybuilders he came to know at the gym where he works out, to whom he is an informal chaplain, as well as the parishioners he serves. The music was mostly provided by a gospel choir, who brought everyone to tears, and whose music blended perfectly with the parish choir's Gregorian chant, with which it alternated. It was a day of harmony, of perfect blending, but with high spots of color, like the paintings of Bonnard. I bought for the occasion a red silk dress with a fitted waist and an elaborate collar. I wore gold shoes. On the altar, flanked by red and white flowers in brass vases, I read the Epistle of St. Paul to the Galatians, which assures that in Christ there is neither male nor female, slave nor free—a blurring of distinctions like the blurring of boundaries in Bonnard, where the edge of an arm melts into a tablecloth, a leg into the ceramic of a tub, flesh into water, the sun's light into the pink triangle of a crotch.

Nola has the long legs, slim hips, and small but feminine breasts of Marthe Bonnard. I know this because a certain part of our relationship centers around water. We swim together in the university pools; afterward we shower and take saunas. She has introduced me to a place where, three or four times a year, we treat ourselves to a day of luxury. A no-frills bath in the old style, a shvitz, a place where we sit in steam, in wet heat, in dry heat, in a room that sounds like something from the *Arabian Nights*: the Radiant Room. We spend hours naked among other naked women, women who walk un-self-consciously, women of all ages and all ranges of beauty, in a place where wetness is the rule, where a mist hangs over things, as in the bathrooms of Bonnard. The preponderance of bathing women in Bonnard's work has been explained by Marthe Bonnard's compulsive bathing. She sometimes bathed several times a day. Whatever the reason for this compulsion, her husband used it triumphantly.

Nola has just come from a friend's wedding in Maine. She was seated at the reception next to a German student, who became besotted with her. He grabbed her head and tried to put his own head on her shoulder. "You must come and have a drink with me at my inn," he said to her. She refused.

"You weren't tempted by all that ardor?" I ask her.

"No," she says. "I saw he had no lightness, that there was no lightness to him or anything that he did."

Bonnard's paintings are full of light, but they are not exactly about lightness, and his touch is not light, except in the sense that the paint is applied thinly and wetly. But he is always present in his paintings, and his hand is always visible. He has not tried to efface himself; he has not tried to disappear.

When I walk into the dining room on the day of my mother's birthday, I see that she has already been served lunch. The staff have forgotten to hold it back, though I told them a week ago that I would be providing lunch. She hasn't touched anything on her tray except a piece of carrot cake, which she holds in her hands. The icing is smeared on her hands and face. I don't want my friends to see her smeared with icing, so I wet a paper towel and wipe her. This fills me with a terrible tenderness, recalling, as it does, a gesture I have performed for my children. If I can see her as a child, it is easy to feel only tenderness for her. Bonnard paints children most frequently in his earlier period, in the darker Vuillard-like paintings, in which it is his natal family that is invoked. In the brighter pictures, children do not take their place as representatives of the goodness of the world. That place is taken up by dogs. In the painting *Marthe and Her Dog*, Marthe and a dachshund greet each other ecstatically in the foreground. In the far background, faceless, and having no communication with the woman and her dog, children run, leaving lime-colored shadows on the yellow grass.

As I wipe my mother's face, I see that her skin is still beautiful. I hold her chin in my hand and kiss her forehead. I tell her it's her birthday, that she's ninety years old. "How did that happen?" she asks. "I can't understand how that could happen."

I have brought her a bouquet of crimson, yellow, and salmon-pink snapdragons. She likes the flowers very much. She likes the name. "Snapdragons. It seems like an animal that's going to bite me. But it's not an animal, it's a plant. That's a funny thing."

One reason I bought the flowers is that the colors reminded me of Bonnard. I don't tell my mother that. Even if she still had her wits, I would not have mentioned it. Bonnard is not someone she would have heard of. She had no interest in painting.

I have bought food that I hope will please my mother, and that will be easy for her to eat: orzo salad with little pieces of crayfish cut into it, potato salad, small chunks of marinated tomatoes. I have bought paper plates with a rust-colored background, upon which are painted yellow and gold flowers and blue leaves. I deliberated over the color of the plastic knives, forks, and spoons and settled on dark blue, to match the leaves. I am trying to make an attractive arrangement of food and flowers, but it's not easy against the worn gray Formica of the table. I think of Bonnard's beautiful food, which always looks as if it would be warm to the touch. It is most often fruit, fruit that seems to be another vessel of sunlight, as if pressing it to the roof of your mouth would release into your body a pure jet of sun. Bonnard's food is arranged with the generous, voluptuous propriety I associate with the south of France, though Bonnard moved often, dividing his time between the south and the north. He places his food in rooms or gardens that themselves contribute to a sense of colorful plenitude. Yet it is very rare in Bonnard that more than one person is with the food; none of the festal atmosphere of the Impressionists, none of Renoir's expansive party mood, enters the paintings of Bonnard in which food is an important component. The beautiful colors of the food are what is important, not that the food is part of an encounter with people who will eat it, speak of it, enjoy one another's company.

Nola and Gary and I enjoy one another's company; I do not know what my mother enjoys. Certainly, the colorful food—the pink crayfish in the saffron-colored orzo, the red tomatoes, the russet potatoes punctuated with the parsley's severe green—is not a source of joy for her. Joy, if it is in the room, comes from the love of friends, from human communion—usually absent in the paintings of Bonnard. I do not think, though, that my mother feels part of this communion.

I talk about the food a bit to my mother, but she isn't much interested in descriptions of food. She never has been. She always had contempt for people who talked about food, who recounted memorable meals. She doesn't join us in saying the grace in which Gary leads us. Nor does she join us in singing the songs that, two weeks ago, she still was able to sing: "Sweet Rosie O'Grady," "Daisy, Daisy," "When Irish Eyes Are Smiling." Nothing focuses her attention until the cake, a cheesecake, which she picks up in her hands and eats messily, greedily. I wonder if it is only the prospect of eating sweets that keeps my mother alive.

When we are about to leave, I tell my mother that I'm going on vacation, that I won't see her for three weeks, that I am going to the sea. "How will I stand that, how will I stand that?" she says, but I know that a minute after I'm gone she'll forget I was there.

I have bought the catalogue of the exhibition, and when I leave my mother I go home and look at it for quite a long time. I read that Bonnard once said that "he liked to construct a painting around an empty space." A critic named Patrick Heron says that Bonnard knew "how to make a virtue of emptiness." Illustrating Bonnard's affinities with Mallarmé, Sarah Whitfield, the curator of the show, quotes a description of a water lily in one of Mallarmé's prose poems. The lily encloses "in the hollow whiteness a nothing, made of intact dreams, of a happiness which will not take place."

Much of my mother's life is made up of emptiness. She does, literally, nothing most of the day. For many hours she sits with her head in her hands, her eyes closed, rocking. She is not sleeping. I have no idea what she thinks about or if she thinks, if she's making images. Are images the outgrowth of memory? If they are, I don't know how my mother can be making images in her mind, since she has no memory. And if her eyes are mostly closed, can she be making images of what is in front of her? The beige walls and linoleum, her compatriots with their withered faces, thin hair, toothless mouths, distorted bodies? The nurses and caretakers, perhaps? No, I don't think so. I think that my mother's life is mostly a blank, perhaps an empty screen occasionally impressed upon by shadows.

Sarah Whitfield says that in the center of many of Bonnard's pictures is a hole or a hollow: a tub, a bath, a basket, or a bowl. A hole or hollow that makes a place for a beautiful emptiness. Nola once described her mother's life as having graceful emptiness, so that a whole day could be shaped around one action. We both admired that, so different from the frantic buzz that often characterizes our lives. I am afraid that the emptiness at the center of my mother's life is neither beautiful nor graceful but a blankness that has become obdurate, no longer malleable enough even to contain sadness. An emptiness that, unlike Bonnard's or Mallarmé's or Nola's mother's, really contains nothing. And there is nothing I can do about it. Nothing.

I don't know what that emptiness once contained, if it once held Mallarmé's intact dreams—dreams of happiness, which, for my mother, will not now be realized. Perhaps she is experiencing the "emptying out" of which the mystics speak, an emptying of the self in order to make a place for God. I don't know, since my mother does not use language to describe her mental state. I try to allow for the possibility that within my mother's emptiness there is a richness beyond language and beyond visual expression, a truth so profound that my mother is kept alive by it, and that she lives for it. To believe that, I must reject all the evidence of my senses, all the ways of knowing the world represented by the paintings of Bonnard.

Bonnard's mistress, Renée Monchaty, killed herself. There are many stories that surround the suicide. One is that she killed herself in the bath, a punitive homage to her lover's iconography. Another is that she took pills and covered herself with a blanket of lilacs. I also have heard that Marthe, after the painter finally married her, insisted that Bonnard destroy all the paintings he had done of Renée. I don't know if any of these stories is true, and I no longer remember where I heard them.

In one painting that survives, *Young Women in the Garden,* Renée is suffused in a yellow light that seems like a shower of undiluted sun; her blond hair, the bowl of fruit, the undefined yet suggestively fecund floral background are all saturated with a yellowness, the distilled essence of youthful hope. Renée sits, her head resting against one hand, a half-smile on her face, her light eyes catlike and ambiguous; she sits in a light-filled universe, in front of a table with a striped cloth, a bowl of apples, a dish of pears. In the margins, seen from the rear and only in profile, Marthe peers, eclipsed but omnipresent. I am thinking of this painting as I stand in the corner of the dining room, watching my mother from the side, like Marthe, the future wife. How can it be, I wonder, that Renée—who inhabited a world of yellow light, striped tablecloths, red and russet-colored fruit, a world in which all that is good about the physical presented itself in abundance— chose to end her life? Whereas these old people, sitting in a windowless room with nothing to look at but the hysterically colored TV screen, their bodies failing, aching, how can it be that they are fighting so desperately for the very life that this woman, enveloped in such a varied richness, threw away? I am angry at Renée; she seems ungrateful. At the same time, I do not understand why these people whom my mother sits among do not allow themselves to die. Renée had so much to live for, to live in, and chose not to live. What do they have to live for? I often ask myself of my mother and her companions. And yet they choose, with a terrible animal avidity, to continue to live.

In a 1941 letter to Bonnard, Matisse writes that "we must bless the luck that has allowed us, who are still here, to come this far. Rodin once said that a combination of extraordinary circumstances was needed for a man to live to seventy and to pursue with passion what he loves." And yet the last self-portraits painted by Bonnard in his seventies are as desolate as the monologues of Samuel Beckett. *Self-Portrait in the Bathroom Mirror* portrays a nearly featureless face, eyes that are more like sockets, a head that seems shamed by its own baldness, the defeatist's sloping shoulders, arms cut off before we can see hands. In the *Self-Portrait* of 1945, Bonnard's mouth is half open in a gesture of desolation; his eyes, miserable, are black holes, swallowing, rather than reflecting, light. At the end of his life, Bonnard was deeply dejected by the loss of Marthe, of his friends, by the hardship of the war, which he includes in one of his self-portraits by the presence of a blackout shade. Is it possible that, despite his portrayal of the joy and richness of the colors of this world, despite his mastery and his absorption in the process of seeing, despite his recognition and success, his last days were no more enviable than my mother's?

My Mother *and Her Bosses*

My mother was never only mine. She had a boss. She was his sec-retary long before she was my mother, and I never doubted that his demands, whose details were vague to me, took precedence over mine.

She went to work for him in 1939, fourteen years before my birth. She was thirty-one and had been working for twelve years when she took the job: secretary to Harold P. Herman, attorney at law. She spoke of those twelve years as Columbus must have spo-ken about the expeditions he embarked upon before he found America: dim sightings, temporary landings, just a glimpse of treasure, and the return to port a shallow victory, without triumph: nothing to display.

She called him, always, Mr. Herman. He called her, always, Miss Anne.

I learned the word "boss" early; it must have been one of the first I heard from my mother's lips, a simple word, a necessary one, like "milk" or "bath" or "blanket" or "behave." Each morning, I was awakened without ceremony, dressed, driven to a place where I would spend the day away from her. She spent her days with *him*. I was miserable at the babysitter's, but aware in my misery of my own importance, which attached to me because of my mother, who "went to business." I did not envy children who stayed home with their mothers. Their lives had a warmth mine lacked, but it was a warmth without glamour, a glamour I absorbed because my mother left the house with me each morning, dressed in a suit, perfumed, carrying a handbag that had money in it she had made. The money I saw always in the form of coins, stamped with the image of an august man, piling up, forming a column, valuable not only for what they could be used to buy, but lovely in themselves.

Early on, the word "work" took on for me a gravity, a luster, like the stone in a monarch's signet ring. "Work" was a word I savored on my tongue like a cool stone, the same cool stone of the monarch's ring, a stone that could be hidden from the light in a box lined with silk or velvet. This hidden place was "the office," the place that my mother drove to. The office, the demesne and province of "the boss."

"Boss" was to my mother a word to be spoken with reverence, but to others a joke word: the image of a fat, bald tycoon, greedy or ineffectual, to be overcome or tricked, but certainly not honored. No, certainly not that. But my mother honored her boss and felt honored by him, honored by their regard for each other and the world's regard for them. For she was seen in the world as being in a partnership—the female part, but without the wife's slightly demeaning domesticity, slightly corrupting sexuality. My mother said "my boss" with the same pride and sense of enhanced value with which a queen might have said "my lord," claiming the same stature as one who claimed connection to a king—not the peasant girl turned princess for love, but someone who had gone through the demanding training required of true royalty (embroidery, diplomacy, languages, dance) and come through proficient and anointed and in charge. My mother said "my boss," and underneath the words, you could hear her calm and proud conviction; you could hear what she was really saying: "You see, you must see, all of you, my worth in the great world."

I had a recurrent dream about my mother's boss. It was neither nice nor honorable. It was dangerous, unclear, coarse, misapprehending: all qualities common to a well-brought-up child's early piecings together of the fragments carelessly left out. The patchwork of which she will make up the misshapen garment: her ideas of sex. In the dream, my mother's boss stripped her naked, lifted her up, and threw her out the window. That was all. No one was hurt, and no one died. The shame was not my mother's; it was mine, for watching, silent, on the side.

In waking life, I saw my mother's boss in the flesh very little. She was with him, axiomatically, when she wasn't with me; when she was not with him, she took me everywhere.

Sometimes when she did extra work for her boss on Saturdays, she would bring me to the office with her. The office was in a building above a drugstore. She had to climb up a long, wide wooden staircase that was a trial for her every day.

It was painful to watch her walk up the wide, creaking stairs, stairs that seemed to me to have come from the Wild West, stairs that might have been leading from a saloon below to bedrooms let to cowboys up above, instead of from the drugstore to the dentist's office. I never saw the dentist, as I never saw any patients; there was only the sound of a drill and the smell, presaging pain, of some anodyne based on cloves. Past the dentist's office, we continued down the dark corridor, to the office on whose door the words *Harold P. Herman, Attorney at Law* were emblazoned in gold on a surface of crushed glass.

Opening the door, my mother would flick on the fluorescent

light. It took some seconds for the room to be illumined, and those seconds frightened me. Suppose they never ended, suppose the lights never went on. We would be trapped in darkness, with only the frightening dental smells and sounds. When the lights went on, an exaggerated feeling of excitement propelled me into the room, as if the threshold were not merely a strip of wood separating the room from the corridor but a marker between realms whose difference in atmosphere, one from another, was enormous, as the trip up the stairs marked a transition equally enormous, from the ordinary world to the world of work.

While I was still standing, my mother would walk over to her typewriter, greeting it as if it were a pet that might have missed her. She'd straighten, unnecessarily, the stacks of white and carbon paper, patting them too, to wish them well. If she'd been told then that one day carbon paper, the typewriter itself would become obsolete, she would never have believed you. She would as easily have believed the prediction that human beings would give up the use of their arms and legs.

After she'd paid her ritual visit to her desk, she would open the door to Mr. Herman's office so I could work there while she was at her desk outside. It was another threshold to be crossed: the one between her small windowless office, uncarpeted, and his large and carefully appointed room, where each object had been selected to make a point. The point was this: the man who worked in this room was a professional, and prosperous. You (and your money) would be safe with him.

I can't imagine who decorated his office; he was not a cultivated man, and I believe his wife was an extremely kind but rather simple woman. So where did the Spy drawings come from: those nineteenth-century English prints that so excited me because they were a glimpse into the larger, older European world, a world I knew was the real, important one, a world that my father was a familiar of, a world that had been promised me by him as my own. Yet this was England, secular, Protestant England, the bewigged duffers muttering words that were indicated in light lettering below their massive forms. There was one that both frightened and pleased me. A hippopotamus of a man, a justice in grayish-black robes and powdered wig, his eyes nearly closed by the pockets of flesh that grew up underneath them, thundered from his unpleased mouth: "That won't do, you know."

I had no idea what the meaning of that picture was, but I knew it was about authority. Not the kind of authority I was most used to: the Pope's, bald and mitered rather than bewigged, an eternal authority built on a law that could not be questioned or argued publicly, and whose punishments were for all time. The justice in his gray-black robes was of an earthly city, and I felt abashed by an authority I could not quite place. I understood that this authority was partial only; nevertheless, it had great scope, and might.

On Mr. Herman's large oak desk was a pen set whose base was black marble, and this too I knew to be a sign of authority. I knew that if I picked it up it would be very heavy, but I would never pick it up, any more than I would write with any of the pens. The pens were meant, not for writing, but for signing, and so their relationship to words was singular. They did not make words; they made *names*.

I sat at Mr. Herman's desk doing a very different thing with words: I was making poems. I wrote my poems in the stenographer's books Mr. Herman provided for my mother. You could say there was a kind of theft in my mother's giving them to me, but we both were happy in our possession of identical books—green-covered, with coils on the top. We both thought of ourselves as workers.

My mother, who was justly proud of her shorthand skills—Gregg, not Pitman, she would say, with the contempt of a virtuoso for a player who still employed an earlier technique—taught me a kind of shorthand for poetry. In high school, she had learned to scan—iambic pentameter was the only meter that she knew, but she was very fond of scanning lines of it, and showed me the half-circle followed by a slash that indicated an iambic foot. So both of us were marking sounds by symbols in our workers' notebooks, and after she had finished her day's work for Mr. Herman, she would come into his office, where I was sitting at his desk, and say, "All set," and we would walk out together, accomplished, spent, into the wide world, silent, each carrying her green notebook, making our way to the luncheonette where we would sit on the false leather seats and order always the same lunch: grilled cheese sandwich, lemon Coke.

Mr. Herman was the son of German farmers. He was an oddity among the Catholics we knew, all of whom were either Irish or Italian, as my mother's parents were. His rise in the world was for my mother the stuff of myth. The miles he walked to college, then to law school (in overalls? with soil-caked hands? barefoot, or in workboots without socks?), then his own law practice, partnership with a Protestant, election to Supervisor of the Town of Hempstead, involvement in the triumphant project of Jones Beach, inaugurated under his watch. Beside the Spy prints on the walls of his office was a photograph of him standing beside Robert Moses, both of them with shovels in their hands. Underneath their feet were the words "Breaking the Ground at Jones Beach Jetty." This was a great puzzle to me: I didn't know what a jetty was, and I couldn't imagine how anyone could break a ground that, since it was Jones Beach, had to be made of sand.

My mother's role in Mr. Herman's religious life was also the stuff of myth. Apparently, though properly baptized, Mr. Herman, unlike my mother, was not serious about his faith: some Sundays he was not even at Mass. Then, one day, only a short while after my mother began working for him, she opened Mr. Herman's office door to see him weeping, his head in his hands. He confessed to her that he'd had for some time a sore on his tongue that had been diagnosed as cancerous. My mother told him he must go to daily Mass and pray for a cure. He took her counsel. He went to daily Mass. He was cured. From then on, he was devout, a turnaround he credited to my mother and her prayers. She became for him not only admirable for her extraordinary secretarial skills, but also sacred, magical. Their placement of each other in the frame of myth—alongside their tremendous shared confidence—made them invaluable to one another. But not just invaluable: lustrous, heroic, singular, beyond compare.

The story of Mr. Herman's cancer is the only one I know about them, because the way they worked together did not produce stories. They wrote up wills and deeds, they went to closings. The more dramatic forms of the law were never theirs. Because their clientele were largely Catholic, they did not, as my mother said, "handle divorce." She said this as if divorce were a particularly nasty, possibly toxic species of effluvia, which they very well knew better than to touch. But after Mr. Herman's death, his partner, who took my mother on, began handling divorce. I had recently become divorced myself, and my mother, kindly, surprisingly, did not treat me as a poisoned thing but was very much, as she said, "on my side." She had never liked my first husband, never wanted me to marry; her romantic dreams centered not around domestic life, but around the world of work. Her most satisfying partnership had not been with my father but with Mr. Herman.

One day soon after my divorce, my mother—who had disastrously learned the word "supportive"—was trying to talk to me about my life. She said she'd come to understand divorce since they were now "handling it." She said to me, in an obviously false, society-matron tone, "In one of our cases something came up that I don't understand, and since you've been divorced I thought you might get it. The wife wants a divorce, and she says it's because the husband wants her to do something called oral sex. What's oral sex?" I tried, gently, to enlighten her. All pretense of decorousness vanished from my mother's tone. She sat up very straight. Her eyes flashed. Her teeth were clenched. "You made that up," she said. "No one but you would think of that. You see why Mr. Herman wouldn't touch divorce?"

As I think of it now, there was another story my mother told about Mr. Herman, and it was about sex. His most lucrative client had been an old German farmer (a relative?) who had made a fortune buying land and real estate when Long Island was turning from farmland to suburbia. He was nearly illiterate, a violent drunk, a widower. I always see him with a face like Teddy Roosevelt's, fatter but with the same carnivorous grin; a huge belly framed by red suspenders. My mother told me he made bootleg whiskey during Prohibition; he brought prostitutes into his house. He had a daughter living in the house with him, Hazel, who, my mother said, "went mental." This may or may not have been a result of her father's bringing prostitutes into the house, but as my mother said, "it didn't help."

When her father died, Hazel was put into the mental hospital in Central Islip. Mr. Herman became her guardian. When he visited her, he would always come back to my mother shaken, and my mother would have to invoke the mysterious will of God to calm him down. "She always tried to jump him," my mother said. "You could imagine what it would do to a man like that. A gentleman." I thought of it often, Hazel in a washed-out housedress, bare peasant feet, red-faced, huge, her kinky hair chopped to a man's length, jumping at Mr. Herman in his gray suit, his black wing-tipped shoes. He had to endure it. She was a millionaire.

These two stories about Mr. Herman, the one about Hazel and the one about his cancer, highlight my mother's role as his comforter. This was strange, because he seemed—and not only to her—the very model of unshakable male strength. If he were architecture, he would have been one of those bank buildings that stood out in the center of a small town: massive, cool, marmoreal, impermeable, safe. Certainly, he seemed monumental to me the few times in my childhood that I saw him. He was tall, and nearly bald, with a kind smile, light eyes, and large, well-shaped hands.

Did the kind smile suggest a vulnerability that his life in the world concealed? On a visit that we made to his house in Connecticut in 1964, on the occasion of my mother's twenty-fifth year in his employ, I too felt myself thrust into the role of comforter.

I was fifteen and feeling awkward. A year before, with Audrey Hepburn in mind, I had bought a green linen sleeveless dress to wear to an important dance. But in the year between that dance and the trip to Connecticut, my breasts had grown. I had forgotten to take this into consideration when I planned to wear the dress for my mother's anniversary brunch. In pictures of that event, my breasts look squeezed into the stiff green linen bodice, and that discomfort set the tone for the whole weekend.

I was disappointed in Mr. Herman's country house. Rough-hewn and simple, on a lake, it wasn't that different from my uncle's house in the Adirondacks, where I'd spent miserable summers as a child. I was equally disappointed in the food; it was my first "brunch," but the food was dull: the first course was a "relish tray" with celery sticks and cottage cheese in separated compartments and something called "watermelon rind," which I'd imagined would be sweet and juicy like watermelon, but which turned out to be not much different from the sweet pickles my mother habitually served with my tuna sandwiches. I don't know what I'd been expecting of the weekend: maybe something like the movie *High Society.* Maybe I expected Grace Kelly to waft in, accompanied by a hyper-casual Bing Crosby in yachting togs. But there were no neighbors, only the family: Mr. and Mrs. Herman and their son and daughter, and their spouses, who had clearly been ordered to attend. I couldn't imagine a possible conversation with any of them.

The evening after the brunch, I wandered out onto the screened porch that overlooked the lake. Mr. Herman was sitting in the darkness smoking a cigar. The red tip flowered like a beacon in the thick air. He turned away from the lake, to me, and said, "Nothing's much good any more, you know."

It was 1964, a difficult year for men like Mr. Herman. The sixties weren't kind to such men; he was too old to be enlivened and enticed by them, or, as we would have said, liberated. But I felt the winds of change blowing me into a freer, more exciting world, and the force of my trajectory might hit even Mr. Herman and my mother. In 1964, I was a Goldwater Republican; in 1968, I was neat and clean for Gene. But throughout all those days, I worked each summer at a job I got through Mr. Herman and his Republican patronage.

This is an untold story of working-class children of the sixties: our double lives, one of yearning for participation in the world of revolution, then the return (on weekends, in the summers) to the life that had to be lived to supplement our scholarships. In 1968, my first year at Barnard, I demonstrated by day and took the train home in the evening to my mother. She would ask, "How was your day?" and I would answer "Fine." "You're not getting involved with any of those weirdos, are you?" *"Of course not, Ma"*—the word "Ma" given an extra, Germanic consonant of irritation, and pronounced, only for these situations, the syllables dragged out in the legato of exasperation, "Mah."

All year I had been shouting, "Hey, hey, LBJ, how many kids did you kill today?" I called policemen pigs, the very men who had been my uncles, my neighbors, the fathers of my friends. There were the months of shocked, uncomprehending silence at the terrible deaths: Martin Luther King and Robert Kennedy.

And then, that summer of 1968, I went back to my job at the Republican-dominated Board of Supervisors in Nassau County, bedrock seat of Republican authority for fifty years. It was my third year there, and my first two had been happy. I was the youngest in the office, although chronologically not by much, and so I was the office pet. Each of the women liked me in a different way, except the second-in-command. With her I entered into a relationship that was to repeat itself during my years of office work: the truly efficient, truly dedicated workers had no time for me; they suspected I got by on charm, and usually they were right. But even the second-in-command who didn't like me understood that I was of value, because the level of incompetence of the others was so high that even my partial attentions left them in the dust. I could easily do my day's work in two hours, and I saw nothing wrong in spending the rest of the day reading and writing poetry at my desk. It took me a while to understand that I should spread the work out over the eight-hour day, and write while pretending to type letters.

Of the nine women in the office, four were named Dorothy;

two known as Dorothy and two as Dot. The others were Lois, Charlotte, Evelyn, Violet, and Ethel: names that have nearly disappeared. Most got their jobs because of the devotion of a husband or a father to the party: only Charlotte and one of the Dorothys seemed to be political themselves; and these were both exceedingly right-wing. But I was special to each one of them; I often had lunch with the oldest of the Dorothys, a cultivated, though not educated, gentle woman in her late sixties who was the receptionist to Elbert J. Mandeville, Clerk of the Board of Supervisors, whose duties were exceptionally unclear to me. I almost never heard him speak; he was bald, bucktoothed; he walked with his head down, as if he was afraid someone was going to ask him to do something. Most days he left early. All of the women liked him; he was undemanding and quite kind. For the first two years that I worked there, on my last day, the girls chipped in for pastries and sodas and had a party for me in the conference room. Many of us cried.

It was a traumatic year, 1968, and I can only explain my otherwise inexplicable behavior that summer as a species of posttraumatic shock. Why else would I have thought it was a good idea to make it public that the Republican Board of Supervisors had for three years been filibustering in order to block a proposal that welfare children be allowed free into county pools? It must have been my guilt at taking money from the Republican political machine, the machine of Richard Nixon, that led me to such a harebrained, indeed suicidally foolish act. I had known the filibuster was going on for two years, but then I had not yet been to college, to the Pentagon March, the Columbia riots; I had known no black people well, and no one I knew had ever been beaten by a cop.

The Board of Supervisors was made up of six middle-aged white men, all of whom in my memory had lush heads of hair and gray summer suits. They sat at a dais behind microphones. There were pitchers of water; each week I filled them, as each week I mimeographed the calendar of events on which they were to vote. That week, I stood up at the podium and made my announcements. Did the citizens know what the Board of Supervisors was doing to black children? Suddenly, I was in a scene from a movie. Bulbs flashed, there were popping noises, and then a rumble like the beginning of a tidal wave. At the door, the Supervisors' press attaché took me roughly by the arm and ushered me into a private room. I was confronted by the Head Supervisor, Ralph G. Caso.

The first thing that occurred to me was that I could easily be killed. *The Godfather* had not yet been made, but the iconography of the Mafia was readily available to the imagination, and, however unjust it was, Ralph Caso fit into it all too easily. He had the high coloring, the too-black wavy curls, the too-white birdlike teeth of an expensive doll. Nothing about him suggested anything that had ever been made of flesh and blood—although the possibility of drawn blood was not far from the surface. He was a symphony in white and silver: the gray silk suit, the white silk tie, the gleaming tiny teeth, the pinky ring with the stone so light blue as to be almost silver. I was afraid to meet his eyes—not silvery, but black, to match his hair. I have no memory of what he said to me. I know he hugged me at one point, my chest to his chest, my cheek against the white silk of his tie.

After he dismissed me, I had to walk back to my desk. The women whom I'd thought of as my friends kept far away from me, wouldn't even look at me, as if even eye contact might be contaminating. Then the phone on my desk rang. It was my mother. I was sure the others in the office could hear her screams. "What were you doing? What did you think you were doing? They called Mr. Herman and told him to fire me. After all these years. Well, you can thank your lucky stars he just stood up to them. Told them to calm down. Told them you were just a kid. Do you know what you could have done? Do you know what could have happened because of you? We could be out on the street. I could have lost my job."

The enormity of it made me feel I had been struck down by a stampeding animal. I wanted to lie on the floor under my desk. I wanted to die. "I could have lost my job." She didn't need to say, "We could be out on the street." Because it wasn't starvation whose prospect devastated us both. It was the loss of place. Who would my mother be without her job? Who would she be if she had to know herself, think of herself, as a person who had been *fired*. Fired by Mr. Herman.

Fired. The image came to my mind: my mother set aflame, reduced to ash. And it could have been my doing. Except that Mr. Herman had saved her. Us. He stood up to these frightening, powerful, furious men. He stood up for us. I saw him tall, shining, heroic, our protector, with his buckler and his shield. I was grateful beyond words. There were no words to thank him, and I didn't try. In fact, I never spoke to him again.

Mr. Herman died while I was still in college. I had gone to Harvard for the summer to study Italian, and, begrudgingly, I had come home for a weekend in early August to see my mother. Her drinking had got much worse. She had, in a drunken state, taken a bad fall and broken her leg in three places; the doctor had confined her to a wheelchair for six weeks. She couldn't go to work. A cousin, who thought me heartless to leave her like that and go back to Cambridge to finish my course, agreed to be responsible for her care. I came home as little as possible.

I suppose it was lucky that I was with her when the call came, saying Mr. Herman had had a heart attack and died. My mother, who never shied away from expressing emotions as primitively as she could, howled and howled at the news. She howled in her bed, she wept in her wheelchair; and I got on the bus to Boston. I left her to my cousin and headed northeast to learn the first sentences of the language of my dreams of a greater, lighter world: *Oggi piove. Si, anzi nevica.*

When Mr. Herman died, his son, who had become his junior partner, took my mother on. But within six months, he passed her on to another of the partners, and took the other partner's secretary.

My mother never knew of my scalding love for Paul Herman. An entirely ridiculous enterprise, it began when I was ten years old. I was meeting my mother at her office after our Fifth Grade Field Day, and I was sweaty and hot and a bit surprised: for once I had had fun at an event for children my own age, an ordinary event for ordinary children, and I had miraculously felt one of them, actually *been* one of them, instead of wretchedly standing on the sidelines yearning to be at home with my books. I had won a sky-blue plastic headband in some race, and I very much enjoyed the bite of its plastic teeth into my sweaty scalp, not unlike the pleasure of biting down on the baby teeth I had finished losing only three years earlier.

My mother was abashed at my dishevelment, so out of place IN THE OFFICE, but decided to make a joke of it when bringing me into Mr. Herman's office to meet his son for the first time. Paul had been away before this time: at boarding school, in college, in law school, and, most recently, in the army. "This is my daughter," my mother said. "She was at Field Day. You can tell because she looks like she just came in from the field." Mr. Herman laughed and said hello but stayed behind his desk. Paul, though, stood and then walked over to me, his hand extended. We were going to shake hands! I felt ennobled, as if he'd struck me on each shoulder with the blade of his sword. He was ushering me, with the utmost tenderness, the utmost graciousness, into the world of adult women. Women who were courted. Women who could expect to be stood up for, their hands taken. And so I developed what was called a crush, and I did feel crushed by it: my breath was different when I thought of him, my heart beat painfully against my ribs. Two years later, when I went to his wedding, an elaborate event at the Waldorf-Astoria, I wept in a booth of the opulent ladies' room out of sheer, hopeless envy of the bride.

After his discharge from the army, Paul came to work in his father's office, but the partnership, so long dreamed of by Mr. Herman and my mother, was an unhappiness. He wanted new ways. Change. Mr. Herman and my mother had not changed since 1939. In an entirely original reversal of the usual thinking about the good effects of army life, they felt that the army had made him undisciplined. "The GI pass-the-buck mentality," my mother called it.

One Saturday, while my mother was doing extra work and Paul's wife was hanging curtains in his office, he and I chatted in his father's room, the only idlers in the group. "I believe in change for its own sake," he said. This was in reference to the curtains. I was no longer in love with him, but I loved him for saying that. As he had, by shaking my hand when I was ten years old, ushered me into the world of grown-up women, that day he opened the Golden door to the New World, and showed me through.

I lost interest in Paul Herman as the sixties progressed. He was married with children; suburban, *straight*. I didn't think of him at all while I was in college. Before he died, Mr. Herman had taken on two new partners, and so there were four lawyers at work in the office, and their secretaries, whereas in the golden days it had been only my mother and him. Paul was the junior partner, the youngest by twenty years. No one was happy with the arrangement, but the grumbling seemed to lead to no change.

I had contact with him again when I was in graduate school. One of Mr. Herman's wealthy clients, who had been taken over by Paul, had died. She had been a woman of cultivation and had a large library. No one knew what to do with the books. Paul suggested to my mother that, since I was a graduate student of English literature, I should have first pick before the library was dispersed and sold up.

In her retirement (she had been a college librarian) the client had moved from Long Island to an apartment on Park Avenue, and Paul arranged that I should meet him and his wife there. His wife, my former rival, was heavily pregnant; I guess she was there to help make decisions about the books. They were so happy in her pregnancy, so happily married, and I was so miserable in my new, adventurous life. My boyfriend was homosexual; he'd phoned me up, tripping on acid, from a party at Andy Warhol's Factory, and, while trying to finish my paper on Matthew Arnold, I had to try to talk him down. My life also had its moments of exhilaration—I had left home, I was in the center of the center—and I dealt with my displacement and misery by a sharp bath of contempt for Paul and his wife.

The library was a disappointment to me. Much of it duplicated my father's: it was strong on the Catholic classics—Newman, Hopkins, Maritain—weak on contemporary poetry (except for Eliot: I took all she had of his), which at that point was what I wanted to be reading most of all. I concentrated on the art books: Fra Angelico, Bellini, Grünewald. Nothing after the seventeenth century, nothing that could not be known as sacred art, had been represented. I shouldn't have been surprised. She had taken my father under her wing, as a kindred aesthetic/intellectual spirit, not so common in those days on the Long Island ground.

Paul took the art books to my mother's house in Long Island; it made my mother happy to have this sign of Mr. Herman's thoughtfulness on the property, even if it was only in the form of boxes in the garage. Then, one night, when she was drunk, she told me about how my father had hurt her in relation to Mr. Herman and the woman who had owned the books. Without telling my mother, he had asked the woman for a loan for one of his Catholic intellectual projects. Like all of them, this one had failed. He had been unable to repay the loan. She listed the unpaid loan as a loss on her income tax. So Mr. Herman had found out all about it, and that was the way my mother had found out.

"I was mortified. But he didn't say a word. But I knew he knew. He had no right to do that, your father. He humiliated me. He put Mr. Herman in a terrible position. I can never forgive him for that."

The next morning my mother forgot that she had told me the story. But it had tainted the books, and so I left them in the garage, not unpacking them for years, until I too was married, housed, and tamed.

Not long after I had seen him and his wife in the Park Avenue apartment, Paul lost a child to leukemia. At that time, my mind inhabited a different universe, and the sorrow of the child's death did not affect me, except abstractly: as a type of the world's sorrow. But I agreed to come with my mother for a memorial service for little Jane.

I don't remember much about Paul's house, or who was there, except that I know Mrs. Herman wasn't—she'd gone to Florida for the winter—and Paul's sister, who had just had a baby, was not there either. My mother and I seemed, somehow, to be representing the Herman family, but no one seemed glad to have us there. My mother and Paul had grown increasingly impatient with each other.

No one talked to us except their next-door neighbor, a Lutheran minister, who had been extremely kind to the family during their tragic time. My mother, deprived of company and not getting enough attention, began to drink more and more. Paul asked the Lutheran minister to say a prayer, of blessing on the food, and remembrance of the dead child. After he did, my mother rose to her unsteady feet.

"Why is there no priest here? Why is a minister saying a prayer for the dead? Isn't this supposed to be a Catholic house? What would your father say?"

She started to walk out of the house, in high religious dudgeon, but as she stepped onto the mat in front of the door she fell. A loud, crashing fall, accompanied by her howls of pain and rage. The shocked silence that accompanied her fell on me like a safe falling on an animal in a black-and-white cartoon. I knew only one thing: I had to get my mother out. Up. Home. She was a heavy woman. I told Paul and the others who approached to help that I knew what to do. But I didn't know what to do—only that I had to get her to her feet. I did, and she collapsed again, like a doll whose joints have suddenly gone rotten. We all understood that she wasn't going to be able to walk. Paul and the Lutheran minister had to carry her into the car. I saw as they were lifting her that she had wet herself. I didn't know how I would get her into the house after I'd driven her home, but I reckoned that I could support her somehow so that she could walk a bit, and that, if she had to, she could crawl.

It was not long after this that Paul left the firm and moved with his family to Connecticut. A few years later, my mother retired. She was seventy-five; she had begun working for Mr. Herman forty-four years earlier. But either she had lost her touch or she was out of touch with the new culture of the firm—or perhaps the legal profession, or perhaps the world. The partner who was not her boss suggested that my mother's time was up, and that if I didn't arrange for her retirement he would do it, and it would not be pleasant. The idea of my mother's being fired ignominiously was unbearable to me. I convinced her that I needed her to help me with my two-year-old, and with the baby I was pregnant with. I bought her a house, two blocks from mine, in the town in the Mid-Hudson Valley where I was living. She seemed proud, even smug, when she turned in her resignation: strutting a bit in her new role as desired grandmother. But she didn't want to have anything to do with packing up her things. One Saturday, when no one was in the office, I packed everything of hers in cardboard cartons and drove them to her new home.

Among the things she told me that she wanted were several boxes of the firm's letterhead, which still had Mr. Herman's name and dates. I don't know if the firm still exists, and if it does if Mr. Herman's name is still included. They would never have removed his name while my mother was still around. But I don't know if, after my mother left, her boss's name became invisible. She had no contact with any of the people she had worked with. In retirement, she fell apart. Without her work, there was nothing she wanted to do. She no longer knew herself, and no one who'd seen her at her desk, typing, talking on the phone, taking dictation from some man who would tell everyone she was a treasure, would recognize the woman that she had become.

My Mother: *Words and Music*

We sang, we suffered, we were there.
Where were we?

—RICHARD HOWARD
"From Beyoglu"

When I think of my mother happy, she is singing. When I think of the two of us happy, we are singing together. Someone once said to me, "All your best conversations with your mother were sung."

What a strange thing it is, singing. So inefficient. Putting words to music. Putting them—where? So time-consuming. How much longer it takes to sing "I love you" than to say it. For one thing, you must come up with the melody, fit the melody to the words. But perhaps it isn't really inefficient, not in the long run, because it is easier to remember words put to music than spoken words, harder to forget them.

Goethe did not believe in setting words to music. He believed the meaning of the words was diluted by the music. I suppose it all depends on what you think words are for.

What did my mother think words were for? She was not a middle-class woman. She did not have conversations. She would have said, "I don't have that kind of time." No time devoted to talk for its own sake, talk that explored or played or followed something as you might follow the course of a stream. She did not describe things. She did not analyze. "I don't dwell on things. I don't harp on things, I don't dig things up like you. I can't afford it." She was impatient with people who spoke about scenery or food, who recounted the plots of movies. "I guess they have nothing to do but waste my time and theirs." "Waste my time." "I can't afford it." Her attitude implied a proper economy. A useful investment. How would time, for my mother, be used well? In work or prayer, she would have said.

But she was not a puritan; alongside work and prayer she believed in pleasure, and she enjoyed skirting indecency. It is a particularly Catholic combination: piety and profanity linking hands (a sign of large-minded and true comprehension of the world), by passing entirely the respectable, a Protestant terrain. For her, I think the pleasure of words was directly related to the joy of insult, its corrective power. All her jokes had a barb, a sting in the tail: many of them had as their targets pretensions towards gentility. One of her favorites was about an Irish couple living on a farm. The wife has ideas above her station; they invite the parish priest for tea, and the woman, clearly the tartar of the couple, warns her husband to be on his best behavior in front of the priest. Everything is going well until the food is laid out on the table. "Sorry, Father," the husband says, "the butter's as soft as shit." Abashed, the wife tries to make up for his gaffe. "Pay him no mind, Father," she says, "he has no more manners than me arse."

One of our pleasures in church was using the time between her early arrival (calculated so she could get her favorite seat, near, but not too near, the front) and the beginning of Mass to make fun of others in the congregation. Someone passed by with a large nose—"How'd you like to have that full of nickels?" she'd say. Critical of women who wore pants to church, she nudged me when someone in tight jeans walked by: "If you had an ass like that, would you come to church in that getup?"

She was on red alert about my pretentiousness: particularly my desire to be fashionable. When, as a young teenager, I begged to be able to wear a straight skirt, jettisoning the endless pleats she favored, on the grounds that "everyone else has one," she said, "When they pay your bills they can tell you what to wear." In the age of miniskirts, she accused me of wearing a skirt so short that "everyone can see where you sat on the ax." When, at some point in college, I started using the words "fabulous" and "super," she would mock me, elongating the vowels: "faaabulous," she would say, "suuupah," holding her pinky in the air, as if she were a fop sipping tea from a particularly ridiculous small cup. When I began smoking Gauloises, she said she refused to have her living room turned into a French whorehouse.

She had an excellent ear for speech that was false, a cover-up. Even in her last years, she never lost this gift. I was with her once in a painting class in the nursing home. I had been asked to accompany her: she was impossibly uncooperative with the teacher. But she'd never had any interest in painting; she didn't know why she should be expected to have it at this late stage in her career. To encourage her, I brought in a book of photographs of Ireland, whose landscape I knew she'd loved. We sat together in front of a picture of a deep-green meadow; my mother picked up a large paintbrush and slathered, unlovingly, swaths of plain green paint. "That's wonderful, Anna," the teacher said. My mother looked at her and said, "If you think that's wonderful, you need more help than I could possibly give you."

In her last year, when she was truly wretched, moving from anxiety to stupor, I talked to a friend who had worked with hospice patients for many years. He said that often what people who were living miserably needed to hear was that it was all right for them to let go of their lives. He suggested I say that to my mother. I held her hand and looked into her eyes. "It's all right for you to let go, Mom," I said. "You can let go of your life now, you can let yourself be with God." She looked at me with her old gimlet eye, focusing as she hadn't for quite a long time. "Why would I pull a crazy stunt like that?" she said.

I am used to thinking that what gift I have for words comes from my father, but in fact my mother used language skillfully, imaginatively, with precision and style. She was well known for writing excellent letters; it was one of the skills her boss, Mr. Herman, treasured her for. He had only to sketch out the main ideas for a letter, and then leave it to her. Once, when she was trying to raise money for the Sisters of Mary Reparatrix (at whose retreat house on 29th Street she met my father), she wrote to Major Bowes, the host of the enormously successful radio show *The Original Amateur Hour*. In response to her letter, he sent the sisters a hundred dollars. This was a princely sum in 1932, and my mother was the toast of the convent, sisters and retreatants alike; it was a fame that never left her; she was remembered for it years later. In 1969, when I went with my mother on a retreat that was a disaster (I was a staunch unbeliever then, but I was determined that my mother wouldn't guess), an old sister, told by my mother that I was going to be a writer, said I was a chip off the old block. "Remember that letter, Anne," she said. "We've prayed for you ever since."

Recently, a distant cousin of mine sent me a letter my mother had written to his mother. It touched me on several levels, including the stylishness of the language and her pride in me. Pride in me was not something my mother allowed herself the words for. When people would say, "Your mother must be very proud of you," I could honestly answer that I didn't know. It is an Irish trait, I think, the reluctance to praise a child, for fear of her getting "a swelled head." Or perhaps it was Italian: fear that praise would bring down the evil eye. My Jewish father had no compunction in naming me a genius at the age of five. The closest my mother ever came to complimenting me was her once telling a friend, "You know my daughter is the third-best writer in America." My friend was afraid to ask her who numbers one and two might be.

But in writing a letter to someone I would have no access to, my mother was free to express pride.

> *Dear Pat:*
>
> *I was glad to get your note—and realize you have much to do. I don't want an acknowledgement of my mass for your mother—but I would appreciate a remembrance card if you have one to spare.*
>
> *You well know how much I loved your mother—so you can well understand how much I miss her. But as I told Margaret, that she was spared a long illness was a blessing we must be grateful for.*
>
> *Knowing your interest in Mary's first book (your mother told me so often) I thought you'd be interested in this "blurb" from England; Random House has sold the rights of publication to the same house in England that published her first book. The book will be out in February so keep your eyes open for it—and spread the news around.*
>
> *I am in seventh heaven being a grandmother. Anna Gordon Cash is a love (as are all babies) but when it happens to be your own there is something special.*
>
> *Anne*

She was a letter writer, a joke teller, but she had a brief career as a creator of fictions when I was a small child. It is true that these fictions were primarily utilitarian; nevertheless, they show a flair that the utilitarian has no need of for its work. She made up a character called Pimples Willoughby who was responsible for all my bad acts. "I don't know where Mary Kate went, but Pimples Willoughby seems to be here again. Mary Kate couldn't possibly be that fresh." I had invented an imaginary friend called Presbyterian, so sometimes my mother would play a game of Giant Steps with me, Pimples, and Presbyterian. Pimples always cheated. She never won.

The cautionary tale that I remember her telling partook of high diction. "Once, there was a little girl playing on the beach with her mother. 'Put down your pail and shovel and come with me,' her mother said. The little girl didn't know why, but she knew that she must obey her mother. In a minute, a tidal wave came, and the pail and shovel were carried out to sea in one second, far from where the little girl could see them. 'And that would have happened to you,' her mother said, 'had you not practiced BLIND OBEDIENCE.'" She used a particularly thrilling tone for those words BLIND OBEDIENCE: I could hear the organ music supporting the words, the notes of portent hovering in the air above our heads.

A creator of fictions, she had no compunction in using untruth to make a point. I used to like to jump up and down on my parents' bed, and my mother couldn't bear it. I was coming out of my dance class once and saw another child coming out of an earlier class. She had only one arm. I asked my mother what had happened to the little girl. My mother didn't skip a beat. "It's a very sad story," she said. "Her mother had told her not to jump up and down on the bed, but she didn't pay attention, and she fell off the bed, and her arm snapped off RIGHT AT THE SHOULDER."

And when I was being resistant about blowing my nose when I had a cold, she once said, "Keep it up, dear, and you'll end up with a nice deviated septum for yourself." I was terrified; I had no idea what a deviated septum was, but it sounded dire. I blew my nose. When, later, in adulthood, I jokingly accused her of scare tactics, she said, "I knew you loved words, and I knew that was the way to get to you. Well, it worked, didn't it?"

When I was divorced from my first husband, she somehow got it into her head that we should have a conversation about my life. "I know that you're a divorcée," she said (pronouncing the word with a long "a" at the end, as if I were the star of a Fred Astaire movie), "and that men find you attractive. And I know why they find you attractive." I was shocked, wondering what the compliment might be: I was unused to a compliment.

"Men find you attractive," she said, "because you're a god-damn fool."

She, on the other hand, was determined to be no one's fool. But when she sang, there was never any danger of any foolishness. Or at least none that she felt. She made up a song for me when I was small that is the clearest indication I can call up of her capacity for uninflected tenderness:

> Did I happen to tell you how much I loved you
> Little Mary Kate?
> Did I happen to tell you how sweet I think you are?
> Did I happen to tell you you're Mommy's angel girl
> And Daddy's little shining star?

I wanted to sing this song to my own daughter when she was small. But I could never sing it without bursting into tears, a kind of uncontrollable weeping that I knew would be upsetting to a child. I can't write the words now without weeping. Why, I want to say to my mother, couldn't you have been like that with me more of the time? Why did you have to wait for song to let me know what was clearly your great, your heartbreakingly tender love?

Perhaps she needed music as a substitute for the real-world risk of unrequited love. Put to music, words weren't dangerous. In music, she allowed herself to inhabit the place of plain romance.

The songs she liked to sing were, not surprisingly, about romantic love. They had no irony, although in life my mother habitually inhabited the ironic mode to protect herself from disappointment. So in songs: her dream of a universe impossible outside the world of songs. A friend of mine, an expert in liturgical music, once said to me, "We sing to feel a world we can only imagine." In songs, my mother felt lodged in safety: she would not, could not be mocked.

Was it because she thought of music as a gift from her father? She spoke of a musical time with him before I was born, of a kind of musicality I never saw or heard. Her father, she said, loved opera. She believed that all Italians loved opera. It wouldn't have occurred to her that some Italians would have said he was not Italian but Sicilian. But he must have known that: he would not allow his children to learn the kind of Italian he spoke, because he said it was a dialect. Impure. And they were in America. They were Americans. There was no need, it would do them no good to learn an impure tongue. Presumably, my grandfather believed that the Italian of the opera he loved was pure.

My mother was proud that her father would get standing room at the Metropolitan Opera, then come home afterwards exalted. And she was proud that she'd learned to accompany him on the piano so that he could sing his favorite arias. She never said what the arias were, and she never questioned why he never brought any of his nine children (not one of them, not once) to share what was purported to be his great love. Did he want it for himself, a treasure kept from the greedy, grubby hands, the open mouths endlessly needing to be fed? His treasure: the language of his childhood, the music of his people. Safe from the children. Kept to himself. Kept away.

They didn't seem to take their father seriously, these nine children that he sired, although they had to pretend to fear him. He died when I was one, so I have no sense of him. Pictures don't reveal much. A small man, inches shorter than his wife. Their wedding picture hangs in my living room. Taken a century ago. She is sitting, he is standing behind her. I have always assumed this was done so that no one would think of her being taller than him. But even sitting, she seems to tower over him. More massive: my grandmother, the Alp.

He was a jeweler. He made jewelry, but also he repaired it. My mother said, "My father was an artist, a real artist." But, unlike many artists, he was able to support a wife and nine children by his art. Yet none of his five daughters seemed to have a taste for jewelry or to hunger for it, or to crave it, as many women do—another common habit—as a proof of their worth, their value to a man, or men. My mother said, "Our dining room was always covered with diamonds," but she was unable to invest this image with any kind of magic. I did not see, when my mother spoke, sparkling jewels upon the dark, varnished wood. It was as if the diamonds she spoke of were industrial: for use on the ends of drills or for some kind of surgery. Perhaps this was because none of the jewelry my grandfather made seemed to have any kind of glamour. It was reluctantly modest: my mother's engagement ring a tiny diamond peeping through a box like a casing of gold; her wedding ring, plain gold, unremarkable; my grandmother's earrings two diamond studs surrounded by some blackish metalwork; the cameos he gave her worn on a velvet ribbon around her neck, or barely visible against the pattern of her gray-and-yellow printed dress, the only one she ever wore for occasions she considered important enough for her to take out, then pin on the cameos.

Yet, for my mother, her father represented the higher things. His love of opera, his artistic livelihood, his fastidious sense of smell, for which, along with his quick temper, he was famous in the neighborhood. Apparently, his first word upon entering the house in the evening was "Garbagio," a signal to the nearest child to take the garbage out. One of my uncles joked: "I was twelve years old before I knew my name wasn't Garbagio." Was this joke bitter? As a family, they would have not allowed bitterness towards parents as a permitted category.

My grandmother, who loved fish, was not permitted to cook it in the house, because my grandfather hated the smell. She had, when she wanted to cook fish, to cook it in the basement. How did she cook it? On a hot plate? Over a spirit lamp? As a treat, her children would take her to a smorgasbord where she could revel in the abundance of fish. My Irish grandmother: five foot eleven. My Sicilian grandfather: five foot six. The joke: that he believed he was the boss of the house. The real joke: perhaps he was. Ruling by his temper, his fastidiousness. The princess and the pea. His sensitive ear. His delicate nose. Auden speaks of his cohort as a group whose "greatest comfort is music / Which can be made anywhere, is invisible, / and does not smell." Did my mother divide the world into the part ruled by her mother—the local, the corporeal, the smelly—and the one ruled over by her father—an odorless space, the music of the spheres?

I never heard my mother accompany her father on the piano. Occasionally, very rarely, she would play the piano and we would sing together. Her touch on the piano was tentative, hesitant, and these were qualities that she displayed in no other area of her life. Or, no, that isn't true; she was tentative and hesitant when presented with a menu in what she would have called a "fancy restaurant." This hesitancy eventually became so pronounced, as she grew older, that she would throw her menu angrily onto her plate and say to me, "I don't care what I eat. You know what I like better than I do at a place like this. I would never go to a place like this if it wasn't for you." So, perhaps in the case of both the piano and the restaurant, she hesitated because she feared she was in a place that was too good for her, where she did not belong.

She played one of two pianos—or, more properly, I should say there were two pianos in the houses of my childhood.

The first: an ugly old upright without the piano's classical (or is it Romantic?) allure. A piano of no sheen, no beauty of conformation; the sound was produced by hammers covered in green felt suggesting nothing of the resonance of strings; workmanlike tools, without magic, hidden behind thin wooden doors that slid—open, shut. The piano was relegated to the front porch, where my uncle Ned slept. The reasons for this were hard to comprehend; there was an empty bedroom upstairs which he was never offered, as if some family pride were marked and sealed by their having what could be thought of as a "guest room," even if there were never any guests. Or almost never; once a year, the two of my grandmother's nine children who lived more than half an hour's distance from her home came to visit with their families. But that was considered grounds enough to relegate my uncle to the porch. Was this a sign, in these eminently practical people, of a hunger for a life marked by a conspicuous misallocation of resources, a conspicuous waste?

The second piano was one my mother bought just for me, when I began taking piano lessons at the age of eight. You could say that my taking piano lessons was another example of conspicuous waste. I studied the piano for twelve years and never made any progress. In part this was because, for the best reasons, reasons that spoke of my mother's yearning for a culture she didn't quite understand, she found me a piano teacher who was too good for me. He was a serious musician, conservatory-trained. He told my mother and me that he had studied with Schnabel, which meant nothing, at the time, to either of us.

I began with Hanon exercises, moved on to a Schirmer yellow book with green print, *First Lessons in Bach,* and then to *Schumann for Beginners.* Then—white pages with Romantic black lettering, "Für Elise." Then some Prokofiev, and then, I don't know, it seemed Chopin nocturnes and waltzes for the next ten years. My piano career stalled when my mother stopped coming to lessons with me. I was thirteen, and all of us agreed—my mother, my teacher, and I—that it had become unseemly for my mother to sit in the room with me, as if I weren't old enough to go to a lesson on my own.

But without her supervision, the musical part of my piano lessons ceased. I don't mean for you to suggest a Paolo-and-Francesca "there was no more reading done that day" moment. No, my piano teacher and I simply talked. About life and art. My mother's quitting the scene of the music room coincided with the arrival of the sixties, my sexual awakening, and the collapse of my teacher's marriage. We had a lot to talk about. He introduced me to Existentialism and Abstract Expressionism: Picasso and Sartre and Beckett swam into my awareness, when I should have been learning new pieces, instead of playing the ten bars of the first movement of the *Moonlight* Sonata—*molto espressivo*—for the eight hundredth time. I regret that I didn't learn more music, but I am grateful, very, very grateful, to my piano teacher for ushering me into the twentieth century—even though it was more than half over—because I had been inhabiting a world that was a combination of a misapprehended Middle Ages and a prettied-up nineteenth century. My teacher brought me into the Brave New World. That it was not the world of music was probably due to my conspicuous lack of talent.

I often wonder if my mother noticed that I was playing the same piece for ten years. Does that mean that she wasn't listening? Or does it mean that the idea of playing the piano was more important to her than any actual piano playing? Or that she knew what was going on and, understanding me in a way I rarely give her credit for, knew it was the right thing? It is always hard to know what my mother understood, what she made of things. Made into what?

What, for instance, did she make of the fact that her father enlisted her as his accompanist on the piano although she had a sister who was acknowledged to be much more musical than she? That prize went to her sister Marie, who was four years younger. "Marie had the voice. That's why my father liked her best." My mother said this without emotion. My mother, always a retainer of old slights, old grudges, old starvations, particularly when she was drunk, never seemed wounded by her father's partiality. It was as if Marie's voice had rendered her a different sort of creature, with different, automatic rights.

My mother was never asked to sing at family parties, but she sang with me, particularly when we were driving in the car. And when I was quite small we sang together for the simple entertainment of it. What do you want to do? Let's sing.

She found songs that she could sing to me as love songs from a mother to a child, transposed, transplanted perhaps, from their original meaning: a message from man to woman, woman to man, but not roughly, not misshapenly, and not with imprecision. And she made up a game to go with the words to "Getting to Know

You." She'd sing "Because of all the beautiful and new / Things I'm learning about you" and then would kiss my forehead when she sang "day," my nose when she sang "by," and my chin for the final "day."

Sometimes she would uncouple the words from their melodies and thread them, as ordinary language, into the conversation: "You know what, I love you a bushel and a peck. Guess what, kid, you're the cream in my coffee."

At night my mother would sing me a song that to me was the sign of how she treasured me. It was called "Let the Rest of the World Go By." I was a hard child to put to sleep; I hated sleep, but I liked her singing those words to me:

> With someone like you, a pal good and true
> I'd like to leave it all behind, and go and find
> A place that's known to God alone
> Just a spot to call our own
> We'll find perfect peace, where joys never cease
> Out there beneath the kindly sky
> We'll build a sweet little nest somewhere in the West
> And let the rest of the world go by

This song didn't seem to be about a man and a woman: it was about my mother and me. And the West was not the West of cowboys, it was the West of endless space, a "kindly sky." A place not of danger but of comfort—contemplative, quasi-divine. My mother was not a peaceful person, but in her arms, embraced by her, resting on her strong bosom, which was a place not of softness but of strength, I did find comfort; and when I had to be separated from her I did feel cut off from comfort. Comfortless. So the song suggested we would never be apart, and yet there would be ample space, endless space, so that her angers would be magically absorbed. Into the kindly sky.

My mother sang me two kinds of songs.

There were the backward-looking ones, the ones that, in their sweetness, in their jauntiness, had one foot in the nineteenth century, that partook of the ideal of a natural paradise before the motorcar, the phonograph, certainly before the moving picture, and most certainly before the advent of talking pictures, movies where the music would be heard.

These songs placed me in a generational limbo: she sang me songs that no mothers of children my age were singing, and I was singing songs no other child my age sang. Partly this was because my mother was forty-one when I was born—almost old enough to be my grandmother. She was a teenager in the twenties, but the memory of the songs of World War I and just before was alive for her. The two songs that I considered MINE were twenties songs: "When the Red, Red Robin Comes Bob, Bob Bobbin' Along" and "Tiptoe Through the Tulips." It seemed crucial to me to sing one of them, and only one, each day, to choose only one of them as my favorite, as if, in choosing one, I was defining myself in some way that would settle on my skin that day. Until the next day, when I felt I had to make the same crucial choice. I too bought into the economy of scarcity, but it was a radical scarcity, or an economy of singularity: I would choose only one song a day to sing, one to be my favorite, one to be MINE. I felt the same anguish of selection when I would have to choose between Cashmere Bouquet and April Showers talcum powder—both desirable to me, one in a pink tin with a bouquet of flowers tied with a ribbon, one in green with rosebuds speckled through.

What did I think would happen if I made the wrong choice or said I couldn't choose? What punishment did I imagine? Why was the threat of these desirables being taken away from me so real? And by whom? This was, I suppose, my version of the economy of scarcity my mother lived by. That it was a currency only in my imagination was neither here nor there. And if I hadn't worked in this economy, would the chosen objects have seemed as valuable? Are multiplicity and wealth a sure ticket to the worthlessness of everything? Did Henry Clay Frick, coming down the stairs of his mansion at midnight to look at his collection when he couldn't sleep, love his paintings less, because there were many of them, than the genteel, impoverished widow poring over her last family portrait saved from the bailiff? We do believe, don't we, that if scarcity is not in itself a guarantee of superior love, then amplitude endangers it. The widow's mite. It is easier for a camel to pass through the eye of a needle. So that, if poverty doesn't exist, we will invent it. As a proof of love.

I think it is that I was desperately looking for signs that would tell me who I was, as I didn't recognize myself at all in the world where I was placed. The choices connected with femaleness seemed hopeless to me, hopeless in their mutual exclusion. So I could choose "The Red, Red Robin" and be cheerful, jokey, perky: this would go along with the choice of April Showers powder, the rosebuds (young, informal, ungathered) as opposed to the beribboned ceremonial bouquet, which would be the partner of "Tiptoe Through the Tulips," which seemed a more serious song to me, especially as my mother would trill the high notes of "Knee deep in flowers we'll stray." I could see myself knee deep in flowers, losing myself; I would not lose myself bob bob bobbing along.

The other songs my mother sang were songs of the city street, *the city street,* Broadway, the Great White Way. "Lullaby of Broadway" was the most obvious, but there were other songs whose lyrics shimmered with urbanity: "(I Like New York in June) How About You?"; "Manhattan" ("We'll take Manhattan, the Bronx and Staten Island too"). And I very well understood that "the city" was where real life happened, it was the place where I would be recognized, where I could be myself. I could see it: it shone on the horizon, silvery, desirable, and my mother and I belonged there because we knew the words to all the songs.

The years pass, years in which, for my mother, there is not much singing. It is the era of folk music, the era of rock and roll, and my mother has use for neither. She says Joan Baez sounds like she's in her death throes and Bob Dylan sounds like a cat in heat; she burlesques their styles, singing along, ruining my listening every time I turn on the phonograph. But even though I've developed new tastes, I never lose my love for musical comedy. We still sing if there is a musical on *The Late Show* that we could watch together, lying in her bed, a can of Planter's peanuts on the bed between us and the dog at our feet. She takes the lyrics of the songs down in her steno pad and then types them up in the morning, and, me holding the original and her the carbon copy, we sing the true, authorized version of the songs, practicing until we get them right, exactly right.

But then I move away, I no longer live with her; I marry. Perhaps in those years she sings when she is not with me, when she's alone. I don't hear it, though, because she is no longer making my breakfast, no longer driving me places, no longer putting me to bed. The situations for her songs have disappeared. And perhaps she no longer loves me as she did when I was a child; perhaps there is not much more for her to sing about. At least not to me.

In the last years of her life, when I put her in a nursing home because she can't care for herself and I can't care for her, I visit her once a week. Each time I go, we sing together, because I know it's something we can do together. And what else can we do in these rooms but sing, these rooms smelling of urine and overcooked food, with nothing lovely for the eye but the decrepit old, nodding or dozing or sitting in a daze? And the ever-present television, so that I have to wheel her into her room, where there is quiet, so that we can sing and hear ourselves. In peace.

We sing the old songs, "Someone Like You," "Bells Are Ringing." As she loses more and more memory, she loses the more recent songs. Songs from the First World War replace the musical comedies of the thirties and forties. She claims never to have heard "Getting to Know You." At the end, she sits with her head in her hands all day and doesn't even lift it when I sing to her, doesn't recognize the songs, doesn't care. And then she dies, moving from a stupor to deadness, a movement that happens in her sleep when I am not there.

What have I taken from her? What have I failed to give her, in being unable to take her into my home, into my heart, for the last, terrible years? To make a home where we could sing? I try to make it up to her by giving her a funeral that is full of beautiful music. A hymn called "St. Patrick's Breastplate," according to legend written by St. Patrick himself.

> I bind unto myself today
> The virtues of the starlit heaven,
> The glorious sun's life giving ray,
> The whiteness of the moon at even,
> The flashing of the lightning free,
> The whirling wind's tempestuous shocks,
> The stable earth, the deep salt sea
> around the old eternal rocks.

I include "O Sacred Head Surrounded," a chorale by Bach from my favorite piece of music: the *St. Matthew Passion,* which it is likely she never heard. Fauré's "Pie Jesu" from his *Requiem.* Fauré, whom I learned of when reading Proust—whom my mother very probably never heard of, and certainly, for all her love of reading, would not have read. So am I really making something for her, or am I making it for myself? Should I have used, for her funeral, only the traditional Catholic hymns I knew she sang: "Tantum Ergo," "Holy God We Praise Thy Name"? Was her funeral my last theft, my last withholding? My last refusal to allow her to be who she was, instead of a citizen of the world I inhabited, which she allowed me access to but could not approach herself? Her funeral may have been too much about me; the priest who gave her eulogy, a friend of mine and not of hers, talked more about me than about her. Would she have liked that? Is that what she always really wanted? I so rarely knew what she wanted. When we were singing, I thought I knew what she wanted: she wanted to be singing with me. I was trying, in the music of her funeral, to make for her, as my last gift, a place in music where we were both at home. Where we could both be happy. More than happy. Where we could both be exalted. Where we could both be the best we might have been, far better than we were. I may very well have failed her once again.

But the music! The music was wonderful. It enabled me to weep. I did not weep at all learning of her death. But I wept when I heard the music. When the music came, I missed her. I wanted her singing, beside me once again.

My Mother *and Her Sisters*

The five of them: the Gagliano sisters. Called until their deaths "the Gagliano girls." I am looking at a formal portrait of them, a photograph taken, it must be, in the 1940s. The three eldest stand in the back, the two youngest in front of them. I try to look at them as a stranger might. This one has cruel eyes, I say; or, How that one has suffered. But that is a foolish enterprise, a false one. They are my mother and my aunts. They have marked my life. They are the female line from which I sprang.

In the photograph, not one of them looks happy. Were they happy women? Would they have said of themselves, "I am a happy woman"? Or "I have always been an unhappy woman"? No, that is not the way any of them would have talked. They did not believe that it was theirs to talk about themselves. They weren't given to introspection; they prided themselves on "not dwelling on things."

They believed in fate, but not in understanding it. No, I don't think they much believed in happiness. Only when the two of them who took to alcohol had drunk too much did they complain. Then they were full of bitterness. Then, of their memories, none were happy.

Handsome, all of them; that is the word that you would use, not "beautiful" but "handsome." Broad shoulders, strong, outstandingly strong teeth. None of them went to her grave (they are all in graves now) having worn dentures. And only one died young, if you consider sixty young. The rest of them led long lives. For the four who died not young: not a good death among them. These formidable women ought to have aged in the way we expect the strong, the healthy, the formidable to age: like great trees, flourishing, then, one day, suddenly struck down. But that was not the way it was; they disintegrated, each of them, a slow, excruciating, long decay.

They are the daughters of immigrants—their father Sicilian, their mother Irish—but there is nothing ethnic- or exotic-looking about them. I guess it is their hair: there's nothing archaic about their hair, bobbed, waved, pompadoured; it's modern hair, American hair. One of them with something on the crown of her head: a ribbon, an ornament? And their clothing: my mother and her sister Lil with appliqués, inserts between the breast and shoulders; my aunt Rita, a row of severe pleats; the youngest, Tiny, in a sailor blouse. And Marie, in the middle—if you look closely, the hem is uneven, as if it was kept up by tape, as if, any moment, it might (the shame for the daughter of a master seamstress) unravel before our eyes.

What can we learn from their names: Anna, Marie, Lilian, Rita, Christine? Serious names, good Catholic names. All named after saints or after the Lord himself, except for one. There is no St. Lilian. Was she named after Lillian Russell, the Gilded Age singer, for whom my grandmother sewed elaborate leg-o'-mutton sleeves, for which she was famous? As if to compensate, she was, at baptism, given three names, Lilian Rose Martha. She was considered the frivolous one of the bunch, the fun-loving one. Was it because she was not named for a saint? And Christine was called always Tiny, pronounced "Teenie." When she left home, she insisted that her new friends call her Chris.

As I look at the photograph, the five of them seem to beg for allegory; they are yearning to be made, at my hands, into types. So they must be: my mother, Anna, always the eldest; Marie, the musical one; Lil, the glamour girl; Tiny, the baby. And Rita: with her cutting tongue, the one of whom everyone was afraid.

My mother was not really the oldest child in the family; she was the oldest daughter. Born before her was her brother Joe, really named Santo, so he signed his name for the rest of his life "S. Joseph Gagliano" and had it legally changed to "Samuel Joseph." Quite early, he cut and ran from the family, marrying young, a Protestant whom everyone seemed to accept readily; she seemed universally loved; she died young. He was said to be handsome and cruelly witty. My mother would recount a joke he made at her expense at a party when they were both in high school. "This guy said my sister Anna wasn't fit to live with the pigs, and I said she was too."

But Joe took no responsibility for the family and its welfare, and so my mother took the place of the oldest son. From the time she began working, when she was seventeen, she turned her paycheck in its entirety over to her mother every week. She paid the family mortgage, and financed the education of her two sisters in nursing school and her two brothers in college. This was considered ordinary; no one seemed to think it at all worthy of comment, or thanks. Later, when the family fell apart, it was my mother's largest source of aggrievement, drunken rage.

The sons were not asked to pose for a formal portrait. Perhaps because of the four sons, only two came regularly to family functions. My uncle Joe absented himself deliberately, and my uncle Anthony lived in Philadelphia, which was considered far away. But in the family, there was a great show of pretending men were important, although it was very well understood that all power rested in the women.

Despite everything she did for him, my mother was not her father's favorite. This distinction went to Marie, because she had the best singing voice. She was also considered the most beautiful, although, looking at the photograph, I don't see why. Can it be that she was the only one of them with blue eyes? Of the five of them, I had least to do with her.

It is difficult for me to imagine for any of them a girlhood, but it is the most difficult for me to imagine one for Marie. When I think of her now, the first thing I think of is her varicose veins. Really dramatic: her calves embossed with hard bumps the size of cherries, so that she always looked diseased, and I was frightened, because we shared blood (I would not then have known the category DNA) and one day my smooth legs might be diseased like hers. She made no attempt to cover them up; she always wore socks, rather than stockings (perhaps stockings were painful for her), and white nurse's shoes. I never saw her wear any other kind of shoes.

Should I have read these shoes as a sign of her despair? Her legs were more upsetting to me, almost, than my mother's crippled ones: at least my mother tried, for a while, for style. But Marie never dressed up. Never made an effort. No visible depression: only an icy coldness. Silent, rather. You were afraid, though, when she opened her mouth, that what would come out would not be good. She was meant to have "a dry sense of humor." She was never without a cigarette.

Born in 1912, she was thus a high-school girl then in the late twenties, but by the time she was ready to enter the world, the Depression had struck. If I think of her as a type, a character in history, a character in fiction, I can become sympathetic. The real woman could never have been made sympathetic. For those of my aunts whom I dislike, it is the case no doubt that if I were writing them as fictional characters I would be more sympathetic, more merciful. But I cannot, in real life, because of how they hurt my mother. And there was nothing I could do to protect her, and I could see that because of them my mother, my beautiful high tree, was destroyed. It was their hatred, their disdain, that destroyed her. There is nowhere else to lay it but at their feet.

But suppose I think of them not as my mother's cruel sisters but as themselves, as women with a youth, as women who suffered and experienced loss, as women of the thirties, the forties, born before or during the First World War, living through the Second, and then Vietnam? Let me begin, then, with my aunt Marie: a character in fiction, or in history. The star of her own biography, not a minor character in my mother's life. Mine.

I will think of her as Marie, born in 1912, before the First World War, starting high school in 1925 or '26: a good time to be starting high school if you are a good-looking girl with stunning blue eyes and a fine singing voice, a well-turned ankle, tall for your time (but not for ours). She is a basketball star, and an outstanding dancer, practicing with her sister Lil in the living room the latest dance steps, the Charleston, the Black Bottom, the Peabody. She comes of age in the late twenties, but she is not a flapper; no, she is too large-boned, too deliberate, too law-abiding to be that. Serious, in some way, so she trains to be a nurse, trains in a Catholic hospital—Mary Immaculate, it is called, in Jamaica, Queens.

And then what happens? She might be expected to make, if not a brilliant, then a solidly successful marriage. Prosperity might be expected to be hers. But she marries for love, she marries for music, a handsome man, perhaps a bit beneath her socially, but his voice is wonderful and he has beautiful hair and a heart-melting smile, and he is passionate and generous and kind, especially to children. Buddy is his name, though his real name is Harold. Harold Hoffman (but no one ever calls him that). At twenty-six, late for the time, they marry. And then: children, five almost in a row. Impossible any longer to think of her as any kind of girl.

The children are all musical, like the girl her father loved her for being. But the real musical talent comes from Buddy's family: his father played with John Philip Sousa, I never knew what instrument—something in the brass family.

One of the things I believe to be most true of family life, whether it is a single mother and her child or a huge extended family, is that the family believes certain habits, practices, to be ordinary, whereas they are easily seen by the outside to be odd, inexplicable, even insane. The musical events at my aunt Marie's house were not insane, but it is hard to recall now why they happened so often. They didn't seem to be connected to an occasion. We didn't go to Marie's for holidays—Christmas, Thanksgiving, Easter were at my grandmother's, and my aunt Lil did Memorial Day, Fourth of July, and Labor Day. I don't remember birthday celebrations: no candles being blown out, no slices of cake on paper plates. Marie was famous for not cooking well—another of life's pleasures, like self-adornment, that she had given up—so my memories of the food she served seem to focus on potato salad, macaroni salad, coleslaw—all store-bought, something my grandmother would have considered a minor scandal, although it was a sign of Marie's power, her authority within the family, that no one criticized her, everyone abashed into silence by her famous silences, her famous cold blue-eyed stare.

Marie's house was one of the most uncomfortable I have ever been in. The hallway separating the living room from the rest of the house was nothing but a large heating grate; often it became so hot that you had to hop across it. I don't remember any of the furniture as being upholstered—although there was a couch we sat on, so it must have been—and the couch was uncomfortable, and I remember believing—although this might have been my invention—that it was made of horsehair and that this accounted for its discomfort. Mostly we were crowded—there were eight or ten adults and perhaps fifteen children in a small room; adults took turns sitting, children stood or sat on the floor. There the Hoffmans performed: Chris played the piano, Chopin polonaises, I remember, and something called, excitingly to me, "Marche Militaire." The boys seemed to know an endless number of instruments and to be able to move with perfect ease from Beethoven to Irving Berlin—later, a bit daringly, including what the family called "jazz." Chris, the oldest daughter, was much praised for downplaying her abilities as a soloist to accompany her brothers and her father when they sang or played the clarinet or trumpet or whatever it was. I remember admiring her for her modesty at first, but wishing I could hear her play more of her exciting arpeggios, her romantic trills.

The rest of us, the other cousins, were given music lessons, but we all understood that we were asked to play either as a courtesy or as a foil, a way of pointing out the real musical superiority of the Hoffmans. We were all collected to provide an audience, and we were happy to do it, because they were good-natured in their performance, they accepted performing for the family as their lot in life, a task, like making the beds or setting the table, something untaxing and mildly pleasant.

Did anyone think of how the cousins who were there only to be foils might have suffered from all this? I suffered in a way that I think might have been good for me: it was one of the ways in which I learned the difference between the real thing, the true valuable thing, the precious thing, and the merely acceptable. My piano performance was acceptable; but my mediocre skill could be made up for by my playing *molto espressivo*. But my most beloved cousin, Peppy, two years older than I, my aunt Lil's son, who had neither talent nor a mother who forced him to practice, was made a fool of at each of these events when he continued to play "Für Elise" year after year, and everyone (twenty perhaps, sitting, standing, leaning against the doorjambs) would laugh. A few years ago, he told me that every time he went home after one of these events he cried himself to sleep, but he would never have told anyone, because being able to endure family ridicule was considered an important sign of character.

Marie's two oldest sons were nine and ten years older than I, and handsome in a Nordic way that was unusual in the family— they had their mother's blue eyes and their father's German fairness—and I found them very glamorous. Particularly the younger of the two, the one who daringly introduced jazz into the family setting. He had curly reddish-gold hair and a confident smile that made a mockery of good behavior—the only one in the family who would have allowed such daring into his smile. I remember one year—he was eighteen, I think, so I would have been nine—he brought his girlfriend to one of these musical events. They were the golden couple of 1958. He couldn't have been wearing a white dinner jacket, but in my mind he is—or maybe he was, because they might have been on their way out to a dance, his prom or hers; I remember exactly how she was dressed. It took my breath away. The ideal of young glamour, straight from the movies, had been brought into our family domain—as if Gidget had appeared to show us one of her dresses before a dance. She was wearing a turquoise chiffon dress with what was called a trapeze. Her high heels were white pumps (permissible: it was summer). Her hair was a stiff, perfect flip. The sharp, focused light on the piano could not stay away from the flecks of gold in the stiff helmet of her hair, and her eyes seemed gold to me; they were pointed, amber-colored, like those of a sleepy, benevolent cat who would curl up in your lap at a moment's notice.

My cousin and his girlfriend were in the music room to show us their new dance routine—some version of the Lindy or the jitterbug: it was too early for unpartnered dancing. My cousin Chris played the piano. The dancers had only a few feet to move in, but they were perfect in their steps, and when he twirled her, the trapeze at the back of her dress, which was attached to the hem, flared and was lifted to the limits of its attachment, like a contained sea wave. I was overwhelmed; I lost myself in the perfection, the desirability of the moment. Abject, abashed, in my cotton skirt and short-sleeved cotton shirt, my white anklets, my flat, round-toed shoes, my long severe braid, my dormant sexless body, I reached out to touch the trapeze, as a scrofulous peasant might have reached out to touch the king to be healed. She brushed my hand off—she was very nice, as well as being magically pretty, so I'm sure she didn't mean to humiliate me, the brush-off was a natural response to an unnatural act—and I sat back on the floor as if my hand had been burned.

I discovered that, forty-five years later, when they were both in their sixties, my cousin's ex-girlfriend contacted him. She was wheelchair-bound: some kind of degenerative disease, it might have been multiple sclerosis. She told him that her husband was abusive, kept her virtually as a prisoner, and that she was afraid. He left his family in Arizona, got on a plane to New York, spirited her away from her brutal husband, and moved in with her to an apartment, vowing to care for her for the rest of her life. The brutal husband accused him of kidnapping, and, somehow (the details are vague), she went back to her husband and he to his wife. I think this is a very sad story. I don't know anything about my cousin's wife, but it could have been just like *An Affair to Remember* if my cousin had devoted himself to his first love, the girl with the gold flecks in her hair and eyes, the girl in turquoise-colored chiffon, rather than his lawful partner. When he apologized to her, the wife, she is reported to have said, "All right, but don't let it happen again."

The musical events at Marie's house lasted a long time; I think they began with lunch and they continued long past dinner. The nice part of the evening came last, when my uncle Buddy would play his guitar and sing. From him I learned what a real voice was, a voice that could heal and comfort and inspire. His songs were deliberately archaic: songs from the twenties or even before,

"Somebody Stole My Gal," "I Want a Girl (Just Like the Girl That Married Dear Old Dad)," and—from some dream that seems from a Willa Cather novel, perhaps taught him by his German forebears who'd lived in the Midwest—"The Hills of Home." When he sang it, I always saw gentle hills covered with new greenery, inviting the weary traveler to partake of a kind of sweetness, a sweetness without judgment, without irony, inaccessible to anyone part of my family since birth. He was a nice man, my uncle Buddy, but he would get very agitated in traffic; when he drove us children anywhere, we knew we had to sit in silence. Even a suppressed giggle could set him off.

If Marie's children made the whole of my generation abashed, knowing ourselves to be visible failures, she abashed her sisters by being the one mother whose children entered religious orders. Three of them: the girl, entering the Immaculate Heart of Mary sisters in Scranton, Pennsylvania; one son entering the Marianist Brothers Novitiate in Mount Marcy, New York, north of Albany; and, briefly, the golden son entering the preparatory monastery of the same order, when he was still in high school. These were the days before the Second Vatican Council brought about liberal reforms in the orders: in those days, you expected that when you sent your children away they would not ever visit the family home; they would be visited in their semi-sacred habitats, and only rarely. We made pilgrimages to visit them—a large cohort of us, aunts, uncles, cousins.

We were not a family who took vacations, so, for us children, it was our first time in a hotel. Three or four carloads of us would drive in caravan through the Holland Tunnel, then south through Jersey and across Pennsylvania. We made only one stop: at the Hackettstown Diner in Hackettstown, New Jersey, where we got the best hamburgers I've ever had. This was the first time I ate onion on a hamburger. It seemed a very adult thing to do, willingly taking on that sharpness, and I exulted in the mix of tastes: the salty flesh, the sweet-sour catsup, the onion that burned and did not burn my tongue.

We stayed always in the Hotel Casey in Scranton, piling into three rooms like Okies: the children sharing beds with their parents, or doubling up on cots. The hotel corridors were grander than the rooms, and my cousins and I would walk up and down them and climb up and down the wide staircases, just for the pleasure. I remember that, from the hotel window, our view was of a large mountain of coal, which I found alarming, and which suggested to me the apocalyptic words in the Gospel of Mark: "the abomination of desolation." It was desolate in its unadorned, sheer minerality, a black pyramid there only to be consumed, to be fed into a large inferno where the flesh of children (teeth, bone, clothing) would be entirely eaten up. And yet it was the sign to me of a kind of dull, Protestant wealth, a wealth without glamour, without the appetite for luxury or even ornament; it was like a hill of black money that refused to bring the slightest joy.

But the convent, its beautiful high trees with their generous leaves; the polished wood, floors and banisters gleaming like tawny satin; the nuns, mostly young, it seemed, in their gradated habits. Postulants were without a veil, dressed as nineteenth-century bluestockings in their ankle-length black skirts that made too much of their shoes. The novices wore the long habit but white rather than black veils, separating them from the professed (real) nuns, whose veils were black. Young women, choosing to keep themselves from the world, with their new vocabularies— refectory, porteress, compline—and rooms that had names we had only read: "parlor," "vestibule," now spoken as if they were part of our world. I dreamed of it for myself: my face framed by the veil, walking quietly, my hands tucked modestly into my sleeves, my eyes lowered; everyone coming to visit me, staying in a hotel ("I don't even want to tell you what they're charging").

When we visited the boys, I found the situation much less glamorous. The trees were pine, the floors linoleum. We were allowed to eat with the boys; we were encouraged to bring them food. We stayed in a motel; no corridors to explore, no staircases to imagine ourselves grand on. And the boys wore their own clothes:

black pants and some kind of sport shirt. And they were about to be brothers, not even real priests. Secretly, although I couldn't share this with anyone, I found the whole enterprise, in comparison with the convent, decidedly second-rate.

But none of that affected my aunt Marie's stature. There were pictures of the three children who had left the house to serve the Church, framed in velvet, on top of the piano, as if they had already died and were awaiting beatification. It is gone now, entirely, from the world, the luster that attached to a family who had "given children to God." Nothing had more prestige: going to Harvard, becoming a doctor, making a million dollars, all those signs legible to ordinary Americans as a proof of success, seemed paltry and superficial compared with the honor of having a son or daughter in the religious life. Did my other aunts question one another? Why had Marie succeeded so brilliantly in sending THREE of her children into the Church? What had been the shape or texture of their inadequacy?

But you see, like her beauty, like her music, her prestige as a mother of religious didn't last. All three of them came home again—the older two not of their own volition. My cousin with the golden girl—he left because he wanted the greater world. But the older two were found unworthy. It was never discussed, so none of us knew why. But, though no one ever spoke of it, the residue of their rejection clung to their skin like a mild disfigurement, not disabling enough to render them unfit for human eyes or human company, but they had lost their sheen. They were only like the rest of us. Maybe a little less, because of what they'd lost.

Somehow, Marie's life dribbled away, from enviableness to nothing much. I lose track of her; I don't invite her to the parties for my high-school graduation, or my college graduation, or to either of my weddings, or to my children's christenings, nor does she send me, on any of those occasions, even a card. When she is in her sixties, her brain hardens, crumbles. She becomes an old woman who wanders the streets. Buddy, who loved her so that he would grab her in company and kiss her, hard, on the cheek, forcing her to say "you pest," the husband with the beautiful hair, the beautiful voice, the heart-melting smile, lives in agony because she slips out of the house, determined to wander the streets. He cannot care for her; he too is no longer young. She is put somewhere, and she dies, and I do not know the details, and I do not make an effort to find them out.

Now I will speak of Tiny, the baby, with the joke name. Of the five only two are given nicknames: Lilian is always called Lil, and Christine is Tiny to the family, beloved as apart from them, spared certain things by virtue of being younger, the first girl after two boys. Treasured, cosseted, by her older brother Ned, who adores her. My uncle Ned: much more maternal than any of his sisters. A caretaker—born or made? Someone had to nurture in that family, someone had to take care. It fell to him. I don't know if he chose it.

The family likes telling the story of his devotion. When Tiny was very young, maybe three, my grandmother had put a strawberry shortcake, covered with whipped cream, on top of a dresser to keep it out of reach. Tiny stood on a chair to lick at the edges of the whipped cream, but somehow pulled the cake down so that it fell on her, and her face was covered with whipped cream. Her older brother, seeing her tears, her abashment, made a joke of it— licked the whipped cream off her face so that her tears turned to laughter, and convinced her (convincing his mother too?) that she would not be punished, that what she thought was a tragedy was, in fact, a joke.

Was he trying to tell her that it would be like that, he would see to it that it would be like that for her, there would be no tragedies, only jokes in disguise? His littlest sister, Tiny. But she will bury the name, claiming adulthood for herself when she marries, the real American marriage, the movement out and up. Tiny is, like Marie, a nurse; they are able-bodied and so can be nurses, and they are intelligent, and work is respected in that family, certain kinds of work. People say that I look like her, but it's not true, it's that they can't bear the idea that I look like my father, that I look like a Jew. And I do not want to look like her: her breasts are too large, her eyes are too mocking; she pretends to be the easygoing mother of five sons, but I know that she is cruel; she has been cruel to me. Of the five sisters, three had a gift for cruelty and nurtured it; the other two suffered too much—unarmored by cruelty, they turned to drink. Tiny would never turn to drink; she would never be excessive; she would never appear unseemly, out of control. She had a certain admirableness, a certain bent for heroism, tied to cruelty; so that I am afraid, as a woman, both to be admirable and not to be admirable. To be admirable is to be cruel, harsh; to be unadmirable is to deliquesce before the eyes of everyone. The world.

She moves away, she moves farther away from her mother than any of them. First Baltimore, then upstate New York. Does she mean to, want to? She is the only one with a rural life.

Did she think to herself that she was freeing herself of certain formalities, certain preoccupations with time-consuming niceties, certain concerns with the way things had to be? Her house was newer than any of the houses the rest of us lived in. I remember, the first time we went to visit her in upstate New York, the Thruway was newly built, and bordering the side of the road were hills of red dirt that made the whole enterprise seem provisional: at once exciting and unsafe, as if perhaps the asphalt wasn't quite dry yet, and our cars would fall through, be sucked up, disappear.

Athletics were important to the family, more important than music, and she married into an athletic family and produced five outstandingly athletic sons. Her husband's brother played for the Yankees, then the Kansas City Athletics, then the Mets. We would listen to the games on the radio; later, we would watch them on the television, feeling we had no choice but to root for his team: clearly we had a stake in it. When I tell some men friends of mine that I had an ancillary relative who played for the Yankees in the fifties, it is as if I told them I had secretly been connected to royalty, or had discovered that Fred Astaire was my uncle, Greta Garbo my aunt. They are appalled and amazed that the connection never meant a thing for me.

So she is living in the country, in her new house, where the wood seems not quite finished and the paint not quite dry. She has her five sons. Two nights a week, she works in the pediatric ward of the hospital. She buys enormous amounts of groceries; when I visit her, I am astounded at the number of brown bags she takes out of her station wagon. She is the only one in the family with a station wagon. She drives through snow in it, to Sunday Mass in a church that also seems, in its newness, not quite authentic to me, not quite the real thing.

She and her husband buy a property in the Adirondacks: a ruined estate that belonged to a man whose name I remember because it seemed so elegant to me, such a promise of artistic Europe: Angelo Patri. Was he really a sculptor or have I invented that? How did he manage to have this estate, many acres of land with five houses built on it, large houses, each large enough for a family? They had names: the Beta, the Traveller, the Casa Mia, known as "the Caz." With my uncle Ned (the uncle who adored his little sister, Tiny) and his wife, Tiny and her husband start a camp for boys in the Adirondacks. The only real contact I have with her is in the summers: we are allowed to stay in one of the lesser houses for a week. When she comes to my grandmother's house for holidays, there is always a crowd, and we have no real interest in each other, so we pay no attention to each other. Except that I am impressed, because, of all the aunts, she is the only one to wear spike heels. Because of her shortness: part of the joke of her name.

She lives only two hours away from my grandmother but visits only twice a year. She and my mother seem to have very little connection: my mother is the oldest, and not much interested in sports. But when my parents married, much to my grandparents' distress she took my mother's side. She wrote my mother a letter, telling her my mother had her support. The vain, smug busyness of the letter-writing mother: "Must close now. Paul is in my arms and beginning to squirm."

The summer of 1958, eighteen months after my father's death, I am, at her suggestion, sent to spend July and August at the camp. The lake on which the camp is situated is called, improbably, Paradox Lake, and the Paradox is that I am entirely miserable there, although it is a beautiful place, with hints of grandeur, elegance, even magic (there are shrines in the woods, a perpetually icy spring where the family's wine and beer are set to cool). The lake is beautiful, surrounded by mountains, the water cold and pure and wonderful to swim in, and I do learn to swim there, and I love swimming, but I am miserable, as miserable there as at any place I have ever been. I have lost my father; not lost, he has been taken from me. I am bereft. I am the only girl. I sleep in a double bed with my grandmother, who is the camp cook. Tiny is the camp nurse; her husband comes on weekends. When he drives up, she runs to greet him, jumps into his arms. I am thrilled and impressed; no one else in the family indulges in that kind of marital exhibit. Not in public. Even my parents had more reserve.

Perhaps my lifelong aversion to anything that falls under the category "boy" began here, at this camp, a boys' camp, a disastrous place for me. I never had anything about me of the tomboy, or even the androgyne, so to be extracted from the world of the female was terrible in this period of mourning. Even now, the smell of pine creates in me a rebellious feeling: as if I will have to assert my rights, to dream, to read the books I want to read. At the camp I learn for the first time that some books are not interesting: *The Last of the Mohicans*. For the first time, there is a book I cannot finish. In one of the houses where parents occasionally stay, someone has left some old *Good Housekeepings*, *Ladies' Home Journals*. I moon over the picture on the back cover of the Breck Girl: I moon over access to female life. But I am supposed to find a place for myself in boy's life. A category that I simultaneously find extremely boring and yet am hurt by, because it insists upon excluding me. Because I am not a camper, not a boy, I am excluded from the boys' activity: their games, their arts and crafts. But that is all right; I have no desire to be among them—their interest in violence, sports, and shit. The plumbing is inadequate, and I am always afraid of coming upon some boy's shit improperly flushed. Once, a kind of joke they pulled on one another, I find some turds left outside the house where the boys sleep, left overnight, then rained on, claylike; I am horrified; and for a while I wonder if the shit of boys is always claylike, whitish, unalive. They seem to think a lot about shit. They accuse my dog of shitting on the baseball field, and they make fun of me when I insist that it isn't him, because his shit—I wouldn't have called it shit, I would have said his BMs or his number-twos—is not that color. But I know that I'm right, that my dog has been falsely accused, like me is innocent. They love laughing at shit, and they seem to love punching each other, and one night they carry my dog into the kitchen when I'm playing cards with my grandmother and say he's been hit by a car and he's paralyzed now, and when I begin crying, they put him down on the floor and he runs around and they laugh: why can't I take a joke?

I no longer know how to laugh. I am grief-stricken; I am a person in mourning. My grief paralyzes me. No one knows that I am not really there, that I am pretending to be alive but am really dead, in the land of the dead, with my father. They know something is wrong: I'm not *with it*. I am not cheerful. My aunt Tiny dislikes it very much that I am not cheerful. Not cheerful, therefore not grateful for this gift of a summer in the mountains, away from the smelly sidewalks and the heat. But I long only for my mother. Each day I cry in secret, but Tiny knows, she knows, and it annoys her. She buys me a postcard of Alfred E. Neuman from *Mad* magazine with his idiotic gap-toothed grin. Underneath it are printed the words "Keep smiling." She tapes it up beside my bed. When I am caught crying, she castigates me. She tells me to toughen up. She tells me not to be so sensitive. Even my grandmother knows she has gone too far. My grandmother, usually austere, judging, cold, says to her youngest daughter, "Leave her alone. Can't you tell her little heart is broken?" My aunt is angry with her mother for having taken the part of a child. An ungrateful child. A child who insists on mourning when she could be breathing fresh air, swimming in the lake, making lanyards. I am miserable, but I learn something very important, that it will be one of the important jobs of my life to honor mourning. To acknowledge that the work of mourning is an honorable job, to insist that its wages be paid, that it be given its due. I never forgive my aunt, I cannot forgive her still, for insisting that I weep in secret, as if it were a cause for shame.

Something terrible happens on that property on the shore of that lake inexplicably named Paradox. My uncle Ray, my aunt Tiny's husband, is on the property with his son in late September, closing up for the season. He is tying up the boats at the shore of the lake. A branch falls from a tree. It hits him on the spine. His son, who is only fourteen, has to get him into the car, and although he doesn't know how to drive, has to teach himself how to drive, out of the woods, up the hill, to get help. When it is spoken of, the same words are always used: a freak accident. The branch was not unusually large, but hit him in exactly the place on his spine so that he will be paralyzed from the waist down, and his mind will be affected. A large man, for the rest of his life he will be a baby my aunt has to tend. But for some years he is put in a rehabilitation hospital in Haverstraw, New York, where he is in bed all the time, and it is the site of another family pilgrimage (Marie's children are no longer in their convent, their monasteries), so on many Sundays the whole family drives up to Rockland County, and we sit on chairs at the side of his bed and make that horrible small talk one makes at bedsides. But he is not dying, and we look for signs of a miracle cure. Once, my aunt Rita leans by mistake against his leg and convinces herself that his leg moved when she leaned on it, and we believe that a miracle has occurred, that he will be walking soon, but it was not a miracle, it was a mistake: he never walks again.

My aunt Tiny is heroic. She raises her five children. She visits her husband. Eventually, because she is a nurse, she is able to take him home, and for many years, she nurses her invalid husband, her husband with the soft brain of a damaged child, the husband whose arms she ran to, whom she kissed publicly, the father of her five handsome, athletic sons. She feeds him and diapers him like a baby, and she works full-time as a nurse and sends all her handsome sons to college, except for the oldest one, who was with his father during the accident, who will not go to college, will not speak to people, will not shave his beard.

She is helped by a friend, a man, younger than she, who lives with his mother and is devoted to her. This goes on for many years, until Ray dies, and she marries the other man and is able to be ordinary again, and work only part-time, see her grandchildren, and be known as Chris.

We had become neighbors after I married—not near neighbors, but we lived in the same part of the world, the Hudson Valley, both of us having moved there, Tiny in 1954, me in 1974, because of our husbands' jobs, hers at IBM, mine at the State University of New York. Was it only twenty years that separated our moves as new brides? Twenty years in which the world became unrecognizable to itself.

My new husband and I go to her house for dinner. Her house is ugly, unadorned, and overlarge. The furniture is uncomfortable. Why did my two aunts who were nurses pride themselves on uncomfortable furniture? I think she served the food on paper plates or plastic plates; I think it may have been defrosted rather than cooked for us. She prided herself, as well as on her uncomfortable furniture, on having given up her mother's domestic thralldom.

She is cold; she does not even pretend to like me. Her husband is kind but doesn't know what to say; perhaps he senses the tense, drawn cord between us, a cord woven of mutual contempt, mutual judgment. I fear her cold eyes, her fortified breasts, her prominent teeth, her hair that reminds me of a country-Western singer, that tough look (where did it come from, like Loretta Lynn but bustier?). She has been through a lot; it shows. I would like to tell her I do not forgive her for forbidding me to weep the summer after my father's death, for hanging the face of Alfred E. Neuman beside my bed. I want to say: Now that we are both adults, I want you to understand that I understand very well that it is wrong for an adult to be cruel to a child, as you were to me. But I say nothing; I say very few words that night.

In the car on the way home, I weep enraged hot tears like a child. My husband doesn't understand. It was a long time ago, a very long time, he says. It's all over now. You've left that world, all those people, for good. They have no hold on you any more.

He is a social scientist, born Protestant, turned atheist. Therefore, he believes in progress, that things can be left for good. He thinks my tears are an affectation, an aberration. He insists, like my aunt, that they stop.

I do not sleep with him that night. I write the first real story of my life. About the summer after my father's death. After this, I write less and less poetry. I feel called to story now; I rename my vocation in this way.

The last conversation I had with Tiny took place in my kitchen. We were waiting for my mother, who was driving up to Poughkeepsie from New York City to visit me. She was uncharacteristically late. I was unwrapping cheese and cold cuts and putting them on plates.

Tiny's eyes fell on a plate; they grew focused, punitive, as if there were something hateful about the meat and cheese.

"Your mother always thought she had more right to things than the rest of us. She didn't let us into her things. Like, when her bridge club met at our house, she'd buy cold cuts for them, expensive cold cuts, like we would never have for ourselves, us kids, and she wouldn't let us have any. 'Don't touch those, they're for my bridge club,' she would say. Our mouths were watering, but she didn't care."

I put the knife down on the counter, because I was afraid of the strong impulse to plunge it deep into my aunt's heart. "What in the name of God are you talking about?" I wanted to say. "My mother gave more than any of the rest of you to the family. She paid for your training and Marie's training in nursing school. She paid her brother's college tuition, the part that wasn't taken care of by scholarships. She paid the mortgage on her parents' house from the time she was twenty-five until the time she married, fourteen years later. She wanted to serve her friends special foods. And you begrudge her that? After fifty years, you still begrudge her that?"

I would have loved to throw her out of my house, to tell her that she was no longer welcome, that she was unworthy of my regard and even my civility, and certainly my mother's loyalty and affection. But I said nothing, because I knew my mother would have been devastated by an open rift with yet another sister, the baby, who had suffered so. I allowed her into my house once after that, another house, another husband, the Christmas after my first baby was born. She gave the baby a very ugly brass Christmas-tree ornament in the shape of a teddy bear with her name and the date of her birth inscribed. Over the years, something has eaten into its surface, so that the polish is degraded, the writing invisible. But I don't throw it away. Because I am afraid of my aunts' coldness, their capacity for punishment, even from the grave. I do not display the damaged ornament, but I keep it, hidden, in the dark, unused.

Soon after that visit, Tiny developed cancer—stomach cancer, the third relative of mine to have succumbed to it, so that I have to check on medical questionnaires a greater vulnerability. And then she died, the first of the sisters, the youngest; the only one not to die in degradation; the most fortunate.

I did not go to her funeral. I don't know what excuse I made to my mother, and, oddly, she didn't press me to go, and we both knew I could easily have gone. Perhaps I said that I had two young children, or that I was traveling for my work: I have the most public career of everyone in the family, and when my mother chose to, she could abash them all with my success. Never did I feel like a better daughter than when I savored on my tongue the bitter taste of that refusal.

I guess my aunt Lil was a silly woman, but I loved her very much; she was the only one of my aunts that I did love, the only one who didn't freeze my heart, the only one of the five with no talent for contempt. When we children were around her, we were happier than we were around anyone else in the family. She could make us forget the family curse, the family judgment. She made us think that it was possible for all of us, any of us, to have fun.

One of her nicknames was "Featherhead." She did not do well in school. Her intellectual failures, combined with the happy fate of her marriage, were for my mother the magnum exemplum of the foolishness of men, a weapon to be used against me, against herself. When I was twelve, she sent me to typing school, because "you're a smart girl, and men don't like smart girls. Look at your aunt Lil. So you better learn to type so you can support yourself, because no man will ever want to marry you."

My mother talked about seeing Lil as a child playing school with strawberry plants and taking a ruler to them. I don't know if she hurt the plants, if she struck them until they bled. I think not. My grandmother wouldn't have stood for that, that waste.

She was, by profession, a beautician. This was a bit shameful in such a serious family, a family that prided itself on its lack of interest in adornment. There was my mother, who worked for a lawyer, who "went to business," who "earned good money." Two were nurses. Rita was a "keypuncher"; she neither made good money nor had an enviable boss, and she kept her salary to herself, but at least there didn't seem to be any pleasure in it, anything lighthearted. It was a form of penance, and that was seen as a good. But Lil, Lil was in the beauty game. Her field was beauty. She did everyone's hair. Including mine. I learned from her, it must have been from her, the pleasure of making up, dressing up, shopping. That the daughter of my mother should enjoy these things is a strange thing, almost a miracle. I owe it to Lil.

She was the first in the family to wear trousers, the first to dye her hair, the only one to make up her eyes. Unlike the others, she would change her hairdos with the fashion: from a Pointer Sisters pompadour in the forties to an Italian boy cut in the fifties, to a Jackie Kennedy bouffant in the sixties. Then she seemed to lose the impulse to change; she kept the bouffant until her death twenty-five years later. She was the only slim one; unlike the others, she was a successful dieter, and the rumor in the family was that she had dieted herself into infertility. The other three who married in a timely fashion (she was the youngest to marry: right after high school, no nurse's training for her, no business school) were models of reproductive virtuosity: Marie and Tiny had five children each, and my mother, married at thirty-nine, had a child (me, the miracle) at forty-one.

Almost as contemptible as the term "featherhead" that was applied to her was the other common family sobriquet: "glamour girl." I always knew that she was glamorous, that she and her husband, my uncle Joe Barquinero, were a glamorous couple. He was from a higher class than she; his father was an engineer, Cuban, an educated man. They were high-school sweethearts; she the champion dancer, he the track star. They were as handsome as movie stars, although his good looks were unstudied and hers were very much a work of art. They were about sex in a way that had more to do with the accessories of sex than with physical passion. They surrounded themselves with the accoutrements of glamour: chrome cocktail shakers, cigarette holders, frosted glasses for cool summer drinks: Tom Collins, sloe-gin fizz. Theirs was the kind of glamour that became, years later, the stuff of camp: stylized, everything made to be in the shape of something else (ashtrays that held cigarettes in birds' beaks, peanut dishes in the shape of peanuts, orange-juice glasses in the shape of oranges, ice buckets embossed with penguins standing in a row). And it seemed to me that that kind of glamour brought with it a kind of freedom I very much wanted for myself, a freedom to ask for, to grasp, pleasure.

In that house, with their son, my beloved cousin Peppy, I laughed and laughed to the point of ecstatic near-sickness. We ate potato chips; we drank soda—there were many flavors, because my uncle Joe—known in the family as "Joe Barky"—worked for White Rock; behind the bar in the basement was a cardboard model of the White Rock Girl, kneeling, bare-breasted (only you couldn't see the breasts), an Art Deco nymph who could slake thirst as if by magic. In the basement refrigerator you could get grape or black cherry or cream or root beer, and, to show their largesse, there was even Coca-Cola, which they didn't get for free. There were chocolates in the shape of stars, there were gumdrops and Jordan almonds. And you could watch television, as much as you wanted; no one would tell you to "turn that thing off" or, like my father, who refused even to have one, suggest that it was bad for you. On Friday nights, we came over to watch *My Friend Irma* and *Our Miss Brooks*. Before "her shows" began, my aunt Lil would do my mother's hair while we kids played in the basement, dressing up in my aunt's old high heels or playing with my cousin's electric trains.

You could never use up the luxury in my aunt Lil's house. You always stopped before you had to—and you didn't have to stop a minute before you were ready. Nothing need be abstained from; nothing need be given up. There was no superiority in unfilled appetite here. No one in that house feared prosperity. The rest of the family felt it was because my aunt just didn't have the sense to. They complained that in that house so many things went to waste. Of all the sisters, my aunt Lil was the only one not plagued by the horror of waste. In order to safeguard against waste, the others were ceaselessly surveillant, and all we children felt our movements frozen and distorted under their surveillant eye, an eye that never closed in rest, or sleep, or ecstasy, but was ever vigilant, ever on guard.

But Lil stood for allowances rather than restrictions. She opened her house as a place where laughter and indulgence were possible. She took me shopping for the dress for my father's funeral, and she paid for it. She gave me my first home permanent, she lent me her mascara (a little brush, a little rectangular slab of black paste) and her eyelash curler, and she showed me how to use them. She sent me to a beauty parlor for the first good haircut of my life. She gave a bridal shower for my first wedding. (Arriving at the end of the shower, my husband-to-be was appalled because the bread was dyed blue and green: the theme colors of the afternoon.) When I got divorced, she said, "It's so exciting. You're getting divorced. Just like the movie stars."

They criticized her vehemently, constantly. But they ate her food and drank her liquor and dressed in her hand-me-downs and never thought to question their right to the enjoyment of things they wouldn't have dreamed of procuring for themselves.

Everything about that house seemed prosperous to me: the white stucco and brown trim (Mock Tudor, though I didn't know the name). Lil and her husband, Joe, were the first to have wall-to-wall carpeting and air conditioning. They were determined to be modern. They wanted to separate themselves from the way of life made manifest by my grandmother's house, a separation unmarked by anger or resentment or revenge, a separation graceful by virtue of their certainty of its rightness. In my grandmother's house, everything referred to the past, everything was difficult to maintain, everything pointed to the virtues of thrift, frugality.

I suppose my aunt Lil had far too many clothes. But she needed them: they were the costumes in the drama she was enacting, a drama of the modern. She was always eager to appear in a uniform, although she had no right to any of them. She sat on the back of a convertible in the Memorial Day parade, waving in a WAC uniform, although she hadn't been in the army, but she was a member of the Ladies Auxiliary of the VFW. And she made them all look good, dressed up and waving. When my cousin became a Cub Scout, she became a den mother, and wore the uniform much more often than she needed to.

She had negligees and satin mules. She had a vanity table, a silver-backed comb, brush, and hand mirror, perfume bottles with rubber atomizers that seemed as if they must be edible, delicious as nougat, or licorice. The two lamps on either side of the vanity mirror had crystal prisms hanging from the edges. The bedroom had wall-to-wall carpeting, dove-colored, and velvety to bare feet. The bedspreads were a silver-colored satin, the color of moonlight falling into a dark lake.

A certain kind of weather always brings me back to that room, a certain kind of coldness on skin cold from summer rain. I don't know why I was changing out of my wet things in my aunt's room. It doesn't make any sense; usually the room was forbidden to us. I must have been ten years old. My body was still a child's but would not be for long. I took my wet bathing suit off and left it on the rug. I dried myself with one of her peach-colored towels that had her initials monogrammed on it in white and navy blue. Then I did something daring to the point of idolatry. How could I have had the courage? If I had been caught, I would have been thought very strange. But I did it. I had to. Somehow the coldness of my skin made me feel that it was of the same material as the moonlight-colored satin. I had to be underneath that satin cover; I had to feel my skin against it. I pulled the cover back—only a little, only enough so I could slip my body in, as if I were slipping a letter into an envelope. And I lay in her bed, and let the moon-colored satin cover me. I stayed for a few seconds, terrified that at any minute she would come in. She never did. And quickly, and as efficiently as a master thief, I pulled the cover up, I took my wet bathing suit from the carpet (it had not left the smallest wet spot), brought my towel into the bathroom, and hung it, neatly, on the rail above the tub. I felt that I had stolen grace; I felt like a clever girl in a fairy tale: the queen in "Rumpelstiltskin" who has saved herself through trickery. Through theft. But what had I saved myself from? What had I stolen? I had saved myself from an unprosperous life. I had stolen prosperity. It had rubbed off on my skin; I could feel the sheen of it. That it happened to be invisible to others was neither here nor there.

Was she really as silly as she seemed? The stories that we loved to tell about her, that my cousin and I still tell, that my children have passed on to their friends, certainly point to a thoroughgoing miscomprehension of the world. There's the story of her response to the Kennedy assassination. We were all sent home early from school, and when my cousin walked in the door, my aunt said, "Sit down, son, I have something terrible to say to you." He thought, "Oh my God, not only has the President been assassinated, my father's had a heart attack." "Something terrible has happened today, son," she said. "Jack Lemmon's been shot." "No, Mother," my cousin said. "It's not Jack Lemmon, it's Jack Kennedy." "I was wondering why everyone was so upset," she said.

There was her inexplicable response when the doctor told her she had to eat more chicken and less beef. "That's impossible," she told him, "because my stomach is shaped like a boot, like the country of Italy." And her remark, after Karen Carpenter's death, "If only she had eaten that ham sandwich instead of Mama Cass, they would both be alive today." When she was introduced to my husband, she fitted a cigarette into a holder she'd bought for the occasion, lit it, and intoned in her best Billie Burke accent, "Tell me, Arthur, for how many years has your mother BEAN in

ORLAHNDO?" When my cousin and I fell on the floor laughing at her, she said, "Well, I was trying to impress him. He's a professor."

But there's the other part of her, which we don't talk about, because we don't like to. Her dark side; her depression, her agoraphobia. A few months after my grandmother died, my aunt developed cancer of the throat. She recovered splendidly, but it changed her. She rarely went out of the house; she made only two trips out each week, to go to church on Sunday and to bowl with her league on Wednesday afternoon. She rarely left her room. She refused to cook; my uncle did everything around the house. They rarely had people in, they who had thrown the famous parties, the Memorial Day picnics, the Fourth of July barbecues. She became, for the rest of her life, frighteningly thin. I think she believed herself at death's door, although she lived another thirty years.

Lurking in the lush, well-cared-for garden of my uncle and aunt's house, there was a snake—a snake who struck and poisoned many of us in the family. I hate thinking about him. I am very glad that he is dead. When he died, my beloved cousin, my aunt Lil's son, sent me a note with the words "You and your children can rest easier now." From him, I learned everything that I would need to know about the hatefulness of men, the frightfulness of men.

George was said to be handsome, but I didn't believe it. He had black wavy hair, like a movie-star gangster; he was well muscled in the torso, short in the legs. A French Canadian. His eyes were full of malice and begrudgement and revenge. When he laughed, it was a snarl or a sneer. He had a cleft chin, like the devil, and one of his teeth was filled with gold, and when he smiled, it flashed dangerous. For special occasions he wore a glen plaid suit; I have forbidden any man who has ever loved me to wear glen plaid. He was a plumber. He liked talking about bodily fluids, bodily products. He liked talking about how he had to hack up my little cousin's shit with an ice pick to get it to flush. He liked to talk about sores filling up with pus, and styes the size of nickels, and people's legs so swollen that they could never walk again. He liked talking about the way his blood spurted when he sliced his finger, and how he had to wear a steel protector over it for what seemed like months and months. He liked to talk about his hypertension.

How did he worm his way into our family? However bad we were, we didn't deserve him. It was through my uncle Joe Barky's kindness; that is the beginning of it, a beginning that is comprehensible, but then it becomes incomprehensible. He rented my uncle's garage, where he parked his truck at night, leaving his car there during the day, picking it up at night and driving it home to the apartment in the next town where he lived with his ancient, tiny mother. When my uncle went away to the war (George was 4-F: hypertension), he asked George to keep an eye on Lil in his absence. I don't even want to speculate on what might have gone on when my beloved, kind uncle was away.

Because there was passion between George and Lil: it took the form of terrible angry fights, screaming fights; he would shout at her, and we children would hide in the basement, knowing it was safe to come up only after we heard his car pull away. What did they fight about? Why was he there every afternoon for twenty-five years, why did Uncle Joe continue to allow him to park his car in the garage, and berate his wife, and shout at her, and frighten the children?

Perhaps even my uncle was abashed by his sheer brute male force. He was brutish—the brutish male. He seemed to have a hold over some women; because of watching this, I knew a certain kind of thing at a very young age about the culpable unwisdom of women, and I vowed that I myself would never be similarly unwise (and I have not been; my mistakes with men have not occurred because I was drawn to the brutish).

I was very young when I realized that he disliked me. He would try to scare me: the kind of thing some adults think is amusing to children, but that is actually terrifying. He would jump out at me from behind doorways; he would try to tickle me. When I saw him coming towards me, I would run behind my father's legs, where I felt safe: he was long-legged, my father, and his long legs made a barrier even George would not breach. I wasn't the only one afraid of him; my beloved cousin's friends refused to come to his house when they saw George's car parked in the driveway.

I knew from a very young age as well that he was very stupid. My revenge against him was to use words he didn't know. There were many to choose from. Once, when he was in one of his rages, I said—to my grandmother, but in his hearing—"Sometimes I think he's schizophrenic." He turned away from my aunt and said, "What the hell do you mean by that? You don't even know what that word means." I did know what it meant, insofar as my information was taken from the popular media of the 1950s. "Yes, I do," I said. "It means you have a split personality. Sometimes you can be very nice and sometimes you can be very angry." I stood my ground against his fuming; when it came to language, I was implacable; it was my fortress, and when I lodged there, no one in the family could hurt me. If there was one thing I was sure of, I was sure of that. Another time, when he was shouting, I said to my mother, "He seems to have lost his equanimity." A word I must have picked up from Louisa May Alcott or a series of books about brave World War I nurses, or perhaps one of the lives of the saints. Once again he accused me of using a word I didn't know, and when I calmly defined it for him, he stormed out of the house and drove away.

The first harm he did us was that he broke up my mother's friendship with her best friend, Kathleen: they started dating, and she abandoned my mother in order to double-date with George and Lil and Joe. He said he couldn't marry her because of his hypertension; in fact, Kathleen was the one who died young, of a heart condition. I think he must have weakened her; I think he wore her out.

And then he courted Rita. And that led to the end of everything for all the sisters.

But what happened to my aunt Lil at the end of her life, I can't blame him for that, much as I would like to, because I hate him and I love her. She did not have a good end, my dear, my most beloved, my silliest aunt. After her husband died, she became more and more withdrawn, more abjectly dependent on her son, whom she tormented by phoning him constantly at work, insisting he come over: she smelled a burning wire, there was a stranger in the yard. Her husband had spoiled her; he had, as my mother said, her jealousy coming out when she was drunk, "waited on her hand and foot." Lil seemed to fade from life, this show-offy, vibrant woman. In her last weeks, she insisted that her son care for her as if she were a baby. She turned her face to the wall. The doctors could not determine a cause of death. Impossible to write on a death certificate: she was tired of living.

Then there was Rita, neither the oldest nor the youngest nor the most beautiful nor the most beloved, Rita, whom I have resisted speaking about but have reconfigured into all the villainous cold-hearted women in my fiction. Yet I have not wished to write about her truthfully, because it has been important for me to retain hatred for her, bitterness, to maintain judgment, superiority, to punish her for the disaster she inflicted on my mother, and so on me. To punish her, in order to prove in writing that something can trump that implacable coldness, that law-abidingness, that vigilance that will not make a mistake and stands silently, not even pointing (which would seem to be a sign of weakness) to the mistakes, the messes of others. I have always known that if I wrote about her childhood I would have to forgive her. And even now I do not wish to forgive. What would be lost if I forgave my aunt? What would be lost if I gave her up as the adamantine model of all that, as a woman, I refused to be?

But then sometimes I thought if I could write about her childhood, if I could describe the sadness, the abandonment, the betrayal of her childhood, I could give up hating her, and this would prove something else about writing: that it could be used to heal, that it is a moral force in an immediate way that I do not for a

moment believe, because I want writing to be somehow unconnected to good behavior, I want it to be irresponsible, as a beautiful
woman is irresponsible in her beauty, as it is not her fault if men
or women fall in love with her, suffer for her, commit crimes for
her sake.

I suppose I am always a child when I am speaking about,
thinking about my aunt Rita—a child who was treated with deliberate cruelty. If I give up being a child, if I acknowledge that her
cruelty did not hurt me in ways that were fatal to my growth and
happiness, I may feel that she had not been punished enough, that
my mother had suffered more at her hands than she had suffered
at mine. And this I do not wish. I will not betray my mother. I will
not leave her unavenged.

But it is impossible not to be shocked, not to be sorrowful at
the betrayal Rita experienced at her own mother's hands as a very
young child, a child the age I was when she was given the opportunity to practice her cruelties on me. For, if I am honest, I must say
that what happened to her was much, much worse than what she
did to me. Like my mother, she contracted polio as a young child.
Terrible to think of: three of my grandmother's children were
stricken with polio, my mother and my aunt severely, my uncle
Pete's case rather mild.

But only Rita was sent away from home. From the age of six to
the age of twelve, she was sent to a school for crippled children—
as my mother was not. What was in my grandmother's mind, to
make this decision—for it was not the kind of thing my grandfather would have had any say about? To send her child for years to
the other end of Long Island, where she would see her family only
on Sunday afternoons, when they came for a visit, the car loaded
down with whichever brothers or sisters there was room for that
week, and baskets and baskets of food. Was my grandmother's
decision to send her child away simply the immigrant's inability to
say no to the possibility of a better life for her child, an opportunity
not to be passed up? And for free! They were being offered something for nothing. My aunt would be trained, educated by nuns,

French nuns—and for the Irish, the French, unlike the English, were the benchmark of civilization. Civilization that was Catholic to its bones, but prosperous, unlike the Irish version, and with more possibility for worldly success. Perhaps it was suggested she would be given the best possible medical attention for free. Whatever it was, she was sent away.

The training that the nuns gave her was, as far as I could see, nothing but a training in fanatical cleanliness—an insistence on obsessive, ferocious, punitive cleaning that searched out each speck of dust as if it were the devil itself, his minion or his sign. The only story I know about the school points to this obsession, obsession to the point of grotesque cruelty. The nuns tied rags on the bottom of the crippled children's feet so that, since they shuffled when they walked, they could be always polishing the highly waxed floors. Rita told that story as an example of efficiency, a kind of thrift. But I heard the story, even at a very young age, as a horror tale—more horrifying because I seemed to be the only one who thought it so.

I don't know much about Rita's young womanhood. She left the school for crippled children; she went to the same public high school her siblings went to. She had a series of jobs that, unlike my mother's, had no whiff of romance about them. She worked for a company that made the parts for oil burners, then as a key-punch operator for a firm that had something to do with advertising, something to do with publishing; one of the perks of her job was that she could get Reader's Digest Condensed Books at a discount price. Perhaps this is another reason for her bitterness. Not only did my mother seem a more romantic figure than she, but she had no place in the family iconography. My mother had her admirable boss and her admirable friendships with priests and her admirable ability to keep the family afloat; Marie was musical, and Lil was glamorous, and Tiny was the baby. But what did Rita have? Perhaps she held on to the power to make everyone afraid because all other gifts had been denied her.

So she became famous for being fastidious and thrifty. I know from my mother that, unlike my mother, who turned her weekly paycheck over to her mother, Rita was allowed to keep her salary for herself. She bought herself a new car, a black 1954 Chevrolet; she was the only one in the family not to buy used. The only new furniture in the house was hers, light-gray deal to match the light-gray linoleum, so that her bedroom always seemed icy to me, uncomfortable, challenging rather than conducive to rest. She was generous to her nephews; she liked playing tricks with them. She would pile four or five of them in the car and then say, when they were stopped in traffic, "I'll pretend to beat you, and you pretend to cry, and let's watch the people's faces." What could she have been thinking of? Was it that she viewed most of the world as, if not enemies, at least fair game for mockery? Most of her joys were rooted in contempt.

She preferred boys to girls because she said they didn't mind being teased, they weren't (my besetting sin) "so sensitive." So she indulged her nephews; she bought them sporting equipment, and she took them out for ice cream. When my aunt Tiny's husband was hurt, she visited them every weekend. I remember her saying that one weekend she took every comb in the house and soaked it in a solution of water and baking soda. She was very proud of that. She would pass her nephews the occasional dollar bill, rolled up in her fist like something dirty. Her nieces, she seemed to imagine, had no need of her indulgence. Or perhaps we were no fun.

But her most striking indulgence was that she bought herself a mink coat. She did this after she had been chosen as a contestant on a TV show called *The Big Payoff*, where the prize (which she did not win) was a mink coat, modeled by Bess Myerson. The format of the show, from what I remember, was that a couple appeared, and the man was asked the questions in order to win a mink coat for the woman. Rita's partner was one of my aunt Marie's sons, who was only sixteen at the time. He was knocked out in the first round. But I think Rita bought the mink coat soon after she was on the show, to confuse people into believing she had, in fact, been a winner.

She was thirty-three when I was born—still a young woman, and said to be attractive, with her thick black hair and light-brown eyes. Her dimples. Yet I never thought her a desirable, enviable kind of woman. Perhaps it was only because I was aware always that she didn't like me. It occurs to me now why that was. She must have planned that she and my mother, two unmarried cripples, would live together, grow old together in the family house. Then my mother married at thirty-nine. That would have been tolerable; by the family's standards, my father was nobody's prize, nothing to be envied. But then she had a child. And Rita had always wanted children. How could she find the sight of me anything but galling, anything but tormenting? Perhaps it would have been better if I had been a boy.

When my father died, my mother and I moved into my grandmother's house. This was a terrible decision, and it seemed to be made under our noses, or not made at all: it was just assumed that my mother and I would leave the apartment, three blocks from my grandmother's house, where we had lived as a family. Was it cruelty, or just an automatic response, given her excessive devotion to domestic order, that made Rita insist that nearly everything from the old apartment be given away: my toys, my dolls, the Alice in Wonderland rug my father had bought me, the tin dollhouse with the tiny furniture, plates, candles, lamps? And all the larger dolls I had. I was allowed to keep one or two small ones, and I was allowed to keep my books, but they had to stay in the room my mother and I shared—they could have no place in the larger house.

And how can I forgive her for having turned me into an indentured servant, for insisting that my Saturdays be spent cleaning, not playing with friends (not that I had any), and not in the library, not reading? Reading, my only refuge for the unbearable loss of my father, the shock of his death and my deprivation of my main companion, my main source of delight. "Put down that book. Do you think we're the slaves around here? Who do you think you are?" Saturday, every Saturday, winter or summer, spent among brooms and rags and dust mops and harsh chemicals and a vacuum cleaner—state-of-the-art—she insisted her brothers and sisters chip in on, which seemed overlarge and overpowerful, as if it too, like the words that came from her harsh mouth, could suck up joy.

She took from me joy and safety, but she gave me invaluable things as a writer: an ear for the tone of hate below the words of reason, an ability to detect the falseness in my speech when I was trying to ingratiate myself to a tyrant who never would be satisfied—an ear for slavishness, the slave's false speech. My own hate fed itself on a recoil from her physical presence: after she took a bath, I would retch. I would retch at the smell of her bath salts when it was time for me to bathe myself. I was convinced I could smell it when she had her period, and the smell made me sick. The smell of her scent—Tweed, it was called—seemed to me all the proof I needed of how she had misconstrued what was necessary to be a desirable woman like my mother (Arpège) or my aunt Lil (Chanel No. 5).

Occasionally, I would relax my guard and the trap would come around my tender limbs. Like the time I told her, excited, that I was about to buy my first bra: "Who do you think would be interested in anything like that?" Or when I happened to mention that I had to write a paragraph comparing and contrasting two unlike things: "Why don't you write about the difference between an upright and a canister vacuum cleaner? Or you wouldn't know anything about that." Not learning my lesson, because I couldn't believe that anything connected to writing would hurt me, I said, at dinner, that I was going to write a composition about spring, and she said, "Why don't you write about spring cleaning?" Not realizing she was mocking me, I did what she asked, trying to please her. When I showed it to her, she laughed that laugh that sounded like a car trying to turn over on a winter morning, a laugh—so different from my mother's, which made everyone want to laugh also—that made you afraid to laugh, because you didn't know, ever, whether what was being laughed at would do someone harm.

"You writing about spring cleaning, that's a hot one," she said. When I won prizes for writing, when the poem I had written about the election of Pope John XXIII was published in the parish magazine, she said nothing, or talked about the athletic awards of my boy cousins. "I don't see what good being a bookworm will do you. You'd be better off getting out in the fresh air and running around the house once or twice." Never have I met anyone else whose expressions, whose slightest words, could dash all joy.

She did great harm. Not only to my mother and to me, but to her own mother. No one told her there were some things she could not do. Why did no one tell her not to tear apart her mother's house, the house her mother had lived in for forty years, when her mother was almost eighty and away for a month in Florida, visiting her sister, having no idea what was going on?

At first, it was only that they were going to put in a downstairs bathroom and a laundry room so my grandmother wouldn't have to climb stairs to go to the bathroom or carry laundry to the basement, where she still used a washing machine with a wringer. But it got out of hand—or it was put in my aunt's hands—and she made plans. How did she do it so quickly—a month only—and without my grandmother's ever finding out? My grandmother's kitchen had been tacked on to the main house, but it was light and warm and comforting; it led to a dining room with a massive mahogany table where holidays had been celebrated and where, when there were no holidays, my grandfather, a jeweler, laid out his diamonds and his tools. The living room, with its ornate gilt mirror, its maroon lamps with Fragonard dancers gamboling, pointing their gilt toes, the antimacassars she had crocheted herself pinned to the tops of the heavy maroon furniture, the oaken floors covered with a pinkish carpet, the flowers faded but inviting, and the fringes, thanks to my grandmother's care, still fresh-looking, intact.

All the nine children chipped in, so they must have all agreed to her plans to have the kitchen pulled off the house, the dining room turned into an "eat-in kitchen" with a "dinette," the front porch combined with the living room to a large wall-less space, her pantry dismantled, my grandfather's workspace, where his bench and Chinese pots full of rich philodendrons ruled like dark gods, would be simply disappeared. Why did no one stop her? Or did they all want to hurt their mother, did they all want to punish her—for her aloofness, her judging austerity, her lack of tenderness, the busyness that could not give a child a timely pat, a needed caress? Was this what they all wanted? Punishment in the name of improvement, in the name of modernization—was that what they all wanted? To murder a hated past?

During the month when the renovations were taking place, the house was full of men—carpenters, plumbers, electricians—and we pretended they all wanted to marry Rita, whether they were married or not. Perhaps they were afraid of her, as we all were. It was a busy time, a hectic time: I don't remember. Miraculously, they finished the job on time. It was all ready for my grandmother's return.

She walked into the house as if she'd been struck by lightning. She said nothing; she went into her bedroom, which had been left completely intact: they must have at least understood that some violations were not permissible. From that moment on, she became old. It took three years for her to die, taking the house over with the smell of her illness, her dying, turning the "eat-in kitchen" into a waiting room for death, full of the accoutrements of illness: the bandages for her colostomy, the machine to suction the phlegm from her throat, cartons of gauze and bandages, jars of Vaseline the size of oil drums.

It was just after the renovations were completed that Rita became George's girlfriend. Is that the right word for it, is that the right way of putting it? Other ways of putting it seem even less right. He courted her; they began dating—one seems, well, too elegant, too gracious, and there was no elegance, no graciousness in that brutal man; and "dating" makes what it was that they did sound too youthful, too lighthearted, and they were middle-aged, at a time when the middle-aged had their own caste, whose lines did not blur over into anything that might be referred to as "young." And I don't recall their doing anything like going to dinner or to a movie. He came to our house, my grandmother's house, where my mother and I lived, where my aunt lived. He came over after supper on Friday, Saturday, and Sunday nights. He sat on the couch with her. They sat close to each other on the couch. Once, I saw him pinch her breast; she was wearing a salmon-colored sweater. His touch was contemptuous; it made a mockery of tenderness, of desire, of the sweetness of female flesh. It said that touch was about punishment, about ridicule: that appetite was a weapon, and, in order that it not be turned upon the appetitive one, it must be used against someone else; it must be avenged.

They watched television. He drank beer. He drank so much beer that, by the time he left, he was so drunk he shouldn't have been allowed to drive.

It is the time now for me to tell the story of that time, but there is only one way that I want to tell it, and several ways that I wish, most passionately, to avoid. It must be said: with his visits a darkness entered our family, and it was miserable for me; I was the child in the house, and there were things done to me, things I should not have seen, ways that I was looked at that I should have been kept from. But this is not the way I want to tell the story, because I escaped, and I have to thank them for making it so clear to me what must be escaped from. That clarity is, after all, a kind of gift. But that clarity was not my only gift, not my only good fortune. I was fortunate in coming of age in a time that was conducive to my escape, when there were other ways of living that seemed open to me, seemed desirable, and not outside my grasp.

For, at the same time that he was getting drunk and pinching the breast covered in salmon-colored nylon-wool blend, Jack and Jackie Kennedy were walking hand in hand down Pennsylvania Avenue, taking their place (our place) at the head of the New World. And at the same time they were offering me the endless possibilities of judgment, of punishment, Pope John XXIII was on the throne of Rome. He was opening windows; he was saying: Don't worry. The world is more open than you think and it is not a place to be feared, despised, to shut your doors from. The air has changed; the storm of the world war has lifted; we must still be afraid of the communists, but maybe not right now. The light is golden; the leaves are sticky, new, yellow-green. I was a lucky girl, to have been the daughter of a loving father, to have come of age when possibility was the order of the day. And so I suffered, but I escaped. So this is not the story of my suffering. It is my mother's story.

My mother did not escape. What they did to her broke something in her that went unrepaired until the day of her death. It all began, though, on that couch, on those Friday, Saturday, Sunday nights, when I was sent to the basement to bring George bottle after bottle of Budweiser, when I had to listen to his ranting and his bad temper, when I had to let him look at me in my nightgown in a way that made me anxious and say nothing, because, as my mother said, "They're letting us live here. We can't make waves."

And my grandmother didn't escape; the house renovations sickened her unto death. What would have happened if my grandmother had not got sick? For, in speaking about her daughters, it is essential I should speak about their mother, and this I have not done. My grandmother: a tall, strong tree, an oak, imposing, something to be leaned on, taking its nourishment from deep, deep roots. Also: casting a shadow. Mother of nine children; famous for her skills as cook, nurse, seamstress, translator from Sicilian into English. Beloved by the children of other mothers, children whom she took in when the mother sickened, when the father ran away, when the parents considered sending the youngest to an orphanage because there were too many mouths to feed. But not too many for my grandmother, never too many mouths, never too little room. Charity, then, implacable as a Roman matron's, the wife of a consul, the mother of a senator. But tenderness? No, only, occasionally, to me, her favorite among the grandchildren, named for her. An immigrant, sent over by herself from Ireland at seventeen, and then never a moment's rest, never a moment free of the anxiety of feeding, clothing, sheltering all those children, who were born, with regularity, every two years, then nursed until the next one came, and the husband, "an artist," not even Irish but Sicilian, a scandal to marry, but she had courage for that: oh, she had courage, she could face anything.

But perhaps she couldn't face what her daughter had done to her house, the house she moved into as a mother of young children—ripped from her, destroyed when she was away in Florida, foolish in the sun. She weakened; her amazing energy seeped away; she was less frightening. Querulous now rather than imposing. She did not, as she once might have done, forbid George the house, she did nothing to silence his rages; she ignored the empty beer bottles. When he appeared, she took to her bed, although it was only eight-thirty, nine o'clock.

And perhaps that is why Rita did it to the house: to steal her mother's strength, held on to for too many years: the old regime. She wanted to be, for once, in charge. She could make everyone afraid: because she could be more silent than anyone and then say one thing, probably something true, that would freeze you to the ground.

In the middle of my grandmother's sickness unto death, Rita does something that, even after all these years, is inexplicable to me. She marries George, secretly, at eight o'clock Mass on a Saturday morning in April. Through an odd coincidence, I am at the Mass, which I would usually never be at (at age twelve, I want to sleep till twelve), but I am going on a class trip to see the movie *El Cid* at Radio City Music Hall. I walk down the aisle with my friend, and try to make sense of the sight I can't make sense of. How can they be there, Rita and George, getting married? My cousin Chris, the witness to the crime. Rita turns around. She sees me. I don't say anything to her. I don't say anything to my friend. On the bus, at the movie, I can think of nothing else. I am terrified. Something terrible will happen, it is nothing I understand, and there is nothing I can do about it.

By the time I come home, at five o'clock, she has already moved out of the house, taken all her things in many suitcases. For two months, my mother and I bear the burden of my grandmother's dying by ourselves.

Here is the part of the story that even now, forty-three years later, I can't bear to tell. My mother is furious that Rita has left her alone to care for her mother. She insists that Rita help. Rita and George come in one night a week, and my mother and I go out for dinner; Rita and my mother are not speaking. And then my mother asks her for one weekend off: to go to the graduation of the son of a friend of hers and my father's in Staten Island. She has not been away in over a year. And while she is gone, my grandmother dies. And my aunt gloats. She says, "I think it was a sign from Ma, a blessing on our marriage. I let George close her eyes."

And my mother wails and says it's a sacrilege, it's a desecration to have let him close her eyes with his filthy hands, and I know she's right, and I think, if it is the truth, if my grandmother blessed my aunt instead of my mother, does that mean my aunt is living the right way and my mother is living the wrong way? That coldness, contempt, the mania for domestic order that destroyed the idea of pleasure, the styptic tongue that stopped our hearts' blood—if that is the way that is rewarded, rather than my mother's imagination and indulgence and operatic excesses— well, then, I am lost, and there is no place for me, for the likes of me, in the world. The generous and the imaginative will be cast down; only the righteous are righteous, and love means nothing, there is only law.

The terrible times start. My grandmother hasn't left a will. My mother feels that the house belongs to her, because she paid the mortgage on it for twenty-five years, while none of the others contributed a penny, and because she is a widow with a child, and Rita has a husband and no children. Rita says she was living there for years, it was her only home, she has a right. The family splits. The two brothers who have distanced themselves from the family do not take sides. Lil and Ned side with my mother. Tiny and Marie side with Rita. Perhaps it is because they are the mothers of sons, and she has been kind to them; she has bought their loyalty. And Pete, the youngest brother sides with Rita. For the rest of their lives, there will never be an occasion on which all the sisters speak to one another.

In the middle of this terrible time, my mother and I come home one night to find all the living-room furniture gone; my mother's papers spilled out of the desk onto the floor; a note from Rita saying she'd paid for half the furniture, and a pile of twenty-dollar bills on the rug. And for weeks, my mother can do nothing about the empty living room and the pile of her papers on the floor—my mother, fastidious about anything official, from the state, or having to do with business and money. I don't remember how it happens, but eventually something legal is worked out between the two of them; my mother will have to pay Rita a certain amount of money every month for years. But we stay in the house, my mother and I, and the house falls apart, it's too much for my mother and me. It would have been better if we'd given it to Rita, sold it right then, moved to a small, pleasant place that was all our own.

After this, because of this, my mother sinks into drunkenness, a drunkenness I am the only witness to, and every night she weeps about her sisters and their ingratitude, and I know that she is right to feel betrayed, that this is another valuable way of knowing: at a young age I understand the taste of betrayal, I understand that it is different from loss. I lost my father, but the wound was clean; betrayal is gangrenous, the limb consumes itself. This has happened to my mother's spirit. It is Rita's fault. I cannot think of her as the child sent away to French nuns, banished from her family, rags tied to the bottoms of her shoes. I think of her face at family parties, pleased, smug, self-contained, while my mother drinks and weeps and makes everyone turn away from her and I must take her home, one of the uncles helping her into the car and driving until I am old enough to drive, and it is all my problem then, I don't ask anyone ever again to help me with my mother.

Mine is the job of hiding her shame. And keeping in my heart the promise: one day I will expose the murderous true heart of my aunt: the Law Abiding, the Destroyer.

She destroyed my mother. What Rita did was the end of her. She wanted to destroy; she was powerful; she did as she liked. She was selfish; she was greedy; she was full of malice; she wanted to punish my mother, and she did.

I suppose that it is possible to say that blame should be assigned not exclusively to her, but also to my grandmother, who should have known her children better than to die without leaving a will. I say to myself that my grandmother was, for all her competence, essentially a peasant, uneasy with the forms and papers of the bourgeois world. But peasants can be shrewd and cunning; why wasn't she? Or was she afraid of Rita too?

I go nearly ten years without seeing Rita, and then I must see her at the funeral of my uncle Joe, my aunt Lil's husband. I am eight and a half months pregnant, but my cousin Peppy begs me to come. "They're all going to be here," he says. I know exactly who he means. If you come, he says, we can laugh at them; if I have to face them alone, they're just too scary. I have to lie to the airline and tell them I'm only six months pregnant, or they won't let me fly. My husband, a Midwestern Protestant with no relatives specializing in flamboyant hate, accompanies me in case I go into labor on the plane. Later, he tells people that before he met them he was sure I was exaggerating about my mother's brothers and sisters, but then he saw what I was talking about. Over my uncle's coffin, George made a threatening fist at my uncle Joe's brother, shouting, "God speaks to me, goddamn it, not to you."

My last sight of Rita was at my aunt Lil's funeral. My cousin had left an article about me out on the counter (he is my greatest ally among them), silently forcing the aunts and uncles to acknowledge my success, which none of them, except my aunt Lil and my uncle Ned, ever did. Rita picked up the newspaper, looked at my picture for a second, two, then crumpled it and threw it on the floor. "I looked at this and I saw it was garbage, so I figured you wanted it thrown away," she said to my cousin, who picked it up off the floor, smoothed it out, and took it out of the room as if it were a wounded animal. My final vision of her was of her taking some flowers off my aunt's grave. "Put those back, Rita," my cousin said. "Why?" she said. "She doesn't need them." For the first time, someone in the family successfully resisted her. "They're not yours, Rita. Put them back." "You always went in for waste," she said, throwing them down and turning her back on the two of us.

After George died, Rita turned to Peppy for help, and because he is kinder than anyone else I've ever known, he would visit her every few months to help her with financial matters. His news of her was increasingly bizarre. She had become obsessed with making plastic rosary beads to be sent to the Philippines; every doorknob, every chair back had plastic rosary beads looped over it. She insisted that my cousin drive five hours to take her on a ten-minute drive to see a building where, at sunset, you could see the profile of the Virgin Mary projected. Another cousin called Peppy to say that when he offered to bring his children to visit her on the way home from Disney World, she refused to see him because she was involved in a boycott of Disney organized by Mother Angelica, the TV nun evangelist, because Disney was connected to Miramax, which had produced *Priest,* a film that was soft on both priestly homosexuality and priests who had a loving relationship with a woman.

Her end was very grim. She lost her hysterical fastidiousness, she refused to bathe. Her house was filthy and stank of cigarette smoke. She stopped using the toilet; she would no longer wear her brace, and moved out of a chair only to hobble to bed or to get something to eat. When she needed to move her bowels, she defecated in empty Cool Whip containers, which she would empty in the kitchen sink at the end of the day. My cousin convinced her it was time for her to move into a nursing home, and spent a week cleaning out her disgusting house and moving her into her new place. When she asked him to stay another day, he said he was on his way to France for his vacation. "Vacation again, pleasure boy?" she said, and wheeled herself away from him in the new motorized wheelchair he had arranged for her to rent.

She caused problems in the nursing home. She developed a sexual mania for one of the male residents and would stalk him in her wheelchair, lunging at him during meals. They had to put barricades up in his room so she couldn't wheel her chair through to get at him.

This is the last story I hear about her. Then she dies. She dies, and my mother is still alive—in a stupor in her nursing home, but at least not a scandal like her sister. And at least alive. Victorious in that. I take it as a sign. I have kept her alive; my love, my care, has been stronger than their darkness. My mother lives longer than any of her sisters.

It is not a good story, the story of the Gagliano girls. It should have been a better story; they should have come to better ends. What was the good of all that vitality, all that rude health, triumphing over polio and every other natural blow, those good looks, that energy, all those bonds of kin and faith? They had everything that most people believe makes for a good life. But their lives did not end well, except perhaps the one of them who died young. They were of no help to each other; even the ones who stuck together couldn't do much to help each other in the end.

What kind of story is this? Is it about the price of immigration, the pressures of respectability, a mix of Irish and American puritanism, the price of dogma too strictly or rigorously applied? Or too little maternal love, too little spread too thinly, replaced by the iron rule of law? It is, in any case, an old story; there will not be a family of sisters like them again.

Shortly before she died, Mary McCarthy was having dinner at my house. Dinner was over, and I moved to sit next to her as we drank our brandy. We spoke about our aunts, about the joy-denying, life-denying women who had blighted our youth. Mary smiled at me—that famous smile, sidelong, sly, complicit, the Catholic girl's slice of purloined triumphalism—and said, "There aren't any more aunts like that. It's all over." And we raised our glasses and toasted each other. "Let's drink," she said, "to something gone for good."

My Mother *and Her Friends*

———————

Unlike her brothers and sisters, my mother had friends. The others seemed to think the family was enough; there were, after all, nine of them, and endless aunts, uncles, and cousins— why look further than the circle you were born into? And for what? Companionship, stimulation, the relief of loneliness? Does this mean that, of all of them, only my mother found the family inadequate?

She made her first friends in high school. It is strange to think about, but my mother, born in 1908, was in high school in the 1920s. The Roaring Twenties. The time when "Bernice Bobs Her Hair." In the year when Fitzgerald's story was published, my mother was starting high school. It was also the year of *The Waste Land* and *Ulysses*. And three years later, *Mrs. Dalloway*. But my mother was not a Modernist.

She wasn't even a flapper. And yet the quality of her friendships has an unmistakably twenties tone. Poems copied out and pasted under photographs in albums of black paper; souvenirs from football games, snapshots in raccoon coats, a program for a Rudy Vallee concert, girls getting together on a rainy Saturday to wash their hair and make fudge. Giving one another nicknames: my mother was Tulip, her friend Millie was Matt, and Clara was called Winnie, or Win.

My mother's two high-school girlfriends were both Protestant, and that was unusual, because no one else in the family had the slightest connection to non-Catholics. They were quiet and pleasant and well behaved; I wonder what they made of my mother, her raucous laugh, her famous temper, the house bursting with children—my grandmother's and the ones she'd taken in—the rich Italian food cooked by an Irishwoman, the endless sewing, the endless laundry. More important, having made friends with what she thought of as real Americans, my mother changed her name informally from immigrant "Anna" to American "Anne." Only after she became the grandmother of my daughter Anna did she change back.

From birth till death, Millie lived in the same house, first with her parents and her brother, Melvin, and then, when her parents died, caring for him, until he died and she remained in the house alone. She would have us to dinner from time to time, and I understood that this was a Protestant house, an American house. The quality of the light was quieter; everything seemed a "brown study"; there was a piano that no one played, on which were photographs of her dead parents; on the walls there were watercolors of cows lapping the water from shallow, cool-looking brooks, or a boat becalmed in silver water. There were no flowers or green plants, and, most important as a sign to me, no sacred objects. I can't remember what we ate, but I know I liked being there. Millie always had a small gift for me, and it was always something pleasing: a toy that was really interesting, a puzzle that was not too hard for me.

Clara married early and moved to Alabama; I saw her only once in my childhood, and the visit made a deep impression on her, if not on me. We gathered to see Clara at Millie's house. I was five years old. I was asked to sing. I think they were expecting to hear some appropriate songs, like "Row, Row, Row Your Boat" or "This Old Man," but at that time my favorite song was "The Theme from Moulin Rouge": "Whenever we kiss / I worry and wonder / Your lips may be here. But / Where is your heart?" Before I began, I said to my audience, "I'm sorry, but I'll have to sing this a cappella." Clara loved this, and over the years she reminded my mother of it, to their shared delight. This was the kind of thing her family would have criticized me for: accused me of being "too smart for my own good," of trying to make fools of them.

My mother made her first post-girlhood friendship when she went to a business school called Drake, seven miles from her home in Jamaica, Queens. There she met Kathleen Hogan. When my mother talked about Kathleen, she always began by talking about her looks: my mother thought her a great beauty. She died before I was born, so I never saw her, but in the photographs she is pretty enough, in a rather temperate way: a kind of Ruby Keeler prettiness with no sense in it of intelligence or vitality, none of my mother's liveliness, her appetite for the world. She died unmarried, and my mother explained this by saying that Kathleen's mother, with whom she lived, was "very demanding." "She kept Kathleen tied to her, which my mother never did," my own mother said, with pride in both herself and her large-hearted mother.

What was important about their friendship was that they went into the city together. Two working girls in the twenties, the early thirties, in their drop-waist dresses, their cloche hats, taking the subway from 179th Street in Jamaica to Times Square to see the Astaires, the Lunts, and then, later, more surprisingly, to Madison Square Garden, where they were devotees of the rodeo. I know this was my mother's idea; she had a romance about cowboys, and

Kathleen doesn't seem to have been a person of much initiative. But was it Kathleen's sweet good looks that brought them to the attention of the two cowboys? Both of them were champions, named Cecil Henley and Turk Greenough, who later married Sally Rand, the fan dancer, who, in my mother's unamused words, "broke his stride for good." You couldn't kid my mother about Turk Greenough and Sally Rand. She would take umbrage, and this was unusual for her—she always liked a joke, even when it was on herself.

The cowboys took them to nightclubs—these two Catholic virgins. My mother remembered going to Texas Guinan's (did her name make the cowboys feel at home?). What was my mother doing in a speakeasy, where the chorus girls were scantily clad and possibly also call girls? Texas Guinan, I learned, was also a Catholic girl, educated by nuns. My mother told me that the cowboys never tipped and she would have to send Kathleen back to leave something on the table while she distracted the boys on the sidewalk. What did my mother say to her parents or her siblings after a night out with cowboys? Were they interested? It is likely to me that they were not.

In a picture taken at that time, my mother, in a cowboy hat, a bandana around her neck, looks uncharacteristically sultry and seductive. What would have happened if my mother had married a cowboy? If she and Kathleen had married their cowboys and moved together to the West, rodeo widows, waiting for their boys with their dangerous occupations to come home?

It would never have happened. It is unlikely that either of the cowboys would have married a cripple, and Kathleen would never have left her mother.

The bonds of their friendship loosed as the thirties progressed. There were two reasons for this. The first is that Kathleen began dating a friend of one of my aunts, and her weekends were spent with him, my aunt and her husband, and other couples, whose configuration excluded my mother. I think this hurt my mother deeply; it was one of the wounds she fingered when she was drunk. She found replacements to go to the theatre with her; she formed a bridge club of unmarried girls, called the Chin and Chew Club, that met monthly at each other's houses to play bridge, and to talk and eat (hence the club's name), but, most important, to contribute money to a fund for theatre tickets. But I think there was another reason for the friendship's weakening: my mother's religious life became more complex, more intellectually demanding, more geographically spread out. The friends she made from this time on were based on a shared religious vision, a shared religious practice.

To understand the friendships of my mother that would be crucial in her life from the mid-1930s to her death, it is necessary to understand the Working Women's Retreat Movement in the American Catholic Church of that time. It was a very good thing for women like my mother; it provided a situation in which their spiritual life could be taken seriously, it brought them into community with one another; it gave them a place to go to get away from family. The retreats would last a weekend, and were usually held in a convent; the women were cared for—their food was prepared, their linens were provided—by nuns, to whom they spoke very little. There was Mass and sermons, private spiritual directions, and public talks by the priest in charge.

Most of the women who made these retreats were unmarried; they were free to travel a few times a year for their spiritual growth and to see their friends. They ranged in education and professions: there was a Radcliffe graduate, an ex-showgirl turned Madison Square Garden usher, several teachers, a bank executive. In the photograph I have of them, they aren't particularly sexually alluring, but, on the other hand, they don't look downhearted, downtrodden. They stand in front of a statue of the Virgin; there is one man: the priest they followed, the object of their romance.

Two of them, the Radcliffe graduate and the showgirl, seemed more part of the world than the others. The Radcliffe graduate, whose name was Mary Elizabeth Fallon, married a lawyer, lived in Larchmont, and had eleven children. One year, the year I was fourteen, she invited me to spend a week at her house in the summer. I was older than her children by some years, but I wasn't expected to babysit—they had a housekeeper who took care of that. I think she found me good company. I remember our reading together an issue of *Life* magazine that had Barbra Streisand on the cover, then going to buy one of her records; I remember our pleasure at her singing, and my delight when Mary Elizabeth told me I looked a lot like Barbra, and would even more when I grew up. She wanted to convince me that I might try for Radcliffe.

Their home, a brick house on a sloping lawn, seemed to me the absolute model of modest elegance. Her husband went in to work at a big New York law firm and arrived home, cheerful, at night (he was a bit older, balding, thin; she was a bouncy redhead with a caustic tongue). I thought you couldn't do much better than that: a man who could buy you such a house, a yacht-club membership, a mink coat, and still take his children on his knee, and never lose his temper. At the yacht club I saw some Catholic celebrities from afar: Walter Slezak, Jean and Walter Kerr, Marie Killilea, who had written a popular book about a saintly crippled girl. I thought that I could be a writer and have a life like Mary Elizabeth. And I could take my place, as she did, at the communion rail, trailing my cheerful children, my cheerful husband: I could be part of the world and not lose my soul. She didn't talk about religion; she read whatever she wanted, pious or not; she seemed to situate herself in American high society without any danger to herself at all.

Her good fortune did not last; her kindness and intelligence didn't save her. She died before she was forty, of breast cancer. Her husband married again; he and my mother lost touch.

My mother saw two of the out-of-town women in the group regularly, when they came to New York from Springfield, Massachusetts. One, Nora McDonnell, a social worker, my mother didn't like. My mother thought her a killjoy, someone with no sense of humor. But her friend Cathy Walsh was beloved by us all. She was another one of those daughters whose fate was to care for an aged mother. She worked in a department store, in the notions department: I imagine her happily selling pins and needles, tape measures, grosgrain, pinking shears. She loved her job, but, then, she seemed to find everything in life delightful. My mother thought she was an angel, and every year while she could still travel, I brought my mother and my children to visit Cathy in Springfield. We would spend the night in her house; she would indulge my children outrageously; she and my mother would happily recount the great old days of their retreat; she would remember meeting my father for the first time, when he taught "Catholic Literature" to a circle of Springfield women. They each paid five dollars for a series of five weekly talks on subjects like Thomistic philosophy or the poetry of Paul Claudel. "He was a genius, your father, but he didn't talk down to us. We all thought he was quite a guy."

From the forties through the sixties, Nora and Cathy made their yearly trip to New York to stay in a "good" hotel and go to the theatre. They stayed at one of two places, the Gramercy Park or the Hotel Commodore. My mother would join them in Manhattan, and they would go to dinner and a show; my mother would bring me home a cocktail napkin and a swizzle stick from the hotel bar. When I got older, I was invited along, and I think my lifelong love of good but modest hotels springs from those outings.

They would order drinks from room service; I would be brought a Shirley Temple. We would talk while we drank, and then head to the theatre, and to dinner. They made a point of eating in "good" restaurants; one year they chose the Top of the Sixes, a restaurant in the penthouse of 666 Fifth Avenue, and to my delight, I was introduced to the idea of "cleansing the palate" with a grapefruit sorbet between courses. We looked out over the city with no question that, although we were only middle-aged women and a child, we had the right to the best the city could offer. We didn't need a man to pay for us; it never occurred to us to wait for that.

It is strange for me to write about these women, for now I must write accurately about people whom I used as fictional characters. My second novel, *The Company of Women,* was about my mother and the friends of hers who devoted themselves to a Passionist priest, Father Dermot McArdle. When I made a fictional character of him, I named him Father Cyprian; I called the ex–chorus girl Mary Rose, but her name was Kay. In creating a fiction about her, I didn't make up the outline of her fate, but I invented an inner life for her—for all of them—which may have been the case or not, but it allowed me an access to them I had no approach to in real life. Did I assault the fortress of their inner lives, these women, who had no practice, seemingly no appetite, for talking about themselves? Did I batter their hearts?

I didn't invent the fact that Kay had married, young, a man who had gone insane and been institutionalized early in their marriage. The Catholic Church would not allow her to divorce him, and Father Dermot supported her in her struggle to keep loyal to the Church. For at least thirty years, she had a boyfriend, Jimmy the Greek, who owned a diner near Madison Square Garden. When she was seventy, her husband finally died, and Kay and Jimmy married.

Kay would get us tickets to the circus, and would take us to supper at Jimmy's diner. She was redheaded and wiry and good-natured and always cheerful. I can only be enraged on her behalf at the sacrifice of her youth. But she was not enraged; I don't think she had rage in her. Is it a good thing or a bad thing that she did not? I still don't know.

Of the friendships my mother made with the women in her retreat group, two were passionate and lifelong, and these two friends of my mother's were important in my life as well. Like good aunts, they filled in the gaps left by my mother and my father. Peggy took my father's place as the person who gave me books and talked to me about them as if they were important. And Jane—Jane opened my eyes to parts of the world I would never have imagined.

Peggy Campbell was the only woman I knew as a child who

had in any way a quality I would call softness. This despite the fact that her body had none of the qualities of softness associated with the female. She was very thin; I remember being shocked when I leaned my head against her chest and felt none of the pillowy bounce I was used to in my mother; I remember my mother telling me, with no small sense of contemptuous wonderment, that Peggy was so flat-chested she didn't wear a bra, she wore an undershirt. Like a boy, my mother said, which is how she was built.

When I was quite little, I insisted on calling her "my cousin," wanting her closer than any name for her like "friend" suggested. She seemed to me the only representative of what I thought of as the valuable feminine pastel world. In my memory, she is always wearing one or another shade of light blue. Some blues, I knew, were hateful—royal blue, navy blue—but Peggy's blues were soothing, like the first drops of rain cooling the eyes after a beastly heat. Though she wasn't beautiful, her looks were very pleasing to me: her swimming blue eyes, which always looked as if she'd just got over crying but wouldn't want to burden us with the details; her always manicured nails, polished in a shade whose name pleased me: Windsor Rose. She had a weak chin, almost no chin at all, and negligible lips; I didn't like looking at her mouth, because for many years she filled in the gap of two missing lower front teeth with strips of wax. Finally, my mother bullied her into going to a dentist, and she was given two false teeth, a bridge, which somehow looked no better than the wax solution she'd lived with for years.

She bought me birthday cards that I loved and treasured as if they were enamels or Persian miniatures. I kept them in a special box—a tin box, a purple background with lime-colored vines, which had once held Louis Sherry candies—and took them out, going over and over them, spreading them out on the floor near my toy box. They were the kind of thing I loved but that no one else understood a girl like me would love: pictures of shepherdesses or Victorian girls in lacy pantaloons and satin slippers, the words "Happy Birthday" in yellow or pink or blue, fragile-looking as if they'd been written on air or water. She bought me books of fairy tales printed in England with Art Nouveau illustrations that favored shades of teal and ochre; little girls with smocking dresses and dimpled knees and geometrically cut hair, little boys who might be little girls, so vividly did they share their sisters' looks and interests. She was one of the only people who had a nickname for me: "Kidlet," she called me, and I enjoyed the feeling of being the kind of person someone would have a nickname for; it made me feel, rare in those years, mercifully not in charge.

And when my father died, only Peggy understood that my one possible consolation lay in reading quietly, incessantly. The day after his death, she arrived to support my mother carrying a package of books for me: one that was particularly absorbing, *St. Pius X: The Farm Boy Who Became Pope,* and *The Trumpet of the Swan.* It was she who gave me my first copy of *Little Women,* and then every Alcott book I asked for; she bought me my first *Jane Eyre,* but advised me to wait a bit for *Wuthering Heights.* It was on our book-buying trips to Doubleday Fifth Avenue that I bought the collected e. e. cummings, and *The Prophet,* and *Franny and Zooey* and *The Catcher in the Rye.* All of these, I understood, were not quite her cup of tea. But she allowed my rhapsodies about J. D. Salinger; she bought me the copy of *The New Yorker* that had his last published short story in it, "Hapworth 16, 1924," published in 1965. She allowed me to read it in Schrafft's while we waited for our orders, and, seeing that I enjoyed the magazine, she gave me a subscription for my birthday. I read "The Talk of the Town" and knew that it was speaking of a world to which I as yet had no access but towards which I was heading at all possible speed. I knew Peggy didn't have access to it either, but I was grateful to her for at least pointing the way.

She read my poetry and praised me for it without reservation. My mother would type up all my poems and make carbon copies for Peggy; she would mail them to Peggy as soon as they were typed, as if she knew that with Peggy, unlike her own family, it was safe to brag about her word-drunk child.

Was it only class that accounted for the difference in affect between Peggy and my mother and the other women in my family? Peggy wasn't working-class; she'd been to college; she had a job as a teacher; she told us about the gifts her husband had bought her before he ruined himself and her, perfumed cigarettes and stockings with her name embroidered on the tops. She had none of the pushing, elbows-out qualities of all the other women I knew. She was incapable of force; her lack of forcefulness almost caused disasters from time to time—disasters from which my mother would rescue her, her knight in shining armor, her bulwark against the thrusting world.

She was Irish, but she'd been born in Kentucky and came to New York with her mother to study at Columbia's Teachers College. She had married young; her husband, a success in the Roaring Twenties, was, by the end of the Depression, a hopeless drunk. She had two sons by him; her family life, unlike my mother's, seemed dominated by males who alternately worshipped and oppressed her, who seemed incapable of making a living, who depended on her for money and yet believed they shielded her from the harsher realities they called the world.

My mother performed some of the traditional roles of the powerful, protective male for Peggy. An event that solidified their friendship was my mother's rescuing her from her creditors. Her husband had disappeared, and before his alcoholic decline and absconding, she had never paid a bill. On one retreat she broke down in tears and confessed to my mother that she was being hounded by bill collectors. She simply had no idea how much she owed, or to whom, and how she could get around the problem. My mother said she'd deal with it. She told Peggy just to make a pile of all her bills. With great shame, Peggy confessed: she had hidden the bills in different places around the apartment. As if she were taking out pieces of spoiled food, or dead animals she had buried behind the wainscoting, she produced the bills. I can imagine my mother, her eyes serious behind her blue-rimmed reading glasses, her competent hands slitting open envelopes as if she were slitting the throats of an enemy, phoning up threatening men and in her professional voice warning them to stop harassing Mrs. Campbell—there had been clerical errors, the checks were in the mail. She wrote out a check for each bill; she made Peggy sign them in front of her; she wrote a firm, no-nonsense letter to accompany each check, and she walked them down to the mailbox herself. For several months, she paid Peggy's bills with her, until Peggy got the hang of it. From that time on, Peggy adored my mother as an exiled princess might adore the loyal steward of the royal estate who would ensure her safety in the harsh new world. She thought of my mother as her protector.

Certainly, her sons could offer her no protection. They were both types of men I found hard to place. Even though the older one died when I was three, he loomed in Peggy's mind, and in the apartment where I visited her, where his photo dominated the piano with its hard, unforgiving stool that seemed to have the imprint of buttocks on it, lightening the wood and giving the illusion of a softness that had no basis in the physical world. I would fool around on the piano—playing "Chopsticks" or "Heart and Soul," later the first pieces of Bach and Schumann I had by heart—and look up at his face, which frightened and compelled me, partly because of his hair, which simultaneously bristled and curved, like a laminated haystack. I knew that if I'd ever touched it there would be no softness, nothing pliable, and yet it was definitely hair, hair that had been tortured into some unnatural configuration I had never seen before: it was so uselessly abundant, as if all the force that had been refused his body had gone into his hair. I knew he was a hunchback, with an overlarge torso that made the lower half of his body look provisional. His eyes were dark and small and piercing, like the eyes of a certain kind of small dog, always ready for the chase. I knew he had been brilliant; he'd learned many languages and was particularly proficient in Latin; he worked with my father on his high-toned but short-lived children's magazine. Most important for his fearful allure: he had died young, hit by a car when he was crossing Broadway.

Was he drunk when he was hit? This was never mentioned, although, like his father, he was a hopeless alcoholic. My mother was impatient with the self-pity that led to his benders; she was tough with him, cripple to cripple, and told him to stop feeling sorry for himself, that nobody wanted to hear him crying in his beer. Apparently, he adored her, and loved the idea of her and my father as a couple; for him, as for members of a certain subset of Catholics, my parents' marriage (the unworldly husband, devoted to the life of the mind; the afflicted yet earthy wife, representing the flesh) was the perfect romance, and my birth the greatest miracle since John the Baptist leapt in his mother's womb.

His younger brother, Bobby, pointed to Buddy's death as one reason for his problems keeping sober, keeping a job. The other was a disease he had contracted in the army—lupus, he said, although, unlike Flannery O'Connor's case, his seemed to limit itself to a rash on his upper lip, exacerbated if he went out into the sun, and perfectly covered up by a mustache, which he always wore. His picture on the piano, a third the size of his brother's, shows him a brooding boy in uniform, with a girlish Robert Taylor look—the surprise, looking at the pictures, was that he, and not his bristling brother, had lived.

Bobby was a cartoonist; he lived with his parents, but he had girlfriends, who were reported to be glamorous in a bohemian way of which his mother disapproved. I think he sold some of his cartoons; I remember one that showed a bosomy blonde sitting on a soldier's lap, but I have no memory of a caption. Once, he made a birthday card for his mother that I found deeply impressive: he had drawn a smiling sausage, and inside it the words "I wish you a happy birthday and that's no baloney." He also worked with my father on the ill-fated magazine; he is listed as the art editor. One cartoon he did is a satire on psychoanalysis; the patient is his mother, looking nonplussed. Why this is in a children's magazine I have no idea. He also caricatured unsympathetic teachers, who beat sparky-looking little boys for the crime of sheer high spirits, a penchant for pranks or high jinks. These sadistic teachers also had his mother's face.

I was of no interest to Bobby when I was a child, and the interest he took in me later was not a happy one. There is a kind of desperate middle-aged man who brings out the sadism in young girls; that was what happened with Bobby and me, and I'm glad it was so far outside Peggy's range that she took no notice of it, had no understanding of it. Every summer after my father died, I spent a couple of days with her in her apartment in the Bronx; we would take the subway into the city, where she would take me to the Metropolitan Museum, to Schrafft's for lunch, and then to the Doubleday Bookstore. The last time this happened was the summer after my junior year in high school, when I was sixteen years old.

Bobby seemed to notice me for the first time, and his mother seemed delighted that he wanted to take me out to dinner, to meet some of his friends and then to go bowling. He had quite thoroughly declassed himself, abandoning his mother's genteel world for the rough-and-tumble world of the Irish Bronx, their bars and grills, their bowling alleys. Perhaps his mother's gentility had been too suffocating to him, deprived him of the oxygen he needed to develop into the man he never would become; I think he found the crudity of his new friends exhilarating, freeing. And what was I thinking of in saying I'd go out with him? Possibly, in 1965, Peggy's pastel, soft world struck me as insufficiently edgy. In those days, I believed wholeheartedly in experience; if I was going to be a writer, I had to experience many different things; there was no such thing as BAD experience; any experience could be put to use. And I was starved for male attention; I had had, at that time, two dates in my life, both of them disastrous. I went to an all-girls' school, and any whiff of maleness, on account of my radical deprivation from it, seemed in some way desirable.

So I allow him to walk me, in my pink-and-green flowered summer minidress, down the Bronx streets to the dark bar and grill, where he orders me my first public beer. He introduces me as his girlfriend. I laugh, and then he laughs—and both of our laughs are equivocal and open to several interpretations: it is up to the listener to determine whether we all know he is kidding—or not. One of the men says, "Jailbait"; it is the first time I have heard the term used in life, although I may have read it, or heard it in the movies. But I never before dreamed it could be applied to me.

We go bowling; he puts his arm around my waist to try to help my form; I make girlishly exaggerated gestures when I throw gutter balls; I never believe anyone would believe girlishness of me, it is so much not my style. But I am girlish with him because it makes him so disproportionately happy to be with this girlish girl, and I both despise him for his happiness and am grateful for it, and I despise Peggy for her happiness in seeing her son happy with me, and feel abandoned that she has failed at least to try to protect me from something that might have been a danger, although it turned out not to be.

Nothing happened, really—nothing physical, nothing that could be seen as traumatizing, even to a young girl. I had almost no contact with Bobby after that; the night before my wedding, to which he was invited but to which, having become almost entirely reclusive and alcoholic, he of course didn't come, he phoned me, drunk, and said, "Just tell me so that I can know. Was there ever a chance for me with you?" I said that he'd always been very important to me, but that I probably never thought of him that way. More as an older brother, I said. "The story of my life, kiddo," he said. Those were the last words he spoke to me. A year after that, he was dead—one of those people who are found days after, when the neighbors notice that the mail's piled up.

Most likely it was because of what happened with Bobby that I never spent another night at Peggy's apartment. But it was probably inevitable that, as I aged, as the world changed, our relationship would weaken. I was getting on to college, and I didn't need her to take me to the city any more. I didn't see her much when I was in college, although certainly I could have—but there was no way I could have lunch at Schrafft's with her after I had been to an anti-war demonstration, or a reading of Sylvia Plath's poetry, or a discussion on clitoral orgasm—and I knew that her taste in litera-ture had cut out everything that was, to me, strong and powerful: anything I might want for my own work and life. So much of the modern world made her shudder: she would visibly cringe when certain things were mentioned, anything approaching drugs, sex, and rock and roll. But the modern world was my world, mine and my friends'; it was my liberation, my ticket to ride, my passport to a paradise, not lost, because never possessed, but possibly to be gained in some vague future by me and my kind. Peggy wanted no part of it, so I avoided her. And this was sad, because for very many years she had been my favorite adult.

Is it possible for a young person to find a way that is very distant from the one she was born into without victims, without cruelty? Peggy died, when I was in graduate school; she was in the back-seat of a taxi when it crashed, on her way from the Bronx to Queens to visit one of her teacher friends. By that time, our rela-tionship had become so attenuated that I could hardly bring myself to mourn. But perhaps there is no expiration date for mourning; I can mourn her now and thank her; I am sure she is a gentle shade, patient in death as in life, and not given to ven-geance, a stranger to retribution.

Jane and Peggy. Peggy and Jane. The two names come together, couple like Fred and Ginger, Nick and Nora, Romeo and Juliet. It was never said, but somehow understood, that when Peggy and Jane came to visit, my parents and I became part of another family, a superior one, a more comfortable one, one where our virtues and gifts were understood and prized and witnessed. Where we didn't have to pretend to be anything but our obviously superior selves. Peggy and Jane loved my father; to them, he wasn't the failure who couldn't support a family, couldn't keep a job; they were involved in the larger project of his giftedness, of reassuring him that his failures were not his fault, but the fault of a crude, vulgar, and unappreciative world.

I knew very early on, although I can't imagine how it might have been spoken of, that Jane Kearney "came from money." She seemed removed from the kinds of anxieties about money that pressed on everyone around me. Unlike anyone else I knew, she brought gifts every time she came to visit, and she came to visit once or twice a month. There was always a gift for me and a gift for my mother, and, for my father, a bottle of whiskey or a book. Once, she made a mistake in her gifts, or I made a mistake and opened the one that was for my mother thinking it was for me. My mother's gift was a packet of hangers, covered with a Nile-green quilted satin. I had never in my life seen hangers made of anything but wire or wood, and I was enchanted; I ran my palms over the delightful surface, the soft satin, the rough stitching clothing the hard wood. I was desolated to find out that these were not for me; my gift was a little pin of a fur mouse. My mother, though, understood, and gave me one of the hangers for myself; it hung in the darkness of my closet, empty (it was much too large for my small things), like a friendly planet in a black sky, reassuring me of a future which I was certain would be much more tender and more opulent than the trap of childhood to which I had been relegated for this term of my imprisonment. I needed hints that one day I would be freed; that I would no longer have to pretend to be a child but could take my place in the world from which I had been excluded by the cruel hoax of my body's misleading form.

Jane's father had made a very comfortable living selling the material used to make the linings of coffins. He had died before I was born, but Jane had some kind of legacy, some kind of cushion that made things possible. I had no idea what the possibilities might be, but it was reassuring even to take a whiff of them in the air that was so much, in my house, a fug of financial worry.

Just this year, all of the involved parties long dead, I found some letters from my father to Jane. Apparently, she had provided some money for a Catholic news syndicate that my father was supposed to run; I can't get the details straight, but it seemed, like everything else my father put his hand to, to have come a cropper. She wanted some of her money back. My father's tone is outraged, betrayed. He asserts his need to be paid in advance on account of being the father of a baby girl, and (an indication of my parents' unorthodox domestic arrangements) insists that he needs more money in order to do the research Jane thinks is required because he will have to "hire a woman to take care of my baby while my wife is out working." Defensively, he writes, "I wish to remind you that although you write that all my projects are 'fly by nite,' I edited two diocesan publications completely for five years with complete satisfaction to the bishop and owners of these publications. I wrote for NCWC news service for three years with complete satisfaction. The only reason I am not doing this work is that, after Pearl Harbor, I was asked to write for 'Victory for Democracy,' and I refused. With a family to support, I cannot afford such luxuries as fighting for the Faith now. I can write for cash only."

It breaks my heart to hear my father speaking in these terms; and I can only imagine how the incident must have mortified my mother, who prided herself on being financially both independent and above reproach. I am angry at Jane for not providing my father with whatever he said he needed. However unjust his request. But Jane, although she loved my father, my mother, and me, wasn't the kind of person to be taken advantage of financially. Did she sacrifice my father's dreams, his cherished fantasies, to her practical good sense? I cannot forgive her for that. I know this is entirely unfair. I can't help it; when it comes to my parents, I pride myself not on being fair but on being on their side.

Jane filled in some important gaps in my mother's competence, as she did the night my father died. Even though her family collected around her, my mother called Jane to be with her. Jane drove to the Bronx from Brooklyn to pick Peggy up and then out to Long Island; only those two paid attention to me. Jane was the one I told that I had a rash on my chest: it turned out to be chicken pox. She was the one who took me to the doctor, told me the bad news:

I was sick, so sick that I couldn't go to my father's funeral. She liked to think of herself as the kind of person who could be counted on to be where she was needed, doing what was needed. When I made a fictional character of her, one of the other characters says that she was famous for always showing up with Kleenex and flashlights. For the next Christmas, she wrapped up a flashlight and Kleenex in a shoebox; I didn't get the reference, but when she explained it, I saw that I had made her happy by publicly praising her tendency to come through.

Each year, my mother and I took our holidays with Peggy and Jane, visiting the priest who had brought them together. Years earlier, he had left the Passionist Order and had gone from one assignment to another, never able to find a comfortable spot: a pastor who understood him, a congregation who would support him. In 1960, he moved back to his hometown of Elmira, New York, moved in with his brother, who was recovering from a heart attack, helped him and his wife financially, did most of the cooking (the wife worked in a factory that made paper boxes), said Mass and heard confessions wherever he was needed. Each summer, Peggy, Jane, my mother, and I drove up there and checked into a motel (at first we stayed in his brother's house, but it became clear we were seen as an imposition). Usually, my mother was the driver in whatever group she was in, but on our holiday trips, Jane drove. My mother provided the sandwiches that we ate along the way, and whiskey sours in a thermos; for some years, I was given the mix without alcohol, then, after I was fifteen, I was given a real drink along with the others. All my mother's friends thought drinking was an important sign of broad-minded adulthood: perhaps a holdover from their Prohibition youth.

On these vacations, Jane was my pal; I was her sidekick. I sat next to her in the front, her navigator. As I became a teenager, she would turn the radio to the rock-and-roll station WABC, for as long as we could pick up the New York signal. Peggy and my mother, sitting in the back seat, groaned at having to endure the punishment of such music. On WABC, the number-one song was played every half-hour, and so, by the time we lost the signal, Jane would have learned the words to whatever the number-one song was, and, defiantly, we would both sing it at the top of our lungs. The summer after my grandmother died, when my mother mortified me by getting drunk in front of Father Dermot, weeping fat sloppy self-pitying tears until he shouted at her that she was disgusting and left the house, Jane put my mother to bed and then took me out to an all-night donut place, allowing me, unlike anyone else in my life, to talk about my mother's drinking. She had no idea of what to do, but at least she allowed me not to go along with my mother's pretense that there was no problem.

When I try to remember conversations my mother might have had with Jane, or to imagine what they might have done when I wasn't there, I draw a blank. What does this mean about their friendship? I know they were important to each other, but I have no idea what the flavor of that importance might have been. I don't like to think that Jane was interested in my mother because she was my mother, that it was not my mother's company she craved but mine.

Jane had another life, a life apart from us, a life made possible by her freedom from financial cares. The expansiveness of this life took an unusual, imaginative, very Catholic form. She became involved with doing good works for criminals. This is one of the complicated—some would say, twisted—rewards of Catholic virtue: it did more than open you up to the larger world. In this case, it allowed, it sacralized, a *nostalgie de la boue*: you could consort with people who lived on the dark side, you could hear their stories, spend time with them, even enjoy them, as long as what you had in mind all along was not only their reform—that would be for Protestants—but their conversion to a world of spiritual richness in which they both saw the error of their ways (that would be for Protestants) and, more important, thanked God for their dark past, because it had deepened their souls, made a larger place for the love of God with which they were now on fire, and in shadow-filled churches, in the first light of dawn, they would fall on their knees, in prayers of contrition.

Jane's connection with the dark side came through her membership in the Legion of Mary, an organization of lay people, mostly women, founded in Ireland in 1921, and exported to America ten years later. Their mission was to perform what were known in the Church as the corporal works of mercy, and they specialized in visiting the sick and those in prison. The Legion was an attempt to create for laywomen the kind of balance between a life of prayer and a life of active charity that seemed to be open only to people who had full membership in religious orders. It required a real commitment. Members had to meet twice a week in their presidium (I was excited by the word, as I always was by a foreign word sneaking its way into ordinary English, like nuts or raisins in the batter of a plain cake) for prayer and meditation, and then, like the nuns of that time, travel in pairs once a week to do their good works.

The Legion of Mary, like the Legion of Decency, invoked military terms, but I never saw a group of soldiers, Roman or otherwise, when I heard the word "legion." I suppose it was such a commonplace for Catholics to think of themselves as embattled, the Church on earth was called "the Church militant," as opposed to the Church in heaven, "the Church triumphant," or the Church in purgatory, "the Church suffering." Who was the enemy, whom we were constantly at war against? In a larger sense, it was the entire modern world, but in a more focused sense, the enemy was communism. Interesting that their word "presidium," used to indicate their small units of membership, is a translation for "cell": the unit for communist groups flourishing at the same time.

Jane's partner was a woman much younger than she named Stella, who, like Jane, came to the house in straight dull-colored skirts, blouses starched to a fare-thee-well that had no relation to the body they covered; both women's complexions were a little oily, their pores a bit enlarged, their whole countenances untouched by makeup. Neither of them wore perfume.

I don't know where Stella disappeared to, but it was soon clear that Jane had gone far beyond the Legion's guidelines in her relationships with women prisoners.

She seemed to have gone out on her own, even breaking away from the priest for whom she had left the Legion (who had himself broken away from the Legion, finding their guidelines too restrictive), a priest who for a while became quite famous in his care of heroin addicts and was known as "the junkie priest." A book was written about him; it might have been a movie. But he and Jane had some kind of falling-out; she thought he'd gone crazy, I no longer remember why.

Jane broke away from both the Legion and the priest, risks enraging her genteel mother, because her involvement with the drug addicts became so personal, so intense. She bailed them out. She loaned them money. The Legion did not approve of this sort of thing, nor did the junkie priest—I think he wanted to think he was the only one to touch these women, or that they had to pay some obeisance to him, which the women were unwilling to give. Jane seemed to ask nothing of them; when they called for her, she showed up. Showing up at police precincts, at the Women's House of Detention (picking up their slang, "the House of D") on Sixth Avenue in the Village, then driving to her mother's large apartment in Park Slope; her mother was a retired schoolteacher, now in a wheelchair, real lace always at her throat, a bandeau held together with a cameo. Showing up the next day, exhausted, for her responsible job as vice-president at a bank at Lexington Avenue and 57th Street, right near Bloomingdale's.

She had a particularly close relationship with one of the addicts. I think her name was Lenore. I can see her very well, Jane's Lenore, standing in our driveway, getting out of Jane's tan Chevrolet, dressed as no one I had ever seen was dressed, except someone in a movie. It is 1959. I know it is 1959 because Lenore is talking about Billie Holiday's death, she is very upset about Billie Holiday's death, and Jane is saying, Well, you can learn a lesson from Billie, you don't need to go that way. I don't know who Billie Holiday is, and why Lenore is talking about her death when she has just come to our house, when she hardly knows us, but I am fascinated by her looks: her dark-black hair in a stiff French twist; her black sheath dress, more formfitting than any dress on any woman I have ever seen; her black slingbacks, which she wears without stockings, something I have also never seen a woman do; her dark eyeliner, which I have never seen a woman wear; and her cigarette, which she puts out on the black asphalt driveway with her black heel and then picks up and puts in her pocketbook. So, although I don't know who Billie Holiday is, I have a sense— something that makes a certain kind of adult adore me, and a certain other kind suspect and hate me—that if I'm quiet for a while I'll get the meaning of the thing that I am or am not meant to understand. I learn that Billie Holiday is a singer and died of drugs, that she went "to Lexington" but it was too late, that it was important to Jane that she asked for a priest before she died, but I know that this is of no importance to Lenore.

They don't stay very long, I don't know why they came—they don't have dinner, maybe a cold drink, nothing alcoholic. I can tell my mother likes Lenore, but after Jane is gone, she says she's worried that Jane's "not drawing the line," and that, "for all her brains, she can be a pushover." I see Jane holding a long piece of chalk, refusing to do or draw something; then I see Lenore pushing her into the sand, like one of those round-bottom clown toys that will eventually right itself, though it will take a while.

My mother explains that Jane is trying to reintroduce Lenore into normal life; she's been in jail; she's going to "Lexington," which is a hospital for drug addicts where Billie Holiday went, and Jane's trying to give her some normal good times before she goes.

Lexington is not a success, and somehow Jane must give up on Lenore; Lenore lies, steals money from her, uses her as a reference, then does not show up at the jobs she has been given, although she is, my mother says, very intelligent, and could, if she wanted to, make something of herself. Then, one day, Jane calls to say Lenore is dead; she was murdered by her girlfriend. And once again I have to pretend to understand something that at first I don't understand—a girl with a girlfriend—and then, of course, I do understand it, know that I have understood it all along, that word—"lesbian"—sounding like a swamp creature, unclean, poisonous.

If Jane's attentions to Lenore were traceable to impulses of Christian charity, it is more difficult to trace the motivation for her friendship with a woman whom I will call Chris. Chris seemed to need nothing from anyone—except, perhaps (though she didn't know it, which only made the need more great), the salvation of her soul through membership in the Roman Catholic Church. I don't know how they met; it may have been through some professional-women's organization—Chris worked in advertising, but she didn't seem to have a job that was nearly as impressive as Jane's. She was very good-looking in a way I had seen in magazines, but not in the movies or on television. She had a perpetual tan, and a fascinating gap between her two front teeth; she was tall and slender and moved boyishly. I don't know whether she mentioned early on that she played tennis, but I always imagined her holding a tennis racquet.

Though she wasn't from New York, I imagined she got the code that was embedded in *The New Yorker*'s Talk of the Town. She had pretty thoroughly shaken off the provincial city where she was born: Rochester, Cleveland, Cincinnati, Pittsburgh, something not too far west, a place whose distance from New York, or lack of farness, would have enabled a yearly trip, a stay in a good hotel, "taking in a few shows," going to a museum, although I imagined Chris most comfortably in the Museum of Natural History—she was boyish in that way. I could read her past lack of financial anxiety, even her past as a student at a small, select women's college in the way she wrote her thank-you notes on plain ivory cards, illustrated with witty little drawings in the upper right-hand corner.

(It was what she really wanted to be, a cartoonist, and perhaps she thought working in advertising—which in the early sixties was one of the most glamorous professions—would be an outlet for her creativity. It was not.)

I can't imagine why she thought it would be desirable to go on vacation with us—Jane, Peggy, and my mother and me—staying in a cheap motel and listening to a burnt-out, bitter priest talk about the degradation of the modern world. Only many years later did I begin to have a hint. I was in graduate school, living away from New York, home for a holiday. Jane asked me if I would meet her and Chris for lunch. I barely recognized Chris: she was heavy, bloated, and clearly in a manic state. During the lunch, she gripped my hand, painfully, under the table, as if she needed something, anything, to hold on to, and I happened to be there. She was verbally abusive to Jane, and Jane was embarrassed, trying to calm her down. I have no idea why Jane thought it would be a good idea for me to join them, only somehow that Chris wanted it. That night, Chris phoned me at my mother's house and confessed her years of mental illness, her years of disastrous lesbian relationships. She asked me if I thought Jane was a lesbian. I couldn't bear even to contemplate the possibility, and Chris's discussing it with me seemed like a betrayal of the most shocking sort. Jane, who had stood beside me, as she had stood beside Chris (who had the grace to assert that Jane had been a bulwark to her during her breakdowns), as she had stood beside Lenore and the other drug addicts—to have this all reduced to a displaced sexual desire seemed to me grotesque. It still does. I believe Jane died a virgin.

She did not die well. And when she died, I hadn't spoken to her for years. I had cut her off; I was angry at her, and I wanted to punish her.

After my mother's retirement, which coincided with Jane's, I moved my mother up to the small town on the Hudson where I lived with my husband and children. It was not a difficult drive from New York, and it was easily accessible by bus or train. Time after time, I invited Jane: for weekends, for holidays. I told her she could stay with us, or with my mother, or, if she wanted to go home the same night, we would arrange for that. I even offered to pick her up in Queens, drive her to New Paltz, and drive her home the same night. She never came. Not once in seven years. But she would call often, calls that I came to dread; she was clearly lonely, and she would go on and on about things that were of no interest to me. I would tell my husband, when he answered the phone, to say I wasn't home. I said I would take one call in four.

When my mother was moved to the nursing home, Jane never visited her, although she took courses at Fordham every semester, so she was twenty blocks from my mother's nursing home. When I accused her of abandoning my mother, she became abject, apologetic. She said she just couldn't see her as she was. I said my mother needed her. She said she couldn't be there; she couldn't do it. This time she couldn't show up. I did not forgive her. I let my mother down in many things, but I was excellent at punishing people who had let her down.

So, of course, I was very surprised when, years later, I got a call from a nurse who told me that Jane had died and that my name and phone number were the first ones on the list she kept next to her bed. I said that I had no idea what her arrangements were, that we hadn't been in touch for a long time, that I thought she had a niece who was a nun. "Would that be Sister Dorothy?" the nurse asked. I said I had no idea.

The next day, Sister Dorothy calls me. I know she's one of "my nuns," one of the ones I can feel kinship with rather than fear, because she says: "You'll recognize me; I'm the bleach blonde. I started to dye my hair so the kids—I taught first grade—wouldn't think their teacher was an old lady. Now I've had back problems, so I can't teach kids. I'm doing religious education at a parish in Harlem. It's fabulous!"

I tell her I haven't seen Jane recently, in seven years. I apologize for that. "She was good to me when I was younger, but I was angry at her for cutting my mother off."

"She wasn't easy," Dorothy says. "When I was a kid, I resented her because she would make remarks to my mother about being German. The Kearney family thought my father had married beneath him, although it wasn't true; but they thought anyone who wasn't Irish was unacceptable. Then, when she got older, she was difficult in other ways.

"She was furious when I took off the habit," Sister Dorothy says, insisting I call her Dorothy, which is hard for me. "She wouldn't talk to me for a couple of years. Then we got back in touch, and, believe me, it was a mixed blessing. She'd get on the phone, and one of the sisters would answer and say, 'OK, Dorothy, you're in for it.' She wouldn't get off for two hours sometimes. She was very lonely.

"I tried to think of ways to help her. Once, one of our sisters left the community, and she needed a place to live. I knew there was an empty apartment in Jane's complex, but I knew if Jane knew it was a sister who was leaving, she wouldn't help. So I told a bit of a white lie. I said it was an old friend who was moving back from another town. Well, that was sort of true. She helped her get an apartment, but she never visited her. She just stayed in her own apartment smoking, watching television. I would visit my friend, because, you know, we realize it's a hard transition, and we'd try to help; I'd bring her care packages, suitcases full of staples, paper towels, toilet paper, stuff like that, and just be with her, so she'd know we didn't think she was a pariah. And I'd go visit Jane, but I wouldn't say anything about my friend. My friend could have helped her out, but Jane wouldn't have it."

Besides my husband and me, there are only three people in the congregation for Jane's funeral Mass. As it turns out, all of them are nuns. Sitting beside Dorothy is an old friend of Jane's whom I had dreamed of in my childhood; she was a Sister of the Good

Shepherd, an order that I had longed to join. Their ministry was to care for "wayward girls"; girls who got into trouble were sent to them by the courts as an alternative to prison. The third nun, in a white suit, is the one who made pastoral visits to Jane in her illness. She gives the homily, speaking about how important "*her* Jesus" was to Jane. This gives me the willies; it seems a transference of the worst, most sentimental aspects of evangelical Protestantism to Catholicism, which usually manages to keep itself from certain kinds of falseness by the impersonality of its formal diction.

I invite all the nuns out to lunch, but the one in the white suit won't come. Dorothy is eager, however, as is Janice, Jane's friend, who is still in the Good Shepherd Order but is wearing a blue skirt and striped blouse. At lunch, Dorothy says, "Well, *her* Jesus didn't do much to keep her from being embittered. He didn't do much to make her last days more open, more loving." Janice says that it is very sad: she gave so much to so many people, and she couldn't take anything for herself. She says that Jane was terribly proud of me; she would always forward Janice any favorable reviews.

"I think I failed her at the end," I say.

"I think she set it up so that she could only be failed," Dorothy says.

They loved me very much, Peggy and Jane; for them I was the miracle child, the hope of the future. But I could no longer love them when I was no longer a child, and this is a failure of my heart. Death made it possible for my mother's friendship with Peggy to remain untarnished, and perhaps dementia made it possible for Jane's failures to have made no impression on her.

They gave me, my mother and her friends, the great gift of a model of women who enjoyed one another, who talked about the world, a world outside their families, who made for each other a place where they could find themselves and become larger than what they were born into. I have many doubts about myself, but I believe that I know how to be a good friend. And I owe that to them. So I have for them a sense of indebtedness, of gratitude. I can only hope that these can do something to make up for the old betrayal: the betrayal by the child unable to forgive the grown-up for no longer being taller, wiser, better, braver, more in charge.

My Mother *and Priests*

My mother would have found two commonplaces of the modern world incomprehensible: that the typewriter has become obsolete, and that when most Americans think now of Catholic priests, their minds turn first to thoughts of sexual scandal.

It is almost impossible to convey to anyone under fifty the glamour, the shimmer, the esteem that attached to priests when my mother was young, right through the time I was a teenager, the mid-sixties at least. Priests were treated like princes—no, like kings. As with royalty, certain metonymies applied. If the king was his scepter or his crown, the priest was his hands. The awe connected with the Eucharist was expressed by the attention centered on the hands of priests. Their hands turned bread and wine into the body and blood of Christ. A priest took special care of his hands: he was allowed that vanity; it was considered neither self-indulgent nor effeminate. A certain kind of Catholic understood that there were white linen towels kept especially for a priest's visit, so that no cloth but white linen would touch his sacred hands.

Nothing was too much to do for them. Even the ones who liked to think of themselves as part of the family—who dropped in after supper for a drink with the father of nine while the mother put the children to bed or did the dishes—they never understood that accommodations were being made for them, that perhaps if they weren't there the husband/father might be helping his wife.

But there were other kinds of priests, formal, elegant, who could only be served on the best china, using the real silver. Visits of these priests were anticipated, treasured, like the visit of a movie star to a small town. These priests tended to favor maiden ladies— often those living with their mothers—whereas their more demotic brothers made their way to sprawling broods.

There was a kind of unmarried woman who worshipped priests; it was, without doubt, a form of idolatry, of the species reserved by the female for the male. But was it harmful, this idolatry? Or, put more precisely, did it do more harm than good? At least it created a romance in lives that would have been otherwise entirely bereft of it. And it was a romance that had a certain Mediterranean vividness, in distinction to the Barbara Pym variety: knitting vests for the curate, making needlepoint kneelers. For Catholic women, priestly celibacy scumbled the matte palette of wistful spinster dreams. Because there was no possibility of marriage as the end of this romance, it was spared a kind of lowering domesticity; it was understood that both priests and women knew they were above, beyond all that, in some stoic realm of spiritual athleticism, or, rather, a kind of exhausting spiritual minuet, where the rules were very well understood and the dance was performed on a small, intricate set of parquets.

Perhaps for these women their position with priests was a bit like being the treasured private secretary to a general: we were, after all, a part of the Church militant, and the devil was always ready to make war, particularly with God's most favored, his priests. And, perhaps because both the priests and the women saw themselves as needing to fight shoulder to shoulder, there was at least the possibility of a meeting of the minds; some priests, the ones my mother treasured, were among the rare men at that time who took seriously a woman's inner life. If the priests' advice was occasionally disastrous, at least the women were consulted, rather than ordered about. And, like war, or at least like life in the military, their relationships with priests brought these unmarried women into a larger world, where the stakes were higher than staying at home caring for your aged mother, your pathetic brother. Certainly, praying with a man whom you revered offered more glamour than the role of drab, caretaking sparrow to the wounded of the flock.

You will say that I am naïve, that many of these women served priests sexually. This may have been true in the Latin countries, but I am talking of the American Church in the triumphalist years of 1920–60, a church entirely under control of the Irish, who had no toleration for the wink-wink, nudge-nudge, "we're all human after all," "a man's a man" comprehension of their southern counterparts. None of the priests I ever knew misbehaved with any of the women I ever knew. You might say I wouldn't have known. Perhaps I wouldn't have. But what I believe is that, in place of the ordinary heterosexual narrative, there was an alternative one for these women and these priests, a story centering on the pride a woman took in being the kind of woman about whom a breath of scandal would never arise; what she treasured was the idea that she was the kind of woman "Father" could be himself around.

My mother's relationship with priests wasn't about assuaging loneliness, since, although she was unmarried for many years, she lived in a large, bustling family and had many friends. In fact, many of the priests that she befriended were people she could do something for. She had a whole collection of missionaries, for whom she would raise money. In the years before her marriage, she and her mother organized fund-raising spaghetti dinners for various priests who were working in what we would now call the Third World.

There was Father John Marie, who ministered to what we then called "colored children," in the far reaches of South Carolina. He had been an Italian boy my grandparents had known when they lived in Hoboken; he sent us photographs of himself in his Franciscan habit, brown cloth cinched by a white rope, bare feet in sandals. He stood, somewhat abashed, surrounded by skinny children with ill-fitting clothes and long, thin black limbs. I confused them with the heroic children desegregating schools in Little Rock, and with the girls killed in the church in Birmingham. I fantasized about befriending them: their high legs, their tight braids. I fixed on one who wore glasses. I dreamed of asking my mother if she could live with us, go to school with me. She would be the best friend I had, in my real or waking life, somehow failed to make. I fantasized that we would both cut open our arms and mix blood, swearing to be sisters, friends, forever.

"Overseas," which was my mother's term for any country not the United States, my mother focused on Father Reginald, who had been captured by the Chinese communists, held prisoner for years. Did it really happen, or did we just fantasize that he was particularly punished—the communists fiendishly understanding the importance of priests' hands—by having bamboo sticks pushed under his fingernails, a form of torture it was extremely easy to make real in a child's imagination? It was one of the geniuses of the Church that they had only to personalize torture in the figure of a priest or a nun—with priests, it was the Chinese and bamboo; with nuns, it was the Spanish Republicans gleefully raping them in the name of Lenin. And how could you—if you were pious, had even the slightest positive memory of a priest or nun who had been good to you, even once—fail to understand that it was your duty as a loyal Catholic to avenge this outrage, to pledge yourself to exterminate communism, with every effort open to you until your dying breath?

Father Reginald survived his capture, his torture, his imprisonment; he left China and moved to the Philippines, far less conducive to fantasy. I thought of it as a place that was always hot, where people always wore straw hats. Eventually, he was named Bishop of the Philippines, and it was exciting when the envelopes from him arrived, with a symbol of his episcopacy: a shape that was something like a biretta with tassels but wasn't a hat. It signified the authority of the official Church. He wrote each month to thank my mother, personally, for her contribution. I think she sent him five dollars a month until his death—at which point there were no more missionaries left for her, no one to whom she could write a check, putting a face with a dollar amount.

My mother's desire to be of practical service to the priests she admired was the source of one of her most long-standing—if least dramatic—relationships with a priest. She had devoted herself to the Passionist Order, beginning with her making novenas at their church in Jamaica, Queens, then moving out and upwards to her making retreats with some of these priests, two of whom she attached herself to deeply, and for life. The Passionist Fathers were a semi-monastic order—that is to say, they lived in community, rather than in parishes (there were exceptions, but these were rare)—and they wore a habit, a long black robe and sandals; over their hearts, a black-and-white heart-shaped leather badge that said "Jesu Passio XPI" (I preach Christ crucified). Their major ministry was preaching; they were famous for parish missions and retreats.

Father Lambert was a Passionist who had had a distinguished intellectual past; he had been a canonist—that is, a specialist in canon law—and trained in Rome. But somehow, by the time my mother got to know him, he had been given the job of supervising the order's lucrative business in Mass Cards and something called Purgatorials. These were leatherette folders with, on one side, a sentimental picture of Jesus or the Virgin, and, on the other side, in stylized script, a promise that the dead person whose name was filled in would have a mention in the order's prayers for all eternity. You could buy one of these for five dollars, and bring it to the funeral parlor, where it was more impressive than the plain white envelopes holding ordinary Mass Cards. My mother made it her business to offer these to everyone she might come in contact with; she had quite a little sideline selling Purgatorials, turning every cent over to Father Lambert. Non-Catholics were often particularly grateful to her for being the middleman in providing a memento that would make them seem not only thoughtful and concerned but in the know.

We would visit Father Lambert occasionally, and what was extraordinary about him was the extent of his ordinary social skills—unusual in a priest. He provided us with cookies and soft drinks as we sat in his office and talked about ordinary life. I don't think the Four Last Things—death, judgment, heaven, and hell— were mentioned once. Occasionally, he talked regretfully about how Harlem—where he had been brought up as a boy before the First World War—had gone downhill. "It used to be a bon-ton neighborhood," he said, and when he said that I imagined people walking streets, sitting on stoops, the women in beribboned hats, the men in light suits with shoes as soft-looking as candy. We didn't talk much about the issues that plagued the world, though; mostly, we chatted. Purposeless chatting was unusual for the priests to whom my mother attached herself.

Father Lambert was small of stature, pleasant-looking, smiling; he had large glasses and walked with a sailor's gait. But it was impossible to think of him as a figure of glamour. He was not extraordinarily handsome, and the two priests my mother was closest to had movie-star good looks. Father Lambert seemed to think life was a rather amusing comedy in which not too many people were up to very much, but for Father Bertrand and Father Dermot, the stakes of every day were very high, although their styles were as radically different as the Gothic from the Romanesque.

My mother knew Father Bertrand before she knew Father Dermot, but she always gave him second place in the hierarchy of her regard. Perhaps it was that he was less demanding, less punitive, more forgiving; there was something of the feminine about him, and my mother liked her masculinity uninflected, as she preferred to believe she was involved in a contest judged by harsh, Olympian judges, a contest in which only the very superior would come anywhere near the prize.

Father Bertrand's feminine attributes expressed themselves in his particular kindness to older women, beginning with his mother. I remember visiting him at his mother's large apartment in Union City, New Jersey; everything about her frightened me. Everything connected to her was overlarge and unfresh. Her apartment, which I recall as being painted or papered a dark rose, was insufficiently lit by fixtures set deep into the high ceilings, with bulbs that had nowhere near the wattage to do their job of illumination—if illumination, rather than obscurantism, was what was actually in mind. She had not changed her style of dress since the twenties; I always see her in a drop-waist taffeta, a rusty navy blue, and when she went out, a moth-eaten fur piece, one of those meant to frighten children, with the animal's head, complete with beady glass eyes, biting its putative tail to make a circlet or a shawl. My grandmother had such a fur piece, but it was sleek; whereas Mrs. Weaver's was ratty, mangy, looking as if it were longing to be put to rest. When I first saw the Tenniel illustrations to *Alice in Wonderland* I recognized Mrs. Weaver immediately in the rendering of the Red Queen. Her features had that kind of over-enlargement that blurs signs of gender: a coarseness that could be either male or female, or both, or neither. She would cough, and the cough came from some deep, ruined place. She would never be really well, if she ever had been—and it was hinted that she had never in her life been "a well woman."

Father Bertrand's circle of older women extended far beyond his mother. One of my mother's services to him was to drive him around to visit the aging maiden ladies with whom he would have tea or lunch on his visits to New York. They remembered him from the years when he was stationed in Queens; he was very good at keeping in touch with women like them. I would be enlisted on these visits to houses where the curtains always seemed half drawn in rooms where daylight had never been admitted, where voices were never raised above a whisper, where there was a kind of bruised kindliness hovering above the soft, old furniture and the faded but good carpets and the china, with a plain gold border or a pattern of gentle rosebuds. What did I do there? What did I talk about? The hours have, in my memory, a kind of dim nullity, not unpleasant. I cannot imagine what was in my mind.

My mother claimed to have certain reservations about Father Bertrand's ideas, although I can't help believing that she absorbed her reservations from my father and from Father Dermot. For my father and Father Dermot, Father Bertrand was a "liberal," although I can hardly imagine what that might mean. For my parents and nearly everyone I knew, the word "liberal" could only be an accusation of being guilty of a certain softness about sex or politics. It was before the days of liturgical reform, so the accusation never had an aesthetic cast.

When he came to our apartment to visit, at the end of the evening my father and Father Bertrand would disappear into my father's room and argue fiercely—or I could hear my father's voice raised. But when they came out—and my mother and I could give up our anxious vigil, ashamed of my father for his raised voice, proud as the female attendants of two duelists, holding their jackets, waiting, waiting—my father would fall to his knees and ask Father Bertrand for his blessing. Which also embarrassed and thrilled me. This was the real thing. "Thou art a priest forever"—it had the irresistible allure of the impersonal. We were larger than our personalities, our histories, our likes and dislikes: we were part of the Church, which had gone on before us, and would go on long after we were gone, not caring much about our happiness, our tastes.

. . .

As I am writing this, I decide, on a whim, to Google Bertrand Weaver, CP. There is, remarkably, an entry about him in *Passionist Historical Archives*:

Father Bertrand Weaver, C.P., St. Paul of the Cross Province (1908–1973) Born Sept. 27, 1908, in West Hoboken, New Jersey, he professed his vows on August 15, 1928, and was ordained on April 28, 1934. He was a strong believer of the defense of Catholic faith and morals and at one point even convinced *Reader's Digest* to print his rebuttal article on something he thought was published which went against the Catholic position. He was awarded $600.00. As a young priest, his poetry was published in *Sign Magazine*.

What a frustrating little nugget this is. It reminds me of a bond he and my mother had: they were born in the same place, within three months of each other. For some reason, this pleased the both of them, as if they'd discovered belatedly they were twins, separated at birth. But that is the only real satisfaction the passage offers me. It is infuriatingly vague. The greatest precision seems to be awarded to the amount—rendered exactly—he was paid by the *Reader's Digest*. The subject of the article, however, is never mentioned. It could be anything from birth control to Joseph Stalin.

Among my mother's things is a copy of *The Sign* magazine, published by the Passionists, the issue dated September 1958, including an article by Father Bertrand. The magazine is a fascinating indication of what was on the minds of middle-to-middle-high-brow Catholics in that period. On the cover there is an attractive black woman, and beside her thoughtful face the words "Integration in Action." The article accompanying this picture is an essay praising the Catholic schools of Raleigh, North Carolina, for successful integration without fuss or fanfare. The captions under the pictures are cringe-inducing: "An average student, Barbara responds to coaching. Negroes rate with whites academically. . . . Relationships in cafeteria are informal. Negroes prefer to eat together because main friends are in own race." However, following the photo-essay is an insightful and forward-looking interview about race with Father John LaFarge, a famous champion of the rights of blacks (a convert, the nephew of the man who gave Henry James painting lessons). Following this article is one on the singer Hildegarde, headed "Hildegarde the Incomparable: Hildegarde isn't just the frivolous, witty, glamorous actress she appears to be on stage. She is a person of depth and character whose greatest inspiration is her faith." I can't help wondering if the author of the article was aware that Hildegarde was, at the time of the writing, rumored to be one of the most famous lesbians in New York.

Father Bertrand's article is called "The Cross and the Heart of God." It is entirely undistinguished. The point seems to be that Jesus' death on the cross is a sign of his love for humankind—hardly late-breaking news. My head spins with the number of quotations he uses, beginning with Isaiah and Jeremiah (called, as they were in Catholic circles in my childhood, Isais and Jeremias: Latinizing them, bleaching their Jewishness). He then moves on to St. Paul, Francis Thompson, Richard Crashaw, Pope Pius XII, Pope Leo XIII, an anonymous Byzantine hymnist, and St. John Damascene (this was a Catholic joke: Who's the patron saint of cars? St. John Damn Machine). Most interesting to me, indicative of the habit of mind that joined him and my parents, is this quote from Chesterton: "We are meant to feel that His [Christ's] life was in that sense a love affair with death, a romance of the pursuit of the ultimate sacrifice." But Father Bertrand steps back from this Romantic brink, warning, "This whole way of talking has to be kept in its proper frame of reference. Neither poverty nor death can be sought for its own sake. To seek negation for its own sake is irrational."

The presence of so many quotes in an article of approximately fifteen hundred words speaks to a certain literary insecurity: does he have no ideas of his own, or is he just afraid they aren't good enough? Alongside the Google entry, the article provides me with certain hints, certain questions: Was Father Bertrand an ambitious young poet, an ambitious young journalist? Did he have dreams to become a writer? My parents' meeting came about because my father read an article Father Bertrand had written, and wrote back, objecting to it. Impressed with his opponent's articulateness, Father Bertrand asked to meet, and they met at the Convent of Mary Reparatrix (perhaps he was stationed somewhere outside New York and this was one opportunity that would be convenient to both of them), where he was giving a retreat that my mother was attending. He introduced my parents to each other. I have no idea how things progressed from there, but without Father Bertrand I would not be.

Everyone remarked on Father Bertrand's looks. He had a sensuous mouth and lazy blue eyes; he had a kind of Richard Burton quality—if you could declaw Richard Burton, remove him entirely from the imagination of sexual danger. Sexual danger, but not sexual allure, for part of the story of Father Bertrand and my mother must contain the fact that when I was a quite small girl, from the age of four to the age of ten, I was madly and desperately in love with him. I yearned for his rare visits; I wrote my first letters to him ("How are you. I am fine. Love and God bless you. Mary Kate"). And he wrote back! Who wouldn't love someone who wrote back to a little girl! I asked for the job of checking the mail every day; I flew downstairs when I heard the mailman, and when I saw Father Bertrand's handwriting on an envelope in the mailbox, my heart raced and leapt.

It was love, it was real, passionate love, a passion that at once had everything and nothing to do with sex. Had he been a different sort of man, the sort of man people now imagine all priests to be, could he have taken advantage of this? Isn't it the abuser's excuse always, "she wanted it, she wanted it to happen"? But what is *it*? Certainly, the last thing I wanted (or who knows what my unconscious mind desired—the last thing I could possibly have been aware of wanting) was some sort of genital contact. But it has occurred to me that for many of us genital contact is only a kind of substitute, a kind of language that comes closer than any other to expressing what is really desired but can't be named, because it is more difficult to access for young girls than sex: by which I mean attention, praise. And I got it from him—attention, praise—from his letters, the occasional present (I remember, coming in the mail, the words in larger lettering seeming magical to me—"Parcel Post"—a miniature red box of chocolates), and his special greeting for me, "You are THE ONE."

I found in his physical presence a kind of masculine glamour that was different from my father's brand of the same product. Although my father was born in Lithuania and raised in Cleveland, to me he was New York: quick-moving, angular; his shoes were brown; his hat was gray; when he laughed he threw himself around the floor; he couldn't get enough of me, his appetite for me was endless, and I could manipulate that, and I could have him whenever I wanted. Father Bertrand, whose antecedents were English (remarkable to us: English and a priest!), gave off a cooler kind of allure, a blue-eyed reserve. I had to wait my turn for him to pay attention to me, as I never had to wait for my father. I would sit among the adults in silence, watching him, entranced by every gesture. I loved the way he held his drinks; I loved the name of his customary choice—a highball—and it seemed that in his hand the whiskey grew more golden, lighter, and the clink of the ice against the glass when he swirled his drink struck me as particularly sophisticated, as did the way he chewed ice cubes, with his front teeth. And perhaps I liked the way my mother was around him, the kind of woman he made my mother into. She became a hostess: pouring drinks, filling dishes with peanuts. She encouraged him to tell stories. I think one of the things that priests did for my mother was allow her to be the kind of conventional woman she was usually reluctant to be, the kind she couldn't be with my father, who was so obviously unconventional.

Father Bertrand would sit back in his seat while my mother served him. He laughed rarely, and his laugh was silent. He never seemed angry or anxious, or in a hurry, unlike my father, who was almost incapable of sitting still, who, when he sat, wound his long thin legs around and around each other so sometimes I was convinced he would be unable to unwind them and be stuck, a comic figure, until someone could help him from his chair. Father Bertrand's gestures had a kind of languor; sometimes when he would stick his arm out to stretch, I would touch his hand. When he was getting ready to leave, I would hug him for as long as I was allowed, dreading the moment when we'd be separated. My father, who usually found my every behavior admirable, didn't like that. I can hear his words, "Don't maul the man." But my mother understood; she mailed my letters to Father Bertrand, she agreed with me about his handsomeness, his kindness. She made the point that, of all the priests she knew, he was the most attentive to old, lonely women.

And after my father died, she understood that I needed a kind of male attention, and that Father Bertrand could fill a gap I usually resented others (my uncles, friends of the family) for trying to fill. I think she understood this because her priests were pseudo- or ancillary husbands—first, in the time of her life where there was no real husband, even on the horizon; second, when my father's inadequacies proved mortifying to her; and third, in the comfortable estate of her widowhood. Because she so naturally used them as ancillary husbands, she understood the sense of having them take my father's place in my life as well. So, after my father died, she made a point of getting in touch with Father Bertrand more than we had. We wrote him more often. She even arranged for us to phone him more regularly than usual; he was a traveling preacher, and stationed in Springfield, Massachusetts, so the calls were long-distance, an extravagance that, to my mother, always approached the wildly heedless.

My mother would make an event of our calling Father Bertrand. We would go, of an evening, to Howard Johnson's for an ice-cream soda. Or I would have an ice-cream soda; my mother, who had no interest in sweets, would get a whiskey sour. Then we would go to the drugstore, which took up the bottom floor of the building where my mother's office was located. We would squeeze ourselves into the wooden phone booth and make our call. It never lasted too long—she wouldn't be insane enough to forget all sound financial principles—but it was an outing. We could easily have made the phone call from my grandmother's living room, but my mother knew better. She had a knack for treats, and she knew nothing could please me more than a call to Father Bertrand.

She understood that some of the most difficult occasions for me in the time after my father died were the days before holidays, particularly Father's Day, when the children in my class would make cards for their fathers. I must have given her a hard time the first Father's Day after my father died, and she was ready for the next one. My mother had a kind of genius for contingency plans, a skill cultivated, I think, in a world in which scarcity in most things—physical and metaphysical—was the rule. In the spring of the year after my father died, Father Bertrand was going to be celebrating the silver anniversary of his ordination to the priesthood. We were invited to the celebration, which would take place at the Passionist Monastery in Union City, New Jersey.

I hadn't seen Father Bertrand since the previous summer, and I was immensely excited at the prospect. And my mother had a suggestion that would make the occasion even more momentous. "I have an idea," she said. "When you see Father Bertrand, why don't you ask him if he would become your Spiritual Father? That way you could make cards for him on holidays. They could just say 'to my Spiritual Father,' instead of 'to my father,' but it would be just as good." I wanted to tell her it wouldn't be just as good (my mother would never follow me into the terrain I inhabited endlessly, the terrain of endless, irreplaceable loss). But I understood that a card "to my Spiritual Father" was much classier than "to my uncle"; it never occurred to me that anyone else would fail to see the distinction, would find the whole enterprise strange.

The day did not turn out well. I stood on the line to get communion from Father Bertrand, but at the last moment, another priest decided to help out and I was shunted over to his line. It would have been my first time to get communion from Father Bertrand, and the opportunity had been stolen from me. Behind my hands, pretending I was praying, I sobbed almost without control. My mother was abashed; she never knew when I was going to break into uncontrollable tears of loss about my father, but she was surprised at this outburst. When I explained that I was weeping with disappointment because I hadn't gotten communion from Father Bertrand, her patience snapped. "It's the Body and Blood of Christ, for Christ's sake," she said. "Keep your mind on what's important. The human being doesn't matter." I knew that was one of those pious lies that had no reality, like the one people had told me, "You have nothing to grieve over. Your father is happy with God in heaven."

At the reception, Father Bertrand seemed to be surrounded by kin, and I had a hard time getting access to him. But I was determined to make my request. He seemed to be spending a long time, too long a time for my taste, talking to his nephew and the nephew's fiancée: he would marry them that April. They were talking about the details of the wedding. I was bored. And I was jealous of his paying so much attention to them. Was it because the bride-to-be was so pretty, in her navy-blue suit with white piping, her navy-blue spike heels, her clever hat that sat on top of her chignon like a particularly witty punctuation mark? Whatever it was, I had come to the end of my tether. I waited for a momentary break in the conversation. I was hoping the bride and groom would move away, but they didn't. And I knew we would be leaving soon.

"Excuse me, Father, but I wanted to ask you a favor. Would you be my Spiritual Father?"

As soon as the words were out of my mouth, I knew that they

were wrong, strange, weird, and I was all those things. In my imagination, Father Bertrand's face would be full of delighted gratitude and anticipation; perhaps I even imagined his eyes brimming with unshed tears. But he merely looked puzzled. And the bride-to-be looked at me with the distaste of the conventionally successful for the pathetic failure who has tried to be original but only succeeded in bringing mortification into the room, like a wet wind or a bad smell.

"Of course," he said, but then someone else in his family took his attention, and we didn't speak again that day. The next week, however, there was a letter from him. It was signed, "from your Spiritual Father." But it was too late. The romance was over. I didn't long for his presence, ever, after that, and he became, from that time on, my mother's and not mine. I must have seen him on social occasions after that, but he was no longer important to me.

After I was grown up, I had only two encounters with him. They were both dreadful, and all the dreadfulness was due to me. The first happened when I was in college, at the wedding of one of my cousins, which he had performed. It was 1970, the year of Cambodia, the year of Kent State. I had spent the spring demonstrating; I had been tear-gassed and pushed by cops, I was in love with a homosexual; more than one classmate I knew had died of a heroin overdose; friends went to basements in the Bronx for illegal abortions; we collected money to help pay for them, and then sat around their beds while they bled, and served them ice cream, and prayed that septicemia would not set in. I was furious at the Catholic Church, particularly for the sexual repression it demanded, the sexual lies it told. I wanted to tell every priest I came across that I knew more of the world than he did, so how dare he tell me, or even suggest, how I should behave?

It must have been that rage, that desire to punish someone for the shame I had been made to feel, that led me to act as I did with Father Bertrand and the young man he brought along to the wedding as his guest. I knew the young man had recently been released from a mental hospital, and bringing him to the wedding was another of Father Bertrand's kindnesses. But I had no impulse to be kind. I flirted with the young man; he was good-looking in a ruined, cigarette-y kind of way; his eyes were sleepy, and that could be seen as sexy if one was really looking for that kind of thing. And I was. I was twenty-one. I remember how attractive I felt in my green silk minidress with an Empire waist and a pattern of dim rosebuds, almost rust-colored, as if the petals of the roses had been mixed with ash. I wanted to dance; I wanted to be seen dancing. But whom could I dance with in a way that would allow me to be seen to be the desirable woman I was, the most desirable of all the cousins—I, whom they had early on written off as living only in the mind, therefore irrelevant, pathetic, beyond notice except for castigation or contempt. I flung my long hair; I scissored my feet in my lime-colored Mary Janes; I wiggled my hips and felt the two layers of silk (slip, dress) grow sweaty against the flesh I knew quite well to be desirable. And of course he fell for it, Father Bertrand's friend, he fell for me. The next day, he called me for a date. I pretended to be shocked: he was much older than I. I insisted that my mother call Father Bertrand and tell him to tell his friend that he had no right, no right at all, to think of me in this way. That he must never call me again. Although how had he got my number? Had I gone too far and given it to him? Or had Father Bertrand given it to him, seeing me as part of the ruined boy's cure? My mother didn't put up any resistance; I think she was frightened at the idea of a madman's doing possible harm to her child, and this trumped even her deference to one of her beloved priests. She called him; he agreed to tell his friend he must have nothing more to do with me.

The last time I saw Father Bertrand, I was visiting my mother on a vacation from graduate school. He was spending a few days with her. This was a sign of the increased liberality of the times; in the old days, he would never have been permitted to spend the night in the house of a woman, unsupervised, the two of them alone. My mother had to go to work; she asked if I would make him breakfast. As I cooked his eggs, I railed against the sexual restrictions of the Church: its stupidity about birth control, abortion; the ridiculousness of priestly celibacy. When, finally, I served him his eggs, I noticed that, although he'd just woken up, he was very tired. He had no inclination to argue with me. He said, "I sometimes don't know if the whole thing was worth it or if it was just a mirage." I was terribly shocked—as if I'd kicked my foot against a mountain, just to make a mark in the surface of the rock, and had instead started an avalanche. I was very glad to be leaving soon, back to my studio apartment and my friends whom I did not need to punish, for whom brutality, in the name of honesty, was not required.

When he left, my mother phoned to say that he had told her, weeping, that he was dying of cancer. "He wasn't himself. He asked me for things he'd never have asked me for. He asked me to let him cry. He asked me if I would rub his back with alcohol. He actually took his shirt off in front of me. Of course I gave him a back rub; he said he was in pain all the time, that he was never free of pain. I just hope those priests in the monastery know how to take care of him. I hope he knows he can come here any time and just do whatever he likes, and I'll do anything for him that I can."

He never came back; he died soon afterwards. My mother went to the funeral. But then she never spoke of him again.

My mother loved Father Bertrand, but she adored Father Dermot. He was, much more than my father, the personification of the male ideal for her. He was a strapping Black Irishman: with a commanding hawklike nose, thin bowed upper lip, jet-black straight hair that, when he was agitated, seemed to stand up on his head like an enraged bird's tuft. He had been brought up on a farm, and it seemed he could do anything—carpentry, electrical work, primitive plumbing—and there were the stories of his childhood, a middle boy of seven slaughtering chickens and killing pigs.

He left the Passionist Order in the early 1950s; it had become too liberal and insufficiently strict. Because Father Bertrand was a

Passionist and I found him on their Web site, I decide to Google Father Dermot. When I find him in an entry, it is linked to me, because a Passionist priest learned that Father Dermot had been the model for the priest in my novel *The Company of Women*. The priest who mentions this says that he owes his vocation to Father Dermot. When I phone him, he says that he met Father Dermot giving a mission in his parish, and, despite Father Dermot's discouragement, he entered the Passionists. When he entered, he learned that Father Dermot had left.

When he left the order and became "freelance," he was able to choose his own assignments; they all fell into the iconography of the cowboy priest. He went first to work among Indians in New Mexico. It's strange that all the details I have about his pastoral life are physical—not a memory that could even loosely be called spiritual comes ever to my mind. So I remember his saying how he had invented a perfectly natural method of air conditioning for the church—it had something to do with natural evaporation. After he left there (the reason for leaving is vague: a liberal bishop out to get him, jealous fellow clergy listening to rumors that he was sleeping with his housekeeper, this last a consequence of his good looks, his masculinity), he went to work among the Indians in Sudbury, Ontario. The detail I remember is that it was so cold he had to sleep with his two boxer dogs in the bed beside him, and then he would wake drenched in sweat and have to insist that they take their place on the floor. He never spoke of the Indians he served with any affection: they were drunks, they were cheats, they only wanted what they could get out of you, they had no natural affection for the Church.

He disliked the military; it was, after all, a secular institution, and he had no interest in secular institutions, but there was something military in his bearing, though he was less like a contemporary soldier than a Roman *miles*; it would be easy to imagine him in cuirass and armor, his bare sinewy thighs bronzed by the Mediterranean sun, marching across the Alps to vanquish Hannibal. Of course, I never saw his bare thighs; I never saw him dressed in anything less than black pants and a short-sleeved shirt. But my mother did have, inexplicably, a photograph of him and his four brothers taken when they were children, standing naked in a row, their hands by their sides, their heads shaved. The children looked orphaned, shamed, and shorn; they looked as if they were about to be murdered. What was my mother doing with such a photograph? Father Dermot must have given it to her. But why?

My mother was not the only woman who adored him; if you adored Father Dermot in the years 1935–55, you had to stand in line behind a queue of women, all of whom were pretending to be patient, deferential, to have no needs at all, but who were seething with desire for his proximity, his attention. If you were one of his women, though, you signed yourself up for a very demanding exercise. It was almost impossible to measure up to his standards. You were bound, if you signed up, to disappoint him, and to disappoint yourself. His disappointed silences were like a blow to the face.

He hated the provisional, the makeshift, all that was not absolute. His favorite term of praise was "orthodox"; his most despised activity was "compromise." The line between those two words—the noun "orthodoxy," the verb "compromise"—was a kind of balance beam in which the soul of the woman gymnast tiptoed her way to glory: the prize of his approbation, which almost never but (and this was his secret) occasionally came.

He was a fascist (he wouldn't mind the category), and because of him I know that Sylvia Plath was right when she said, "Every woman adores a Fascist, / The boot in the face." Like all fascists, he prized a romanticized past; he disliked the modern, the urban, the cosmopolitan; his greatest fear was disorder; he had a real sense that the mob, a horde of unwashed creatures ruled by their appetites, were at any moment about to come over the hill. He pretended also to despise "moneymen," but, viscerally, it was the uneducated masses that disgusted him. I would say "terrified," but fear was not something he would ever admit to in the panoply of qualities it was possible for him to embody.

And yet, because of him, I know Plath was wrong when she talked about "the brute / Brute heart of a brute like you." Because, if he had been brutish, he would have been less powerful, less seductive—and, if you interpreted him a certain way, less danger-ous. In fact, his manners were courtly, caressive. I remember the first time I met him. It was the year after my father died, and I had grown up hearing valiant tales about him, as a Scots child might have grown up hearing about Bonnie Prince Charlie. My mother and her friends Peggy and Jane were staying in one of the houses on my aunt and uncle's camp in the Adirondacks, where I had miserably been staying all summer. Father Dermot would join them for a week.

I was sent to wait for him at the entrance to the property and to show him the way to the house where he would be staying. He drove up in a beige Karmann Ghia; it was the first foreign car I had ever seen. He stopped the car when he saw me, and opened the door, gesturing for me to get in. "So you are Mary Catherine," he said. I don't think anyone had ever before called me by my full baptismal name, and I felt, for the first time, correctly demarcated, placed. I can remember the thrill of that, the sense of perfect right-ness, like a Bach partita or a poem by George Herbert or Dürer's signature: AD at the bottom of a drawing of a lion or a squirrel. I felt as if someone had finally found the outfit that perfectly suited my true nature, my true identity, as if he had ordered custom-made for me a finely cut coat made of the purest wool, durable, lined in satin, with ornamental velvet buttons of a vivid, rich, con-trasting shade.

We drove up the hill in silence. The women stood at the door, their hands at their sides, perfectly silent, waiting for him to approach. They knew it was important not to make a fuss. For that week they sat at his feet (only I did, literally; they sat around him on the porch, on wicker chairs) and listened to him talk about God and the United States and Faith and Morals, the corruption of the modern world, the corruption of the Church, the corruption of politics.

I think he worked very hard not to show favoritism among all the women who had collected around him during the two decades when he had their attention, and I don't think he particularly admired my mother more than anyone else, but she had something they didn't have: she had married my father, she had borne his child. He had advised my parents not to marry; he said that my father's vocation as the St. Paul of his age could only be compromised by the responsibilities of family life. Oh, he had no problem comparing my father to St. Paul. Father Dermot's regard for my father, his love for him, his admiration for him, was an Alp compared with the gentle hills of what any of the women could inspire in him. When my mother wrote, after my father's death, complaining of her troubles, he wrote back one of the most brutal sentences I have ever read: "Say nothing of your sorrow. Your sorrow is nothing next to mine. You have a child of his loins. I have lost everything." What he felt for my father may or may not have been a homoerotic passion, but even if it was, that was only part of it. He was in love with my father's conversion from Judaism, with his intellectuality, with his extremism, and the price he paid for it. My father fell into the saints' life pattern of the holy failure. Like many Catholics, Father Dermot treasured failure. Success was for Protestants: a sign of a mediocre nature, of "compromise." This is one thing that has changed about the Catholic Church: no one of any stripe, whether of the right or the left wing of Catholicism, romanticizes failure any more.

But because his feelings about femaleness were so complex and so contradictory, his relationship with my mother was uneven and confusing—or would have been confusing to her if she had thought about it, if she had imagined that she had the right to expect anything of him, if she thought for a moment that he wasn't giving her what she deserved. "Justice"—"deserving"—these were not part of the grammar of her relationship to him. She was happy just to be near him. If he acknowledged her, however briefly, that was all to the good. But it was surplus value: it had nothing to do with ordinary day-to-day economies.

The unevenness of his relationship to my mother was based on the complexity of his position as a priest. On the one hand, he had, being the kind of priest he was, to assert the sacredness of marriage and motherhood for women—although, once again, being the kind of priest he was, with an appetite for metaphysical high flying, he didn't have to assert that it was the highest calling, the superior one. But he couldn't possibly be seen to despise maternity—although he did say to me once that if I ever went into labor I must not cry out, however bad the pain was, because I must be above the weakness of women.

If he had been an allegorical painter recording the women around him, he would have painted my mother as the fleshiest of the lot—which, in fact, she literally was. Perhaps he would have painted her like a fat Rubens, or gorging on grapes or the legs of succulent fowl. My mother's unignorable fleshiness created, in Father Dermot, contradictory responses. Part of their understanding of each other was that they were not "straitlaced." They liked telling each other dirty jokes, often but not always scatological. I remember my mother, barely able to ask her question through her laughter, demanding to know what exactly the Psalmist meant by "let my horn be exalted." He once told a story about the "good old days," by which he meant the Middle Ages, when candidates for a monastery were observed from below, unseen, by their superiors, to make sure they had "sufficient testicular development." As each one passed, the superiors would note "*habet*" (he has them). But one, Father Dermot said, inspired the superior to cry out in a loud voice, "*Haaabbbett.*" Once, when I was going through a particularly squeamish phase, I asked Father Dermot to speak to my mother about her coarse language. He made a point of using as much coarse language as possible in every sentence that followed and telling me, "If you have half as much character as your mother when you grow up, you'll be lucky." He repeated that when I was visiting him once and was stung by a bee on the sole of my foot. He made me bathe my foot in what seemed to me nearly boiling water, and when I refused he said, "Your mother would have the guts for that. I see you don't." One night, though—it was the terrible time after her mother's death when her family turned against her and she felt she had lost everything—she drank too much and fell into a puddle of blubbery self-pity. He was disgusted. He told her she was "behaving disgracefully" and got up and left. She lay in her bed and howled like an animal.

How to explain the pleasure that ensued from the vacations, the pilgrimages my mother and her friends made to him every summer, just to be near him, to listen to him talk. They came to him as loyal courtiers would to a ruined prince in exile. He had failed at everything they had seen him try; each step he took was less large, less ambitious, less grand than the one before. He had moved from his work among Indians to trying to find any place at all in any parish that would have him. He had left Miami—we never knew why—and then established himself in Jersey City, in the rectory of an old friend, who had also left the Passionists. But they too had quarreled, and Father Dermot had left in the dead of night, telling no one, then phoning to say he had moved into his brother's house in Elmira, New York. His brother had had a heart attack, and at least he knew that there he could be of use.

I don't know how it was decided that Elmira would then be our yearned-for and desirable holiday venue; I don't know how my mother and her friends Peggy and Jane settled on their plans: that we would stay in Elmira for a week, just to be with him, to let him know that he wasn't forgotten, that he was honored, treasured, that his words were still the gold coin of the only realm that they believed to be real.

When it was clear to us that we weren't welcome to camp out at the home of Father Dermot's brother, we made plans to check into a motel on Route 17 just outside Elmira. Each year, when we arrived, we would call Father Dermot, and quite soon he would knock on the door, in his black pants and sport shirt, unless he was coming from a sick call or confessions, in which case he would be in clerical black with his Roman collar. But he would quickly take off his jacket, his collar, his black serge bib that tied in the back like an apron, and put on a more comfortable shirt. We would make drinks for him; I would spread soft cheese on crackers and open bags of chips and cans of nuts. And then what? He would talk and we would listen. We would break for meals, but sometimes Jane and I were sent out to Kentucky Fried Chicken to bring something in. Nobody wanted to tear herself away from him even for a minute. Eating was considered a regrettable distraction—to be got out of the way as quickly as possible, with as little fuss as could be arranged.

For the life of me, I can't remember one subject he discoursed on. All those hours of talk, talk, talk, and not one subject. Only a sentence or two—"You can talk about the future because it's a blank wall, nobody's written on it, you can write whatever you like. But the past, the past is a wall everybody's written on, and what's there is there, you can't make of it what it's not." I had always thought of that as somewhat profound, but now that I write it out, it seems empty, silly. Was he an empty, silly man?

Among my mother's papers I've found some sermons of his that she had taken down in shorthand and then transcribed. They are sermons from the 1930s. She filed them as she would have filed one of her boss's clients' transactions: she used an old legal-file folder, punching holes in the top of the pages and attaching them with a special clip. The name of the client is in her handwriting, crossed out; "Father Dermot" is written below. For the first time, I read these sermons now. I can't read them without seeing his face, hearing his voice, so I can't judge them properly. They're not as bad as I expected: they're not crazy. They're not as good as I might wish: they're literate, but not outstanding. They are an assertion of the truth that the Catholic Church has a monopoly on truth:

That Christ entrusted his plan of life to the Catholic Church is an historical fact that can be proven historically. As foundation for her claim, the Catholic Church presents the overwhelming textual evidence found in the Bible, the pages of history, the signature of God in the miracles at Lourdes, and other places. Catholicism can give the answers to all problems only because it has been entrusted with the answers by its Divine Founder, Jesus Christ, and because the mind of the Church is not composite of many human minds, but the mind of the Holy Ghost, according to the promises of Christ, "He will teach you all things."

I can see that this would be reinforcing for someone whose wobbles were only minor, but it seems pretty thin stuff for someone anguished by doubt in the Church's veracity. He seems to have never wobbled, however:

Catholicism gives an answer to every question that burns in the souls of men. It explains the mystery of life and death. It gives an adequate commentary on the problems of suffering. Labor, poverty, wealth, capital, sex, marriage, birth control, divorce, sin, evil, government, all—all these vital matters have their solution in Catholicism.

With such passionate rhetoric, it could only seem churlish to ask, "Father, could you tell me exactly how this is done?"

In a sermon entitled "The Church and the Poor," he praises the Catholic Worker Movement, a surprise to me because I never heard him do anything but rail against Dorothy Day. But that was the sixties; in the thirties he was writing:

When the Catholic Worker Organization down on Mott Street and others of that noble type, carry on the fight for the workers of America, let them hesitate to tag them Communists, unless they are prepared to call the greatest modern popes socialists and communists and assert that "the miserable condition of millions of the poor and the revolutions that have sprung from those conditions are ascribable chiefly to the crime of the wealthy."

He even goes so far as to allow for some reasonableness in the cause of the Spanish Loyalists:

> If the programs outlined by Leo XIII had been carried out in Spain, the incredible ordeal through which that country is passing would have been avoided. But leaders in Spain, both clerical and lay, permitted criminal social abuses to continue, until the workers and the poor, in desperation, gave ear to the cunning and deceitful propaganda of the agents of Sovietism, and its blind and satanic fury turned upon their own churches and reduced them to heaps of ashes.

I don't know how to understand him from his sermons; I don't understand his turn to the right, his sulfurous anger and sense of betrayal, his black prognostications. He was a disappointed man; he saw the Church he loved giving away the very ground he stood on; he had none of Pope John XXIII's hopefulness about the future; he lived in dread. He had no audience. By the time he was living in Elmira, no one in the congregations of the Masses he was occasionally allowed to preach at would have dreamed of taking his sermons down in shorthand. He had been tamed, his wings clipped. Often he said that he had nothing to live for, that he longed for death.

One year, without telling us where we were going, just telling us to follow his car, he brought us to a desolate spot, an area marked by nothing, uninhabited and overgrown with grayish starved brush.

It was the land he had grown up on. He took us to the old founda-tion; his house had burned down fifty years earlier; his mother had been forced to leave. He told us that he had bought an acre of the property, that he was able to do it out of his meager earnings because it was "dirt cheap." Of course it was; I have never seen a land so undesirable. For the next few years, we would, on one of the days of our visit, bring a picnic lunch to the property and eat there, sitting in our cars. In those years, I thought of myself as a poet, and because I thought poets loved nature, I had to pretend to love it. I would take long, self-regarding, self-loving walks in the area, but I never enjoyed myself. The mountains were distant and forbidding—but unremarkably so. The trees were meager, un-accommodating, and ungenerous: tough, unloved, surviving somehow, taking the little moisture that they needed from the earth in which were planted their deep, sullen roots. I was uncom-fortable, because burrs were always sticking to my clothes, and no matter how assiduously I picked them out, there would always be some abrasive matter irritating my tender places. But when I walked back to the women sitting in their car, across from Father Dermot sitting in his car, and I saw how pleased they were that I had gone on a solitary walk, it was worth it. What did they think I was doing? Praying? Contemplating? Writing poetry? Mostly I was feeling inadequate, because I didn't know what to look at and I was distracted by my irritated skin. But my mother and the women would offer me water, and Father Dermot would put his hand on my shoulder, and I knew that I had succeeded in acting out the part they needed, and which I knew very well how to play. If I could be the child Father Dermot wanted, then my mother could be the woman who'd succeeded in his eyes.

When it was time for us to leave, I would be sent to walk him to his car. And he would always hold me and then turn away sharply. We could all see that he was crying. And those tears floored us all: that such a man, the embodiment of stoic masculinity, was weeping because we were leaving (particularly because I was leaving, I who was the sign and incarnation of their hopes, my father's child, "the fruit of his loins"), weeping tears dragged helplessly but reluctantly out of that stern nature. The fierce attempt to keep them back was only a proof of the strength of his emotions, the depth of his loneliness, the extent of his suffering. None of us would allow ourselves to cry. We breathed deeply. We sighed; we put our suitcases in the car and slammed the trunk down with a particularly forceful bang. We knew we wouldn't see him for another year; we were ennobled by the difficulty.

As it turns out, though we didn't know it, we weren't the only ones making pilgrimages to Father Dermot. There was another from the old group, one of the old retreatants. Only she did the radical thing: she retired early, bought the five acres surrounding the one he had bought for himself. She arranged to have two cinder-block houses built, side by side—one for her, one for him—and a third, an outbuilding—a chapel. This was a terrible blow to my mother and her friends. They never liked Mildred. She was a rawboned, red-faced woman, lean, sinewy, with gunmetal hair pinned tight to her head in a harsh French twist. They said she had "no sense of humor." She was "straitlaced." And now she had triumphed.

We still went to Elmira for a week in the summer, and we stayed in our motel, but now we had to collect every day in Mildred's house, and she was part of the circle that sat and listened. Only she would get up and go out and work around "the land," asking Father Dermot pointed and detailed questions to underscore the fact that they lived there together, although she owned the property. But it was she who allowed him to return, as his last home, to the land of his birth. It had been years since he'd lived in a rectory; it seemed impossible for him to get along with his fellow clergy; he had been boarding, unsatisfactorily, with his sister-in-law and her sister; now he had a home. And it was all because of *her*.

In the car, we all talked about what a pain in the neck she was, how she ruined our time with him, how we could tell that she bored him to death and he couldn't wait for company to relieve him of the burden of being alone with her. But we were trapped. If we were going to see him, we had to see her. We all knew, though, that the great times with him were a thing of the past.

And then, one year, it was 1970, he and I fought. We fought about Vietnam. We fought about Daniel Berrigan. He hadn't wanted me to go to Barnard; he wanted me to go to the University of Louvain in Belgium, where I could get an "orthodox" education. But he hadn't made a fuss about my going. He had no idea of the reality of my life; I might as well have gone to college in outer space. But I wouldn't be quiet as he railed against Daniel Berrigan, insisting he was a dupe of the communists, a traitor to the priesthood. I think I was fairly mild in my objections; I know I was polite. But he would brook no discussion. He slammed his drink down on the table, and the whiskey spilled over the sides. "I won't have you speaking like that in this house." "All right, then," I said, "I'll leave," and I walked into the dark. I told my mother I would never go back—and it was, in fact, the last time I visited him. We had no contact after that; I married without a word from him, and then, soon after that, he died. I don't think I wept much—he seemed like the part of my life I had gratefully got rid of by marrying an English Protestant and moving into the secular intellectual world. What is odd is that I don't think my mother wept much at his death, and for the rest of her life—she lived almost twenty years after him—she rarely spoke of him. So what was the meaning of that love? Or had he relinquished his claim on her love by living with Mildred, or by banishing me from his house?

She never loved another priest like that again. There were reasons: she was older, the Church had changed. In the years when she lived in the house I bought her in the town where I lived with my husband and my children, her last years outside a nursing home, the parish priests were kind and attentive to her, and she was fond of them, but they had no hold on her imagination. And on the day when I had to tell her I was putting her into a nursing home, and I called the young priest she'd been fond of to comfort her, she refused to see him; he came around anyway, but she'd drunk herself into incoherence; she shouted at him from the bedroom to keep away, and then she cursed me and God and her fate. I knew she had lost everything, given up everything, if she'd behave like that before a priest.

My Mother *and My* Father

They should never have married. Anyone could have seen they were wrong for each other, and everyone did see it: almost no one would have told them that marrying would be, for either of them, for the two of them, a good idea. They flew in the face of everyone's advice, of every imaginable branch of wisdom. Of course it didn't work.

What did they make of each other at first meeting? What did he make of her? What did she make of him? What they made was—me. I am the product of a mistake. But not of the ordinary kind. Or perhaps all misalliances are originals.

Their mistake was based not, as in the common run, on physical attraction, but on an idea of eternal salvation. They believed in hellfire, and a vocation that it was sinful to ignore. In following their vocation—a call they believed had come to them from God—

they were saving each other's souls. They were marrying to do God's work. They were shoring up the Church. They were giving it a future: me.

So their judgment wasn't clouded by sex, although they were both good-looking—sexy, even. But if you were to say they were a handsome couple, there were certain things that needed to be overlooked, or got beyond. My mother's misshapen body, and the fact that my father frequently failed to wear his dentures. So, if the stars were in the right alignment—which is to say, if she was sitting down and he had decided that day not to appear toothless— then you could say they were both good to look at: my mother with her jet-black hair, famous white skin, huge gray-green eyes; my father looking like every girl's dream of the starving intellectual: high cheekbones, full, promising lips, dark eyes suggesting all the fruits of the intelligence.

I cannot understand how my mother got access to that dream. Did she have a secret reading life? I wouldn't know, because for her reading was something you did, not something you talked about. I don't know if she read a word my father wrote, if she knew he was working on a biography of Paul Claudel when he had the first of what would be a fatal series of heart attacks in the New York Public Library. She would have heard of Paul Claudel—his name would have been on the lips of some of the priests she admired. But I can't imagine her ever having read his poetry or his plays. So maybe that was the route: the priests she admired read books and talked about them in their sermons. Perhaps marrying a man she thought of as an intellectual was as close as she could get to marrying a priest. The old medieval jointure—cleric, clerk—priests were the only literate ones in the community. Perhaps my mother made an old mistake. Or perhaps she found my father physically attractive, and he convinced her that his bookishness was part of his appeal.

They seemed to me more elegant than other people's parents, the only parents I knew who might have been in the movies. They dressed up more; they were almost never casual. He never appeared on the street without a hat; she had a winter coat, cinched at the waist, trimmed with fur at the collar and cuffs; he wore brown wingtips; she had gold compacts. They had a chrome cocktail shaker and six matching glasses, chalice-shaped and always shining. If I were casting movie stars to play them, she'd be played by Gene Tierney, he by Charles Aznavour. But perhaps every child who loves her parents casts them in a movie as their ideal selves.

I don't know the year they met, how long they knew each other before they married, but I think it was several years, maybe five or seven. Which would mean they met during the war. But the war was something that seemed to go over both their heads, something they rarely thought about, and never spoke of in my presence, although others did. But I think of them dressed in wartime clothes—my mother in tailored suits, her hair waved, pompadoured; my father in pinstripes and fedora.

They were, neither of them, in their first youth. My mother would have been in her mid-thirties and my father in his late forties, although she thought he was in his mid-forties: he lied to her about his age. Despite their age, they necked publicly, embarrassingly, on the subway, in the movies; I have this on good authority from friends who were children at the time. For two people whose marriage was ruined by shame, they were, in their early passion, shameless.

I am glad for them; I am very proud of that. To have parents who were heedless, passionate—all the more admirable, lovable, rare, for their not being in their first youth—that is something to be proud of, after all, something to be strengthened by, something replenishing, encouraging. Not everyone has been given that. Having denied me the ordinary gifts—security, consistency, a sense of safety, a normal childhood—having failed to provide, so to speak, meat and potatoes, they set my place with sweetmeats, piquant sauces: sugarplums, champagne, and caviar. Who is to say that I was not well served?

I always knew that there was passion between them. He brought her gifts that showed he thought of her as desirable: one I remember especially, a rose-colored satin slip, bordered in rose-colored lace at the neck and hem. And he wrote her love poetry. Two lines of one poem are engraved in my memory: "Never in all the annals of recorded time / Existed such sweet pretext for a rhyme." Is it an act of Oedipal vengeance that I have lost my father's poems to my mother? Vengeance or jealousy—I have written poems to lovers but never had one, not even one, written to me. Except once in high school, and I believe that it was an English assignment recycled to impress me. So my mother, with her misshapen body, was the recipient of love poetry; I have not been. Perhaps that is because I have scrupulously avoided involving myself with writers.

Sometimes I would catch them in an embrace, kissing each other full on the lips, lingering kisses, like kisses in the movies. This mortified me and mildly enraged me; at the same time, it reinforced my idea that they were more glamorous than other people's parents, more fully adult.

What was the relationship between their sexual desire for each other and their constant fights? I don't think a day went by when they didn't fight. One of their treasured stories about me (but they were both mythomanes where I was concerned, the myth revolving around my signs of early intellect, my verbal precocity) was that, while still in my high chair, I uttered the complete sentence (my first) "I don't like arguments." I remember running up and down the hall when they would fight, then separate, finished for the moment with each other, and begging them to make up. Running up and down, back and forth: hopeless, they wouldn't make up, not even for me. They treasured their rage, their grievance; it was part of the story of who they were.

Were they one of those couples who went to bed satisfied but exhausted after the nightly wrangle that began in insult and ended in a conjugal embrace, then woke each morning ready for the day's meal of fresh blood? Whatever the details of their sexual life, my mother—who never had trouble with dualisms or contradictions—told me that sex before marriage was disgusting, but that after marriage it was wonderful, that my father was "very thoughtful, very considerate, he made sure I had a nice time." I remember her saying, "You can get through a lot of stuff in bed." She told me once that my father had said that, in a Catholic marriage, sex was a sacramental: a sacred object, like a pair of blessed rosary beads or a statue of the Sacred Heart. It is hard to consider the metonymy without laughing: Hey, baby, wanna see my sacramental? And blessed by whom? How? Perhaps he meant that the act was a sacramental act—that is, an act that was in itself like a sacrament, the catechism definition of which is "an outward sign instituted by Christ to give grace." That too could induce giggles—how exactly did Jesus institute the sacrament of sex?—but, nevertheless, it is a good antidote against dualism; as my father's Jewish forebears might have said, it couldn't hurt.

I know that it is difficult if not impossible for most people to imagine their parents having sex, but my parents' sex life presents a puzzle for me that is, I think, particular. How did my father react with passion to my mother's misshapen body, misshapen to the point of being distressful to look at, perhaps even grotesque? I can imagine that, for her, having nothing to compare him with, and relieved simply not to die a virgin, then grateful to him for allowing her to be the mother of a child, and given the fact that my father was experienced, considerate, loving, she would have enjoyed him as a lover. But, given the fact that he was experienced—he'd been married before, to a woman whose photographs I've seen (because her son sent them to me), a Zelda Fitzgerald–type flapper girl—given the fact that he'd had a life as a Cleveland playboy in the Roaring Twenties (I heard two people talk of his success with women), what could it have been like for him when he lay beside my mother, when he caressed her, contemplated her before the act of love? It is true, she said she thought that it was disgusting for people to have sex naked, that an important part of a marriage was good lingerie, so perhaps he never saw her naked. But that's not possible, is it, that I saw my mother naked and my father did not? Or did his passion for her, born of their shared religious life, translate itself into a sexual ardor so strong that the realities of her body were obliterated, drowned out? My mind refuses to dwell on any of this in a way that would produce an answer. That sort of dwelling, that assumption that I could find an answer, seems to me the height of prurience. I must leave them alone. For my own sake. Theirs.

They met in a convent; they were introduced by a priest. Aside from this, I don't know much about their courtship. But I know a great deal, it seems, about their wedding.

It came to be somehow that these two people, who knew each other mainly in the company of priests or of maiden ladies devoted to priests and the spiritual life, she a cripple, he without a job, got themselves to the point where they were necking publicly on subways and then planning to marry. Not only planning, but in fact doing it. A story my mother liked to tell about my father. The week before their wedding, he sent her a letter, each word printed in capitals: "I'M SCARED SHITLESS."

If my grandmother was appalled at the news of my parents' marriage, that has not come down in the annals. My grandfather's horror is well documented, although I can't remember how my mother told me about it. It wasn't one of the stories she told in her deluges of drunken self-pity and resentment, although it is a story that enrages me and turns me punitive. That my grandfather, the villain of the piece, was dead when I was still a baby is neither here nor there. I am punishing him now. For a writer with my temperament, there is no such thing as a statute of limitations. It is one of the consolations of a difficult way of life.

He refused to go to their wedding. They were married, not from my mother's home parish, where she was a kind of celebrity, but from the church where Father Dermot was. How was this decision come to, that they would travel eight hours in a car with my grandmother, my aunt Rita, the bridesmaid, and my father's friend Jack Delaney, the best man? Certainly, it would have seemed more convenient, more obvious, for Father Dermot to make the trip? Were they embarrassed, did they think the spectacle of their marriage was embarrassing?

Only last year, someone who had known my mother in the parish wrote to me: "We were all so surprised that your mother married your father. She was so good looking, she had such a good job, he was older and Jewish; we didn't know what to make of it." And she was someone on my mother's side. What did her enemies think? It was an odd match, a difficult match; perhaps, for her family, an embarrassment. And, it must not be forgotten, a financial blow. Since the day she started working, in 1925, she had given her whole paycheck to my grandmother. She had paid the mortgage for twenty-two years. Now the others in the family would have to divide the load she'd borne.

Did they decide not to marry in the parish because they wanted to give my grandfather a good excuse to stay away? He was always able to rely on his weak heart to spare him from whatever he wished not to face. And, in fact, he died of a heart attack three years later. For whatever reason, they left the home of my grandparents, the house where my mother had lived since she was twelve, and piled into my mother's black Oldsmobile. As she walked out of the door, my grandfather put into my mother's hand a note written in his elegant copperplate: "You will work till the day you die."

I am looking at the snapshot of their wedding. By far the dominant figure in the picture is my grandmother, standing beside my father, but nearly twice his size in her print dress (everyone else is in solids), her hat with the tall feather. Only my mother's corsage vies with her for the eye's attention. My mother is beaming. My father looks somewhat stunned. My mother is wearing not a white wedding dress but a blue velvet suit. I remember the suit that I never saw her wear, but that she kept in the closet: her wedding outfit, we called it. We would take it out from time to time, and lay

it on the bed. I would run my fingers over the smooth nap, rough-
ing it, then smoothing it down again. It still smelled fragrant, of
her perfume, as if the wedding had happened only the day before.

Their honeymoon was a trip to Chicago, where my mother
had never been. But the priest who married them, Father Dermot
(who did not approve of the marriage, but nevertheless presided),
accompanied them on the first leg of the trip, from Dunkirk,
which was near Buffalo, to Cleveland. I want to believe that he got
out of the car before their first night as man and wife. Where did
they spend it? Did they make it from Buffalo to Chicago in one
night? This was 1947, before superhighways. This is probably
unlikely. So where did my mother lose her virginity, preserved as it
was till she was nearly forty?

I want to pretend that she spent the night of her wedding in
the Palmer House, the hotel my father had selected for them.

Fifty-eight years after their honeymoon, I am in Chicago giving a talk and I visit the Palmer House. Excited, trying to imagine
myself as my mother, thrilled not only to be in a strange city, a
grand hotel, but frightened, elated—she is going to lose her virginity to this man. Tonight.

I imagine her walking up the stairs to the grand lobby, passing
the Victorian bronze Romeo and Juliet (does she see herself and
my father here, only luckier?). The huge ceiling is painted with
mythological scenes, everything vividly colored, every surface
ornamented, everything emblazoned—everything meant to be a
proof of American opulence, the American tribute to Europe: we
will copy you, but we will go you one better, we will take your ideas,
we will ape the most extravagant of your periods and gild them
even brighter; we are after all Americans, and it is the Gilded Age.
The first Palmer House Hotel lasted only a year, 1871, and was
destroyed by the Chicago Fire. Potter Palmer, one of the people
who were determined to turn Chicago from a cow town to a civi-
lized city, lost his fortune in the fire, but recouped it, signing only
his name as a guarantee for the largest loan to be made in North
America up to that time. He rebuilt and reopened his hotel in

1873, but the one my parents stayed at was only twenty-three years old, a new version built in 1924.

I look up at the ceiling, trying to be my mother standing in her last minutes as a virgin. Did she look up at the central medallion, a Venus, her cloak a quote from Botticelli's clamshell, surrounded by coy, badly modeled cherubs, one covering her breasts by hands folded in prayer, one bare-breasted, leaning against a column?

My mother didn't approve of the nude in art, but perhaps she made an exception in this room, on this night. Did she think that her life would, from now on, partake more of this sort of opulence: the bronze horsemen, the green velvet curtains, the ink-colored marble urns, the marqueted chests with the heads of Napoleon on either side? The carpets, blue, rust, crimson; the huge, sparkling chandeliers.

I will not follow her up on the elevator for her first night with her new husband. This was nothing, thank God, she ever talked to me about. Most of the details she mentioned when she spoke about her honeymoon were comic. They went to see a burlesque show, and Henny Youngman was the opening act. My mother prided herself on my father's pride that she was the kind of woman you could take to a burlesque show; she'd enjoy the comedians and not pay too much attention to the naked ladies, believing they were not really the point, only an excuse for the comedians, a way of gulling the naïve public: she, however, was the knowing one, sophisticated enough to know that sex was just a joke. How did she experience sitting beside my father watching nearly naked women hours after she had had her first experience of sex? She would have felt that those women had nothing to do with her; she would have believed that they were of no interest to my father, that he and she had some sort of understanding that put "all that stuff" in its proper place.

Their honeymoon was studded with mishaps. My father backed the car into a police paddy wagon; the police were understanding of the honeymooning husband. But the next day, he misplaced the car and had to go back to the police station for help

finding it. My mother and father became adopted by the policemen: one can only speculate what they made of this strange pair,
my mother and my father, so turned around by the experience of
their honeymoon that they could hardly make their way without a
guide, a hand.

Halfway through the honeymoon (a week only), my father
came down with whooping cough. The hotel doctor cared for him;
he had to be piled into the car, and my mother had to drive them
home. This is not the kind of story my mother was bitter about;
she enjoyed seeing them as a screwball couple (Cary Grant and
Irene Dunne in *The Awful Truth?* Cary Grant and Katharine Hepburn in *Bringing Up Baby?*), unable, even for a week, to fit into the
ordinary iconography, the expected mold.

So their honeymoon is over, and then what do they do? They come
home, she goes back to work, he looks for a job and does not find
one. Or will not take the ones that he can find. They try to figure
out how to be a married couple, and it is not the easiest thing,
because neither of them is much interested in domesticity. So how
does my mother understand what it is to be a wife? To be a wife to
this man? She does, occasionally, cook for him, but not particularly to please him, only to nourish him and to make do until the
real meals come around, the weekend meals, the holiday meals,
cooked by her mother.

Food meant nothing to my father. If he was absorbed in a book
or a project he would regularly forget to eat; my mother would
unpack his briefcase and find several days' sandwiches left to rot
or dry. There were some foods he seemed to like: boiled chicken,
any kind of potato. She would leave cold potatoes in the refrigerator for him, which he liked to snack on, dipped in salt. She liked
telling the story of how she tricked him when he asked her to
make something she didn't like the idea of cooking: salmon loaf.
"Instead of saying no to him, I made it so disgusting he never
asked again." She would buy, at his request, jars of Rokeach

gefilte fish: a throwback to the faith he had rejected with such vociferous energy, such rage. Neither of them cared about decoration, although I remember our apartment being pleasant, the furniture comfortable, certain objects (a light-blue chenille spread; a globe with a false rose trapped in water that was crowned at the top by a single bubble that never moved, not a quarter of an inch). So, if he wasn't interested in food or the look of a home, what did he want in a wife? Sex? What she wanted in a husband was clear: she wanted "a good provider." And this he could not be. When they both understand this, it is the end of their happiness.

Do they try to conceive a child? Do they believe they can conceive? Is the idea of conceiving conceivable to them? She lives three blocks from her mother, in an apartment, which she pays for, and she pays a girl to come in once a week to help her clean. She is no longer the daughter in her mother's house. She has her own furniture, her own dishes. At first, she does her laundry in her mother's washing machine; then her brother and sister-in-law forbid her to use her mother's washing machine; they say they are paying for the water, and it's not fair to them. I know this makes my mother cry, and when she tells this story (it is one of the resentments she drags out when she is drunk), she always says that my father was very good at comforting her at that time. After that, she did her laundry in the kitchen sink, scrubbing everything. (Except the sheets—she brings them to the Chinese laundry; they are returned in brown paper, tied with string. We never say a word to the Chinese launderer, or to his wife, or to his children. Not one word in over fifteen years.)

Do they fight about money, or does that only happen after I am born and they have to begin thinking of themselves not as a couple but as a family? We are a family; we know we are connected to one another as we are connected to no one in the world, and we are proud of that, although we understand that we are, if not odd, at least not ordinary. Perhaps not even normal—though we do not think of ourselves as deformed, diseased. Rather: Outstanding. Underappreciated. Undervalued. Misconstrued.

The myth is that I am conceived on my father's birthday. Were they surprised to learn that she was pregnant? My mother, forty, soon to turn forty-one, a cripple, with a misshapen, unbalanced body. The story is that everyone else was surprised, but they believed when they married that they would have children. I don't know whether or not they actually were surprised; I do know that they were thrilled. This is one thing about my parents that I never doubt: that they were thrilled at the idea of me, the prospect of me, and with my actual existence. So I guess people had to be thrilled for them. Or at least pretend to be.

Her pregnancy is a great event. It is the beginning of the change of their identity: their transformation from romantic to miraculous. Those who resisted the idea of my parents as romantic found it easier to understand them as miraculous. Because there she was: surprisingly fecund, like Sarah, mother of Isaac, or Elizabeth, mother of John the Baptist.

The pregnancy was understood to be risky. She was told that, because of her leg (or was it her heart?), she could gain no more than fifteen pounds. This results in the only nice story I know about my grandfather in relation to my mother. Each day, she came to her mother's house for lunch, and he would serve her cottage cheese and lettuce and a glass of milk in a fancy goblet, using the good silver and a linen napkin to set her place at table.

They choose my name. At first my father wants me to be named Monica, after the mother of St. Augustine. My mother pretends to go along with him for a while. And then, as she becomes more visibly pregnant (more visibly fragile, vulnerable?), she suggests that I should be named Mary Catherine, after her mother. Of all the grandchildren, not one has been named for her. With his usual enthusiasm, his usual ability to forget what he had once desired, my father takes up the idea of my being named after my mother's mother. And the mother of God. They choose for the date of my birth (my mother will be having a cesarean) December 8, the Feast of the Immaculate Conception. One of the least lovable days of the Church calendar. People mistake the meaning of the feast: it isn't that Jesus is conceived without sin, it's that Mary is joined to him as being the only nondivine human being conceived without sin.

My father is over the moon at my birth. When the nursing nun comes to tell him he is the father of a daughter, he falls to his knees and kisses the hem of her habit, then drags her down to the chapel, where he insists that they sing the Te Deum together in Latin. Te Deum: the Church's song of victory and praise.

Then they become parents; they have to do normal things, make normal purchases—a high chair, a playpen, a bassinet, a crib. They hire a diaper service. They find a babysitter for me. But that is about the end of us as a family like any other, as ordinary parents and child.

Because, after that, we are not a family, but a couple of three.

But in the couple of three, the most important are my father and me. My mother had a vision or an understanding; it must have been when I was very young, it might have happened in my infancy. She perceived that I was more my father's than hers. Was it a look in my eye, or the fact that I was brown-eyed and had a large nose? That I was Jewish-looking (but my dark looks, like my father's, could have passed for Italian)? Somehow, as if she'd been whispered to by an angel, my mother, without resentment, stood back and gave me to my father. Gave up her place as first in his regard. I won the Oedipal game without even needing to sign up to play. She believed that my father and I were people of the word, the mind, and she of the flesh. It was something she never questioned; she never once accused me, even when she was drunk, of loving him more than her. She seemed to understand that it would be natural that I did—not a cause for bitterness, but a source of pride, at her own discernment, her own commonsensical acceptance of fate.

What did we do as a family? Or as a couple of three? It is important to remember that we didn't have much money, so we didn't do many things that people remember doing with their families. We almost never ate out. We rarely went to the movies together; my parents very well understood that I despised cartoons and any entertainment understood to be intended for children, and my father's ambivalence about Hollywood made the choice of movies difficult. Hollywood was the source of American corruption, and yet he loved movies that didn't take themselves too seriously—Laurel and Hardy made him laugh to the point of helpless coughing. He was fond of Mae West, particularly partnered with W. C. Fields, and, inexplicably, Marilyn Monroe, which embarrassed me, because I didn't like her: I was afraid for her; she seemed excessive to me—too blonde, too smiley. I didn't know that what was excessive about her had to do with sex—I don't think the word would have been mentioned in my presence, and it was not, for the years my father was alive, a meaningful category for me. At least, that is, to my conscious mind.

I remember one movie we all saw together: *Three Coins in the Fountain.* It is difficult to understand that my parents would choose this movie to share with their five-year-old daughter. Did they think it would be educational, with its views of Rome? I don't know the reasons, but really it was a perfect choice. My mother would have loved the Dorothy McGuire role: the accomplished secretary marrying her older, dying boss. Avid as I was for details of female allure and adornment, I would have loved the costumes: Jean Peters' full skirts, laced espadrilles, large hats; Maggie McNamara's high heels and cunningly tailored suits. And my father? Perhaps he was hoping for a glimpse of the Vatican, bathed in mist from the vantage of the Pincian Hills.

I always enjoyed sitting in the backseat of my mother's car when we would drive to visit people. The car was large, the upholstery luxuriously leathery; I could stretch out on the backseat and pretend I was in a hotel room, speaking into the window crank and pretending to call Room Service. My mother, in the front, would pretend to knock on my hotel-room door, and pass me a cracker, a handful of peanuts, a piece of gum. I was always drowsy in the back of the car, pleasantly so, as if being driven by my parents, who, remarkably, didn't fight in the car, were a kind of barbiturate that would allow me to hover above my life, as if it were a good, long, leisurely dream, and soften the colors, the angles of it, so that nothing was difficult and nothing could do harm.

We rarely visited people with children, probably because my parents' coevals would have had grown children, and also because so many of my mother's friends were spinsters. What did I do on these visits? I was quiet, but I wasn't bored, because I was not excluded from the conversation, even if I had nothing to contribute to it. My idea of hell was, at any occasion, being seated at the children's table. I had nothing to say to other children, but I was perfectly happy listening to adults, taking in information, making up stories on the crumbs of suggestion I could take in like the pistil of a plant absorbing pollen from the air. Occasionally, I would be asked to sing or to recite a poem, and I understood very well that my successful performance made my parents feel that everything in their lives was worthwhile.

Every holiday and many Sundays were spent with my mother's family, and I didn't mind being one of those children, because I could be with my cousin Peppy, and we could laugh ourselves sick at nothing, at everything, and I left my parents with no sense of unease to be with him. I remember that my father would often absent himself from the activities and sit in a corner and read until I came over and asked for his attention. He was happy to play with the children, and when an adult was required, he would always take the part. It is remarkable to me that my mother seemed to accept that; she never accused him of bad manners, of thinking himself superior to her brothers and sisters, nor was anything ever said by any of them. I think they understood that he was odd, and since he couldn't make a living, there was no need for them to feel inadequate because he was more intelligent, more educated, more in the center of the world. I don't know what these events were like for my father before I was born, but he simply took his place beside my mother as the parents of this child, a child like any of their children—his passport to the normal world.

We did take one vacation as a family—or, rather, we made a pilgrimage. Some priest had told my parents that the shrine of Ste. Anne de Beaupré in Quebec was an especially good place to go to pray for jobs. The prayer was meant to be particularly efficacious if the petitioner made his request while climbing up the stone steps to the basilica on his knees. So my father, humiliated by his joblessness, would humble himself further by making his way on his knees up hundreds of stone steps. It must have seemed right to him, though; his joblessness was a torment to him, to all of us: a central wound in the family identity. Each night, I prayed with both my parents, "God bless Mommy, God bless Daddy, God bless Granny, God bless all my aunts and uncles and cousins and friends, and please get Daddy a good job." It wasn't just any job I was praying for, it was "a good job," and I understood very early that this would be something having to do with words. With getting paid for words. My mother asked everyone who she thought had any spiritual clout to pray for her husband to get "a good job."

Didn't it occur to her that this might have been humiliating for him? She never seemed to have the wifely instinct to protect her husband's ego. She was too practical for that, and her relationship to prayer was too straightforward. It would have made no sense to fail to enlist anyone who might have spiritual clout; it would be like a Broadway producer failing to contact wealthy backers for fear of looking greedy or inadequate or poor. My father was contemptuous of my mother's kind of prayer. He said, "My wife prays for a black Oldsmobile and gets it." The source of this story was that, during the war, when cars were scarce, my mother wrote to General Motors and said that she was handicapped and needed a hydromatic car to get to work—and one was provided for her. I think my father liked the idea of being married to one of the Catholic peasantry, someone who'd imbibed the faith with her mother's milk, but he was also capable of using these qualities against her, to point out his superiority when she was attacking him for failure to make it as an ordinary husband, father, man.

So we drove to Canada. My mother packed a picnic basket so we would save money, but the food she produced was delicious: ham sandwiches with a sweetish mustard that didn't seem to burn my tongue, Ritz crackers, pieces of Nestlé's Crunch doled out like treasure. She made a game of it; she would say, "I've got a hunch," and I'd reply, "I want a piece of Crunch." As a special treat, she'd bought individual cans of something called apricot nectar. I loved its sweet thickness, but I also loved its name: nectar, not juice, something from a magic place outside the nutritional range of the everyday.

I was terribly disappointed that we stayed not in a hotel but in a motel, a narrow room with plaid bedspreads and wallpaper made to look like knotty pine. In the morning we had pancakes, which were called flapjacks, over which we poured maple syrup out of a glass container with a lid that flipped back and opened a space the size of a dime, but rectangular. And the cream for my parents' coffee came in individual glass containers, the size of two thimbles, which I coveted with all my heart.

As well as being disappointed in the motel, I was disappointed that when we crossed the border into Canada people weren't speaking French. I loved the sounds of the French words for the places we were going to visit, especially Cap de la Madeleine, which sounded to me like a dancer tapping down a flight of stairs.

In the morning, when we got to the basilica, my mother and I stayed in the lower chapel, praying, as my father made his way up the stairs on his knees. I said my prayers in a French accent, pretending that I was praying in French. My mother held her silver rosaries in her beautifully shaped hands. When my father came down to the chapel to get us, he looked refreshed, young, triumphant. Back at the motel, my mother bathed his raw and bloody knees with iodine, then bandaged them. I was proud, but confused; I thought my father brave, like a soldier, but my mother's unaccustomed tenderness seemed strange, as did my father's lofty, calm acceptance of her ministrations.

My parents had planned a special trip for me on the way back home. We would stop at Storytown, a recently constructed poor man's Disneyland that was north of Albany. I don't know how they learned of it. It wasn't the sort of thing they usually knew about— something made for children—and they might have thought it was the sort of thing, like cartoons, I might have had no truck with.

But there was not a moment of disappointment from the minute we got out of the car. Now I realize it wasn't much, just some painted cement monuments to various fairy tales and nursery rhymes: the Old Woman's shoe, Cinderella's pumpkin, the Mad Hatter, the March Hare. It was newly opened; there were piles of red dirt along the cement paths, pristine in their recent dryness. Most children in America were in school that day. Was that the reason we were the only ones there? Or was it that people had not heard of Storytown yet? It was unlike us to be ahead of the pack, but I think we were.

The emptiness made the place seem sacred. I believed that it had been entirely created for me, that my parents had thought it up, and actualized it only to delight me. The figures were much larger than I. Slowly, reverently, I went from spot to spot, climbing up on them, sitting down, having my picture taken. It wasn't as if I thought I was part of the stories; rather, I was honoring them, honoring their place in my life. I did like nursery rhymes and fairy tales if they were read to me, instead of being flattened out and oversimplified in cartoon form. And the overlarge statues allowed my imagination scope and range: I was in charge of the narrative; they were dumb, only I and my parents inhabited the world of words.

I was entirely happy. I felt that my parents and I—this couple of three—were admirable, enviable, my father with his bandaged knees, my mother serving apricot nectar and Ritz crackers with salami slices, me on Miss Muffet's tuffet, smiling as they told me to say "cheese" and my mother snapped her Brownie with the mysterious red dot in the back, its numbers vaguely indicating progress in the course of the event.

It cannot be denied: their marriage was a mistake. Their mistake was not the result of passion dried up or spent or withered on the vine, but of a spiritual ideal that did not serve them as they'd believed it would. But this spiritual ideal, with the culture that surrounded it, was what drew them together: it was the strongest thing they had, except for their love for me, which they understood as its fruit.

My mother never talked about her religious life, and she was such a mixture of the coarse and the refined, the banal and the entirely original, that it is hard for me to know what her inner life, her life with God, might have been. I know that when I saw her praying, when I looked at her face when she came back from communion, it seemed transformed to me, ennobled: I knew she was going through something important, vital, true. I don't think she read religious books, certainly not the kind of theology my father did. He knew his Augustine, his Aquinas; he was devoted to the figure of Thomas More: I was to be named Thomas More if I had been a boy. He read contemporary theologians, mostly Germans, whose names she wouldn't have been able to pronounce. Nevertheless, they met each other, greeted each other, recognized each other in this place whose expanse was much greater than their individual or joint biographies. They believed in the love of God; they believed that Christ died for them, for the love of them, and to redeem their sins. They thought about this every day. They were part of something great, they knew that, but they wouldn't have thought of themselves, as Protestants might have, as the elect. They really weren't interested in those who were outside the fold: they might have granted them a kind of distant, abstract pity, or, in my father's case, an anger at "invincible ignorance." If he had the sense to recognize the truth of the Church, why didn't they? But their focus was not on those excluded; it was on their own inclusion in an entity that potentially included everyone, and whose requirements were only minimally connected to behavior. And radically disconnected from respect-ability and success. If you asked them what they were part of, they might have said the communion of saints or the mystical body of Christ. Their terms, the terms they lived by on a daily basis, were that grand.

I know that they enjoyed praying together, the rituals of public prayer: they loved kneeling together at Mass; walking back together from the communion rail, they were radiant and proud. They reveled in novenas and days of recollection and benedictions and processions. They liked marking their calendars, not by national holidays, but by saints' days, holy days of obligation. So my father might head a letter to my mother, "The Feast of St. Francis," "Assumption 1955." They believed themselves to be in posses-sion of a truth that was eternal and unchanging in its application: what they both despised was relativism; compromise with stan-dards that were "worldly" was the thing they both abhorred, prided themselves, as a couple, on not falling for.

It ought to have carried them through; it ought to have sus-tained them. But it didn't. What the Church provided them with could not stand up to the abrasions of the real world, which turned out to be more made up of dailiness than their faith had led them to believe.

For one thing, my mother must have been constantly exhausted; she wasn't young to be the mother of a baby at forty-one. And she was handicapped, and she worked all day and had no help but a girl to come in a few hours a week to clean. I don't remember my mother appearing fatigued, or complaining of fatigue, but even if she didn't acknowledge it, she must have been worn out. If they'd had money, I believe they might have done all right. Money was more important to them than they believed; they died, both of them believing money meant nothing to them. But that was not the truth.

When I say it wasn't the truth, I don't mean it was exactly a lie, because my mother didn't care much about money, nor did my father, and yet they were both ashamed at his inability to make it.

And what she did care about was being free of debt, being visibly solvent, a woman, a crippled woman, who could keep the wolf from the door. And there was my father, the wolf (in sheep's clothing), ravening her portion, so hard-earned, her reputation for being trustworthy with money, a faithful steward.

Like many failures, my father always believed his ship was just about to come in, and I can only believe that he was convincing, not only to my mother but to her friends whom he convinced to lend him money, and who then had to ask my mother to make good on his debts. She kept a letter that he wrote her that I hate reading; I hate his abjection even as I understand her rage:

Dear Anne:

This is what I have been waiting until you seemed calm enough to tell you.

I have a deal ready to close on the magazine as soon as Sam Campbell and Jack Delaney return to NY. But the terms of the deal have been so that I must get my stock and equipment out of hock at 19 W. 27 which will take $125. If you will make a loan for this amount at VS Bank I will proceed. If your answer is no I know nowhere now where to turn and you must help me find some solution to the problem of this family. To give up and simply stay home with the baby is impossible— it would result in a tremendous explosion. I know that you have financed me (really the family thru me) before and all by the mysterious will of god (nobody has ever accused me of laziness or incompetence in my line of work) the projects failed.

There are only 2 alternatives now:

1. Keep on the same crucifying road (through which we have yet been miraculously preserved for 7 years)
2. or Surrender to despair.

Write me at GPO Box 679 New York City your answer. If it is yes I will borrow money somewhere and come to

Paradox Monday night to drive you back.
  Love to both of you—always D.

My parents, my desperate, miserable parents. And I "the baby," who, if I am the only meaning in my father's life, will cause an "explosion"? Does this mean a breakdown? Has he already had one? I know that he disappeared to the attic of a friend's house for some time once, where he could only sit with his head in his hands and weep.

I read that letter for the first time only a week ago, when I was looking through my mother's things for the poems my father had written her, which I once had and now cannot find. Why did I lose those pages, and why had I never read this one from my father? An accident of the unconscious? An accident of a plethora of paper? If I had read that letter when I was younger, I would have been entirely on my father's side. I would have felt his misery, and thought that a good wife should never permit her husband—and a husband so gifted as to write a letter of that power—to go through what he went through. Now I can only weep for both of them. I understand her shame, her disappointment, her anger: he had done it before, he would do it again. They are still calling me "the baby," although if they have been married seven years I am five.

What should my mother have done? What did she do? Did she borrow the money? The people at the Valley Stream National Bank, for which her boss was counsel, admired her, so they would probably have given her a loan for $125 in the blink of an eye. But would she have had to explain that it was money she needed to get her husband's things out of hock? I don't think she borrowed the money, because the last magazine he started folded in 1954, and the letter was written in 1955. He had two more years to live.

He had had heart attacks before she met him, before she married him, but I don't think his physical weakness was something they ever talked about. Physical weakness attached to her, except that she was vain about never getting the colds that plagued me and my father. But just before Christmas of 1956, he had a heart attack, a minor one, in the middle of the night. I woke to find them sitting in the kitchen. He was groaning; I had never heard anyone groan before. She had poured him a glass of whiskey. He was sitting with his hand on his chest. I heard him say, "My heart is killing me." I was frightened; I asked him what he meant. "It's just an expression, honey," he said.

But it wasn't: his heart was killing him. Just three weeks later, on January 14, we got a call from Bellevue Hospital. My mother called her mother and her brother-in-law. They drove her to the hospital. I was bundled up and brought to my grandmother's house to sleep. It was the last time I ever saw the apartment where we had lived as a family, a couple of three.

With my father in the hospital, my mother became the kind of wife she was always meant to be, perhaps the only kind she had the gift for being. I can only imagine the esteem in which she was held by the doctors and the nurses: the crippled wife and her difficult journey. Certainly, she was heroic in the parish. Each night after work, she drove through the Midtown Tunnel to Bellevue, eating as she drove the sandwich her mother had packed for her that morning. Returning then to her mother's house, to be fed a warmed-over supper at ten. I was not allowed to see him; she was the courier between us, his letters and mine, full of false cheer, false promises. He would be home soon.

He did not come home. Less than a month after he was hospitalized, he had a third heart attack. The call came at midnight: I awoke a minute before the phone rang, sensing something. My mother cried in her mother's arms. I was stoic, silent.

The next day, I contracted chicken pox, so I was sick, very sick for the funeral arrangements. My mother did organize one visit to the funeral parlor for me: her brother carried me in my pajamas. I tried to get into the coffin to be with my father; I tried to hold his stone-cold hand. Before he was buried, I was given the ring off his finger. Not a wedding band: an image of the Virgin, the miraculous medal, turned into a ring. I wore it as soon as I was big enough; my mother seemed to have no interest in it.

She gave us over to her family. She allowed them to clear out our apartment. I can only understand that she wanted it over quickly: that part of her life, our lives, the part that had to do with my father. She didn't protest that the effects of that life were packed away, in her mother's garage, only to be unpacked when, years later, I would make a home of my own. I use them now: her wedding china, informal, a pattern of red, white, and blue checkered fruits, as if they were made of gingham, in the center of an ivory plate with a red border. And the silver—really silver plate— her father gave her for her wedding, the card still in it, "For Anne con rispetto." I know this was a family joke: my grandfather, in a rage, would clamor for the respect due him. I ripped the card up to punish him for the card he put in my mother's hand the day of her wedding: "You will work till the day you die." A message entirely without respect.

My mother only talked about my father when I initiated it. Funny stories about his absentmindedness, his impracticality. Vignettes of his insane devotion for his only child. Nothing about his work; vague praise for his intelligence. I believe that she did not mourn him, and for many years this was a source of both resentment and superiority for me. I was the mourner, the real widow; she played the part, but only when she remembered to. I thought of him first thing every morning and last thing at night. I dreamed of him, I talked to him; sometimes I thought I saw him on the street. I think he was in her mind only rarely. Clearly, she enjoyed widowhood more than she did wifehood. Back home with her mother now, she was served; certainly, she didn't have to work so hard. And the shaming aspects of my father had been washed away by his untimely death. She didn't have to worry about money; it seemed, miraculously, that he died without debt.

Soon after he died, my mother got a call from a woman saying she was his sister. My father had told us both he was an only child. She wanted his body so it could be buried with his family in the

Jewish cemetery in Cleveland. My mother was firm, polite: he was a Catholic now, he would be buried in a Catholic cemetery. It didn't seem to bother her that she'd been lied to. Years later, when my first book was published, a man called to tell me my father had been married to his mother. He remembered my father as a loving and devoted stepfather; after his mother divorced my father they'd kept in touch until my father's death. My mother never knew my father had had another wife. She died not knowing: I never told her. If she had known, she might have registered it briefly, then relegated it to the old attic of the things in her life she didn't want to deal with, and so forgot.

My father was buried, in fact, in the plot of her family, his name not on the gravestone, buried among people who tolerated him at best. For years, I was angry that she had allowed this, and forty years after his death, I moved his body to another cemetery, to a grave whose stone bore his name. In the plot, which is small, there is room for only two bodies; the other four places are for what are called cremains. Before my mother died, I wondered whether, when the time came, I would name her as the other body, allow her to share my father's corruption—or whether I would insist that she go up in flames. Leaving the shared decay to him and me. So it would be my father and me, worm food; and my mother and my husband, ash. But in the end, we buried the body of my mother beside the body of my father. I came to understand that it was only right. They were, after all, husband and wife.

My Mother *and the* Great World

My mother had a vision of the world that was much larger than that of the people she lived among. It was a vision that included categories as disparate as the stylish, the incorporeal, the impractical, the grand. It was a river with many streams, the most important of which were Hollywood, Broadway, and the Roman Catholic Church. And an idea of Europe that had nothing to do with an actual place.

My mother dreamed of things her family wouldn't have dreamed of dreaming. They prided themselves on not being dreamy. They thought of themselves as practical. Dreams were foolishness, and they would have called the substance of my mother's dreams foolishness, if they'd dared. But they didn't dare, because she was the breadwinner for her parents and seven of her siblings, and they only began to call something foolish—her marriage—when she was no longer turning her salary over to her mother to pay for all their needs.

I try to understand how my mother came from the family she came from. People always say that it's hard to understand how I came from the family I came from, but, really, it's much easier than trying to understand my mother's path. Having a dreamy mother, a mother who seemed practical but who actually put very little store on what things cost, what money could buy, what was useful, I found it easy to dream. And, having a father whose life was nothing but a dream, how could I not have been a dreamer? But my mother—she's the real mystery, the real miracle. She was, after all, the child of hardheaded immigrants, pious, thrifty, law-abiding, punitive, ferocious, judging, and perhaps a bit (but only secretly) abashed. She would say things that might have come from their mouths, such as, explaining her decision not to buy a new hat or a second cup of coffee, "It's not necessary to my salvation." Salvation, a concept that was lively and local for her, but used in this case as a joke. Once, when I was anguished by what my peers might think of me, she advised, "When they pay your bills, then you can worry what they think about you."

It is true, she wasn't given much to desire for this world's goods, and she certainly didn't care what people thought of her. But practical—no, she wouldn't have married the man she did, she wouldn't have allowed me to live as I did, if she'd been practical like the others in her family. Sometimes, her old anxieties broke through, or perhaps it was envy of me—that I didn't have to be burdened as she was. So she would occasionally say things like "You look up at the sky and fall on your ass, I look down at the ground and find diamonds." But we both knew she didn't mean it; that it was important to her, one of the important ways she knew herself, to work in the real world so that my father and I could rise above it.

So why wasn't she like the rest of her family? I think, though I have no evidence for it, that the difference happened because she went to the movies. And they did not.

My mother didn't often speak about movies that she had seen when she was young, or movies that had made an impression on her, because she wasn't used to thinking of movies as being important or serious—like books or anything emanating from the Church. They were entertainment, and if you were gripped by the things they presented, well, that was almost a joke. She made a bit of a joke of her love for Gary Cooper, which is one of the few things I know about her and the movies before I was born. In a scrapbook made when she was in her mid-twenties, which would have been the early thirties, there is a photograph of him, put in just anyhow among the others of her family and her girlhood friends. What attracted her to Gary Cooper was his height, his slimness, and his taciturnity. She never said a word about his face.

My father once ripped up a *Photoplay* featuring Gary Cooper that she had bought as a treat for herself. He said he was ripping it up not because he was jealous of Gary Cooper but because it was trash, trash sent from Hollywood to corrupt and stupefy. My mother pretended to believe that he was making a moral point, but I believe she really thought he was jealous, and that pleased her. It pleased her very much indeed.

One of the greatest days of my mother's life was the one on which it was announced that Gary Cooper had converted to Catholicism. My mother's joy made her radiant; she sat triumphant as a bride. "I always knew he was a Catholic underneath it all," she said. She never mentioned what it was that had tipped her off. If the news had come to her that Gary Cooper had been one of Hollywood's leading womanizers, she would have denied it, as she did the reports of Bing Crosby's alcoholism and child abuse, as the baseless accusation of malcontents, probably with a cleverly hidden anti-Catholic agenda.

My mother's relationship to movies was guided by the list created by the Legion of Decency. The Legion of Decency had two
major functions: begun in the 1930s to combat sexual licentious-
ness in movies and the communist influence, it provided a list of
current movies ranked according to their safety or danger for
Catholics; at one Mass each year, we all had to stand up and take
the Legion of Decency Pledge:

> I wish to join the Legion of Decency which condemns vile
> and unwholesome moving pictures. I unite with all who
> protest against them as a grave menace to youth, to home
> life, to country and religion. . . . I condemn all indecent and
> immoral motion pictures and those which glorify crime or
> criminals. I promise to do all that I can to strengthen public
> opinion against the production of indecent and immoral
> films, and to unite with all who protest against them. I
> acknowledge my obligation to form a right conscience about
> pictures that are dangerous to my moral life. I pledge myself
> to remain away from them. I promise, further, to stay away
> altogether from places of amusement which show them as a
> matter of policy. Considering these evils, I hereby promise to
> remain away from all motion pictures except those which do
> not offend.

I remember standing next to my mother as if we were saying
the Pledge of Allegiance, puffed up with pride and determination
to avoid these evils—although I had absolutely no inclination to
see anything with any sexual content at all, and anyway, there
would be no way for me to get into a theatre without an adult.

Each week, the *Brooklyn Tablet* published the list of films
under the Legion Guidelines. There were four categories: A1, suitable for all audiences; A2, suitable for adults; B, morally objectionable in part for all; C, condemned. I had no idea what "morally
objectionable in part for all" might mean, but it seemed a serious
and sober reckoning. Class C, "condemned," though, made me

shiver in my shoes. I could see the roll of film unrolling, hurtling down to hell, along with its directors, its stars, the careless audiences who had taken it in. Most of the films on those lists were foreign; two, *Mom and Dad* and *The Moon Is Blue,* seemed to be on there for at least a decade. No one I knew had ever seen them.

My mother checked the Legion listings, but I don't think she would have balked at going to a film that "glorifies crime or criminals." She had no interest in explicit sex, "a highly overrated pastime," she said, thinking herself highly witty for the locution. But she wasn't a puritan; she followed her own enjoyment, and she didn't think there was anything wrong with enjoying herself, as long as her enjoyment wasn't a "near occasion of sin."

Sometimes, the Church and the movies came together for my mother—most often when she discovered that a movie star she liked was Catholic. Certain Catholic magazines vied with each other to feature these stars, printing articles with titles like "A Catholic and a Star." Bing Crosby and Grace Kelly were the king and queen of such features in the 1950s. Grace's marriage to the Prince in 1956 was an occasion for Catholic women only rivaled when John Kennedy entered the White House with Jackie, his fairy-tale bride, on his arm. The magazines also featured lesser luminaries: Loretta Young, Pat O'Brien, Dennis Day, Ann Blyth. Spencer Tracy was occasionally written about, posed with his wife and deaf son. If anyone knew about what he was up to with Katharine Hepburn, they were keeping it to themselves.

A big problem with movie stars for my mother was that they had such a tendency to divorce. This became particularly vexing when a Catholic star strayed, especially if it was someone my mother liked. Frank Sinatra's divorcing Nancy for Ava Gardner was a particular crisis for her. But she didn't flinch. When Sinatra came onto the radio, my mother would turn it off like Carry Nation chopping down a saloon door. "He's got Ava Gardner, he doesn't need me," she would say.

Because of Ingrid Bergman's divorce and its attendant scandals, my mother felt that some comment was required of her that justified her watching *The Bells of St. Mary's* when it came on TV every year around Christmastime. Comment was required because while Ingrid Bergman was playing the saintly Sister Benedict, she was leaving her lawful husband to take up with the Italian director Roberto Rossellini. Each year, when *The Bells of St. Mary's* was played on *The Early Show,* my mother said the same thing. "I watch it for Bing. I will always love Bing. But why that bitch had the nerve to think she had the right to play a nun while all the time she was planning to run away with that Italian, I will never know."

It never occurred to my mother, though, to boycott the movie because of Bergman's behavior; for one thing, Bergman wasn't Catholic; for another, if it was good enough for Bing (who was almost a priest, having played Father O'Malley so convincingly), it was good enough for her. And how could she give up that moment when the two of us sat in tears when Father O'Malley tells Sister Benedict that she has a touch of TB—"just a touch"—and that if she ever needs him, she should just dial O for "O'Malley."

But she was proud that at some points she was able to "draw the line." She refused to endorse *Song of Bernadette* because Jennifer Jones, who played the saint, was divorced. But I think that was because she didn't like Jennifer Jones that much; there was no conflict for her in taking the high ground. And she didn't go to the movies for piety; she knew where to go for that. Her religious life was serious, and there was no need—in fact, it was a kind of defilement—for it to be mediated through Hollywood.

After my father died, my mother and I rarely went to the movies together. Perhaps because, living with her mother and my aunt after his death, my mother lacked the courage to take me to the movies she knew both she and I would like. She would never sit through a kiddie movie with me; she very well understood that I wouldn't like it, and she wouldn't waste her precious free time. I remember one of the few outings we made to the city after my father died; it was to see the movie *Gigi* in Radio City Music Hall.

A crisis came when my mother saw the high staircase—carpeted in red, but nonetheless problematical for being cinematically elegant. I saw her hesitate, check like a horse wondering whether or not to take a fence, then brace herself for the ordeal. I wanted to cry—because I knew how hard it was for her, and because I was so proud of her, aware of the heroic proportions she had taken on in the eyes of the people who watched us, crippled mother, eight-year-old daughter dressed to the nines (matching white fur hat and muff, red-and-black velvet dress with patent-leather Mary Janes). But did I also want to weep in self-pity for not having a mother who could take the stairs in a single bound? As my father would have been able to.

None of it mattered as soon as the lights went off and we were settled safely in our seats. My mother's focus of delight was Maurice Chevalier: "He has that crooked smile," she said, each time he shamelessly mugged for the camera. I had no idea that Gigi's sexuality was being brokered by her grandmother and her aunt; I loved Leslie Caron with her schoolgirl hat and books gathered by a strap, her cinched-waist skirt, and then, transformed, hair piled up, a vision in white. I adored Louis Jourdan; his move from big brother to husband. I found Hermione Gingold vaguely embarrassing; but my mother adored the older couple's duet: "I remember it well." It was as if we divided the couples—she would take Chevalier and Gingold, I Jourdan and Caron—and we were both completely satisfied, both of us knowing there were no men like that—like either one of them, the ironic Chevalier, the world-weary yet passionate Jourdan—in America, where no one dressed like them and there were no Parisian trees. The day after we went to see *Gigi,* my mother bought me a beret. "You look so French in it," she said, with pride and real delight.

It was easier for my mother when the movies she wanted to

see were on television. This was particularly true in the years when we were living alone: 1962–69, after my grandmother had died and my aunt had married and moved away, and before I moved to my college dorm. We didn't go to the movies much in those years. There were two reasons for this: as the sixties progressed, my mother became less mobile; walking became more difficult; she needed braces whereas before she had got by with a built-up shoe. And there were fewer new movies that she liked. Many of the stars she loved were dead or too old to be in movies any more; besides, too many movies "went in so much for all that sex business. Which is not my cup of tea."

But when there was a good movie rebroadcast on *The Late Show*, particularly if it was on a weekend, we would lie together on her bed, the dog at our feet, as happy as we'd ever been, as we could dream of being. Among our favorites were any of the *Thin Man* series (that was her idea of a marriage: minimal domesticity, maximum wit). Another favorite was *It Happened One Night*: Claudette Colbert was my mother's kind of heroine, not too pretty or too obviously sexual, neither matronly nor girlish, on her own, needing to be tamed. Certain movies could be counted on to be played seasonally: *Holiday Inn*, which had both Bing and Fred Astaire, was on at Christmas, and on St. Patrick's Day, another of my mother's heroines, Maureen O'Hara, appeared with John Wayne in *The Quiet Man*. Only once, *The Late Show* presented us with *Love in the Afternoon*, a trifecta for us: the dying Gary Cooper courting the scandalously too-young-for-him Audrey Hepburn, daughter of a private detective played by the crookedly smiling Maurice Chevalier.

But most prized by us was anything with Fred Astaire. I am slightly embarrassed to say that our favorite Fred Astaire movies were not *Top Hat* and *Swing Time* (although we adored those) but two later ones, *Funny Face*, with Audrey Hepburn, and *Daddy Long Legs*, with Leslie Caron. We dreamed over the dresses; we raved over the dance steps; we sang along with the songs.

Was it an accident that so many of the movies we loved were

set in Paris? Was my mother telling me that the good life required a trip across the ocean, a new language, a new set of behaviors and clothes? A trip to a place where she would never dream of going, where she would nevertheless allow me, encourage me, to go.

Before I was born, my mother regularly went to the Broadway theatre. It was there she developed her treacherous, and unacknowledged, Anglophilia. Hatred of the English was required by all my grandmother's descendants. She'd had an uncle who had been kidnapped by the Black and Tans at the age of three, the story went, right under his family's nose. When Queen Elizabeth was crowned in 1952, my grandmother ordered me to join her in front of the television and do Bronx cheers to the tune of "God Save the Queen." Once, when I was five, we were visiting an English friend of my mother's. I said at table, "I hate the English." My host told me his heritage. "I'm sorry, sir," I said, with a queenly politesse. "But I still hate the English."

So, yes, she was firm in her hatred of the English, but she loved them onstage. Onstage, they lost their connection to her mother: they became part of a world her mother need never participate in, even acknowledge. She spoke lovingly of seeing the Lunts in *Private Lives.* When it was reprised on Broadway with Maggie Smith, she asked me particularly if I would take her to see it. She firmly believed the Lunts were English; Lynn Fontanne was actually born in England, but they are listed in their biographies as American actors. I wonder if this would have pleased or disappointed her.

But the exception to the rule of English hatred situated itself most particularly in relation to two musical comedies, *The King and I* and *My Fair Lady.* My mother saw Gertrude Lawrence in *The King and I,* and she spoke about it often, with a kind of hushed awe. "She was a lady. She was a real lady." And when she miraculously got to see *My Fair Lady* the first year it was on Broadway, she came home agog with the dry desirableness of Rex Harrison. "He talks the songs, he doesn't sing them, but you forget that, you just can't take your eyes off him, you want to listen to him the whole night. That man knows how to wear a suit." So she could make an exception, my mother, if someone was stylish or witty or well dressed. It was an exception no one else in the family would have been able to make.

I said that my mother had a dream of Europe, but it was a garbled dream, garbled in a particularly American way.

But what kind of American was my mother? The kind, I think, who justified the suspicion of another kind: that Catholics couldn't be real Americans; they had a divided loyalty, and the one to Rome always trumped it. When she worried about communism, for example, it was as a threat to the Catholic Church, not to the United States of America.

My mother mostly thought "American" was a synonym for "Protestant," and so she approached the territory marked by the name with either wariness or polite indifference, depending on the context. She was entirely unpatriotic; not to suggest that she was treasonous, but only that the concept of patriotism had no interest for her. There was never a flag in our house, or any kind of bunting—there wouldn't have been room for it, and it would have been out of place alongside the crucifixes and the pictures of the Sacred Heart, the Virgin, and the saints. She did, once, take me on a trip to Washington, D.C., where we saw the Lincoln Memorial, the Washington Monument, the White House, and Mount Vernon. This was something no one else in her family would have done, although we stayed with a cousin who was a D.C. fireman. I don't remember her saying a word about anything we saw, except that she was surprised that the statue of Lincoln was so big.

Whole regions of the country were of no interest to her: the South and the Midwest, where she believed there were no

Catholics, only bigots or bores. She would have liked to see the Far West—largely, I think, because of her fascination with cowboys.

For non-Americans, she had an efficient and austere ethnography: one trait for each ethnic group. The English were cold, the French were sexual, Italians were warm and generous, Irish were saints. There were some surprises: she believed, for example, that Iranians were particularly interested in sports, and Canadians were lazy. Sometimes, as in the case of the lazy Canadians, there was some small basis in her experience. "We had to try to get ahold of the Surrogates Court up there in Canada somewhere, and every time I called they were closed. Wednesdays, closed. Tuesdays, day off. A lazy people." But mostly, I gave up trying to trace the source of these perceptions, as I gave up trying to understand the Trinity.

So, if my mother's Europe wasn't a place on a map or a place in time, what was it? My mother would never have used the word "style"—it was something she would have put under the heading of "phony." But if by style we mean a series of habits, a notable and noteworthy standard by which things are judged acceptable or unacceptable, desirable or undesirable, then Europe was a style. The style was based on generosity, spontaneity, witty dialogue, courage at standing up to power, well-cut clothes, and a habit of bursting into song. And a connection with the Catholic Church that seeped into everyday life—a people whose holidays were not Thanksgiving and the Fourth of July but Pentecost and Assumption.

This was my mother's Europe. It was made up of four countries only: England, Ireland, Italy, and France. England was the only Northern or Protestant country she thought about. She wasn't drawn to Northern evasiveness, tidiness, honesty, and good manners. Scandinavia was entirely outside her sphere of interest. When I introduced her to a Swedish friend, she said, "Your people commit suicide a lot, right?" She thought of Germany as entirely Lutheran, and then there was the war. So they were Protestants or

Nazis: no sense going there. But even some Catholic countries failed to engage her. Spain and Portugal, since she was unrelated by blood to anyone from there, and since she had no interest in bullfights, only glancingly caught her attention. Eastern Europe was to be prayed for, particularly Poland and Hungary, where Cardinal Mindszenty paced the parapet of the residence in which he was for years under house arrest, but you would never think of going there or believing you had anything to learn from them.

She liked the Mediterranean habit of shouting and weeping, then begging for forgiveness and falling into the offender's arms. All of it surrounded by food, the important elements of which were pasta, wine, and cheese. These sets of habits, of course, were connected in her mind with Italy. And with her father.

My mother's Italianness, or her relationship to things Italian, was as different from its Irish counterpart as her feelings about her mother were different from her feelings about her father. For my mother, as for all her siblings, their mother was the real thing, the rock, the source: home. Their ideas about their mother, much more than their notions of their father, were connected with their idea of God—omnipotent, demanding, parceling out a love that was the reward for good behavior rather than lavishing it unearned. I think there is a conviction, hoarded like a shameful and yet valuable secret in the breasts of Irishwomen, that men are something of a luxury item. This is the way my grandfather was regarded. My grandmother was reason; he was emotion—expressive, affectionate, impulsive, fastidious, with a famously bad temper that was here and gone like a summer storm. He was five foot six; she was five foot eleven. I think a great deal must have followed from that.

Unlike the Irish relatives, the Italians carried with them a hint of scandal. There was my great-aunt who had an affair with her husband's brother, and—unheard of among Catholics in the twenties—divorced one brother to marry another. And in the background: the story of some uncle called Uncle LaPanz, or Uncle LaPanza. He was a mob hit man, famous for slitting stomachs: apparently he would cry out *"la panza, la panza"* (the bread-basket, the breadbasket) as he wielded his knife. But on top of it all: the sensual pleasure, the high emotion, the amorality, like the dome of St. Peter's brooding over the city of Rome, was Italy's identity as the home of the Pope, the Prisoner of the Vatican. I think my mother imagined him in white, on his throne, canonizing saints and eating pasta and drinking wine, God's representative on earth, but with a secret appetite for strong-flavored cheese.

Paradoxically, although she knew many more people born in Ireland than in Italy, and spent much more time with her Irish than her Italian relatives, her idea of Ireland came much more from the movies than from any people she might have sat with at table, or in the same pew at Mass. Hollywood and Ireland were linked in a shared romantic conspiracy—a conspiracy in which Italy did not seem to have a part. And she would never have gone to see "foreign movies"; it's impossible to imagine her seeing any of the Italian neorealist films. "Foreign movies" were something she would have suspected as "phony." And, then, so many of them were condemned by the Legion of Decency.

So her idea of Italy didn't come from the movies, nor did it come from stories about the old country told by my grandfather or his relatives. My grandfather was determined to keep things Italian out of the house. He refused to allow his children to learn Italian: they were in America now, they were Americans. Neither of my grandparents was given to talking about the past; it was a sort of bad investment, the details of which they didn't want revealed to anyone, even the family. As with many ethnics whose parents were reluctant to tell stories, my mother's notion of Italian culture was passed on to her in food. Her mother, who had a kind of genius for making the best of a bad situation or a situation of scarcity—or perhaps her palate was simply born refined—not only learned Sicilian but became an expert Sicilian cook. It has only now occurred to me as odd that my grandfather allowed his wife, but not his children, to learn his native tongue.

My mother didn't want to see Italy for the art or the architecture or the history. We would have been better off if, when I was planning our trip to Italy, I understood that. She didn't want to see Italy; she wanted to see the Vatican. She wanted to see the Pope.

The trip to Italy was not a great success. I met her in London, where my English husband and I had been living for a year. I had arranged for her to be accompanied by a younger cousin, a sweet and cultivated woman, mother of seven, who had dreamed all her life of seeing Europe. We flew from London to Rome, and my mother was already cross, because she didn't like my husband, and the strain of pretending she did, of having to be grateful to him in his own country, the country of people who had oppressed her mother's family, quite wore her down. My mother never felt a responsibility to hide her unhappiness, certainly not from me; she made no attempt at the stoical traveler's false, yet sometimes invaluable, good cheer.

Her first glimpse of Rome was a disappointment to her. Maybe it would have been better if she'd seen some Rossellini, some Visconti, before her trip, instead of relying on *Three Coins in the Fountain*. The real Rome of 1976 frightened and overwhelmed her. She found the traffic and the noise intolerable. I had arranged to rent a wheelchair so that she could see the sights, but she refused to leave the *pensione* on the Via Gregoriana, just at the top of the Via Veneto. After a few days of watching the chair wait empty in the lobby of the *pensione*, I decided to return it. Trying to relieve my despair, I made my husband push me down the Via Veneto, and when we got to the bottom, I jumped out of the wheelchair and cried, *"Miràcolo."* But no one looked at me; I had the feeling they'd seen the same thing many times before, and the joke had gone tired for them.

I spent the days sightseeing with my English husband and my cousin. I was miserable; I'd been having a love affair with a man in London, a Bertie Wooster who adored me, and made me understand the starvation rations I'd been living on—no extravagant praise, only grudging approval when I'd jumped through a sufficient number of hoops, hoops that could prove I wasn't a vulgar American. I cried every night in the bed made of two single beds, pushed together, covered over with a tight white sheet; I cried looking up at the ornate ceilings, cried as I opened the shutters every morning for the view of the roofs of Rome. I wrote my lover letters that I hoped would show my wit, my brilliance. I remember writing him a sentence: "The pink geraniums flaunt themselves on the balcony like movie stars." I never got to eat in a restaurant; I let my husband and my cousin go, and I brought cold food to my mother's room, where we sat on the bed, grimly, eating bread and cheese and waiting for our audience with the Pope, the unglamorous and unbeloved Paul VI.

That was the only success of the trip. Because she was handicapped, my mother was allowed to sit in the first row of pilgrims, and the Pope bent over and gave her a special blessing. She looked stunned, and for hours she kept repeating, as if she'd just suffered a blow to the head, "He smelt like raisins. I was that close to him, and I'll never forget it: he smelt exactly like raisins."

We took a tour bus to Florence, and my mother stayed on the bus while my cousin and my husband and I raced through the Uffizi, then to see the *David* and the Fra Angelico frescoes. She did enjoy the dinner in the restaurant, however, and, satisfied by good food and wine, she held my hand in the darkness of the *autostrada* on the trip back to Rome. The radio played Neil Diamond singing "Song Sung Blue," and she told me it was a wonderful trip, she'd never forget it.

The trip to Italy wasn't her first European trip; I'd taken her to Ireland three years earlier. That was a much more successful trip; the truth was, my mother and I were much better on our own than in the company of others. Alone, I could bury the reality that our relationship was strange, unhealthy in its too-womblike closeness; I could endure on my own the anguish of her alcoholism: it was my problem, and no one need pity either of us if I kept things to myself.

Where did I get the idea to take her to Ireland? The year was 1973; I was living away from her for the first time, in Syracuse. That year, my third in graduate school, I had moved from a master's program in creative writing to a doctoral program in English literature. I was also moving, although I didn't know how thorough the move would be until later, from poetry to prose. I wrote the occasional short story, but I didn't consider myself a fiction writer, believing that poetry was the superior art, that I was more interested in a form with fewer words, so that each word would receive my utmost, my undivided attention. It was the height of the women's movement, and one of the by-products of the women's movement was that we began to think we had to reconstruct our relationships with our mothers: to cut them some slack. Was that the reason I suggested that we travel together—to be part of the romance in the air of mothers and daughters rediscovering each other as women throwing off the yoke of male domination, going off together, falling newly into each other's arms? In any case, I had the summer off—and I suggested we take a trip together. She paid for everything, of course, and I think she made the travel arrangements; it was the kind of thing we both agreed that she was better at than I.

What was she traveling to? What did she think she was traveling to? Perhaps, most important, to her mother's home, and since she worshipped her mother, she worshipped the land of her birth. But the Ireland she worshipped had no basis in fact. There were some phrases she took from her mother and her mother's sisters and her friends: "It wasn't from the grass he licked it," explaining heredity. A way of describing someone with "a hen's-ass mouth." Answering the question "Do you know where x is?" by the phrase "Look where the monkey put the nut." Most of the phrases and behaviors that she associated with Ireland involved contemptuously putting someone in his place. She wouldn't have said that; she would have called it a sense of humor. But mostly, the Ireland of my mother's dreams was a drama starring her mother, Maureen O'Hara, and Barry Fitzgerald. And a few priests, sent over to America for education or evangelization.

It was my mother's first time on an airplane, and she was aggressive and insulting to me, as she always was when she was afraid. "Where the hell did you get this damn-fool idea to put me on a plane? I didn't live this long to die in a plane crash." I pretended I didn't hear her and buried myself in my book. As I recall, it was *Howards End,* which I was reading for approximately the tenth time: the literary equivalent for me of comfort food.

After we'd buckled our seat belts, a very tiny old woman sat in the empty seat beside my mother. "I'm sorry to disturb you," she said, "but when we take off, might I hold your hand? I'm terrified of flying." Immediately, my mother rose to the occasion. "There's nothing at all to be afraid of," she said. "These pilots know what they're doing. They're experts in the field. They wouldn't let them fly if they weren't very good at their jobs." The woman held my mother's hand for nearly an hour; she was Irish, and she worked as a waitress at Schrafft's, which thrilled my mother—it was perhaps her favorite dining spot in the whole city of New York.

When we arrived at Shannon and I was about to take the wheel behind the rental car, we discovered I wasn't allowed to drive it: I was under twenty-five. This was an instance of my mother's genius for improvisation, for taking without a hitch the fence no one had seen. "Of course I'll drive," she said, prepared for the wrong side of the road as if she'd done it all her life, as if she'd had a secret past in England, perhaps as the girl chauffeur for Rex Harrison or Alec Guinness.

We drove; we sang; we ate our meals in the bedrooms of our B&Bs, the kind of food we really liked, snack food: brown bread, Irish cheese, washed down with our stash of Harvey's Bristol Cream. I've found the journal she kept of the trip: not a specific is mentioned; under every day nearly the same thing, "Scenery gorgeous, people great, M and I laughed a lot. Beautiful shrines; the faith is strong here, you can see it on the roads."

We made our way to the town where my grandmother had been born, a town in County Longford named Ballymahon that she had left eighty years earlier, the first in her family, traveling alone at age seventeen, then bringing her mother and five siblings over, paying for them all on her husband's tiny salary. We knocked at the rectory beside the parish church; a fresh-faced young priest made a copy of my grandmother's baptismal certificate and drove us to a place where he believed my grandmother's family farm might have been located. It was tiny, perhaps only an acre, the pebbledash house indistinguishable from any around it, the view unremarkable, the land lacking distinguishing features. But my mother would have kissed the ground if she could have. I, however, was not convinced that it was really my grandmother's birthplace; I suspected, though I had no evidence, that the fresh-faced priest brought every American tourist there. And what was the harm? He saw to it that they left happy.

If, for my mother, Ireland was the movies and her mother, for me it was the seat of literature, and one of the stops on my pilgrimage was Sligo, to the grave of William Butler Yeats, a poet whom I worshipped as a god. His grave had for me the power of the shrines to the Virgin or the crucified Christ that, dotting the Irish roads, so pleased my mother. I left on Yeats's grave a branch of gorse, the omnipresent wild yellow flower that grows everywhere along the Irish countryside. I read my mother "A Prayer for My Daughter." "That's fine for now, while she's a baby," my mother said. "When she grows up, he'll find out he doesn't have that much say over what she does or who she is."

I still remember the name of the woman who owned the B&B outside of Sligo where we stayed that night: Jewell Lindsay. She was a young, athletic-looking woman with short strawberry-blond hair and a warm, good-natured disposition, practical but welcoming. Like so many young women, she was immediately taken with my mother, as was her little boy, who liked the funny faces my mother made, the shapes she made out of bread crusts, her laughter when he showed her a drawing or a toy. My mother was momentarily disappointed when Jewell had to correct my mother's automatic assumption that she was Roman Catholic; I don't think that it occurred to my mother that there was something called the Church of Ireland, that there was a church that attached to the Irish Nation that was not the Roman Catholic Church. I could see my mother make a decision: she liked Jewell, she was not going to hold it against her that she was Protestant.

We took our evening meal with Jewell, and she told us we were welcome to sit in her living room—which she called "the lounge"—in front of the peat fire, for as long as we liked. She told us that there was another guest, another American, who was staying with her for several months. He had retired; he was moving to Ireland, building a house in Sligo, but construction had been delayed. But he had to be in Ireland, because he was bringing his dog with him and the dog had to be in quarantine for six months: this was a law required of all dogs coming from foreign parts. He wanted to be near the dog so he could visit it in quarantine.

I don't remember his name, but I remember his looks, and that both these and his manners were undistinguished. He had a bad toupee, a kind of mole color, and bad false teeth. He was small of build; his shoulders were stooped, he wore Sansabelt polyester pants and beige loafers with chains. He had neither wit nor charm—so there is no explanation for what happened, what my mother and I did, what I believe he made us do. Somehow, he set us against each other; he made us compete for his attention. This had never happened before, not for one minute in either of our lives. I had never known my mother to be interested in a man, and she carefully shut her eyes to my sexual activities. My mother flattered him outrageously, told him how interesting it was that he was retiring to Ireland, that she would love to do it but she didn't have the guts, how wonderful it was that he was so devoted to his dog, she had a dog herself and she would do exactly the same thing, but it was a rare man that would be so concerned for his dog. For my part, I kept offering him cups of tea and slices of buttered bread; I moved my body seductively; I gave him meaningful glances and stared at his mouth when he spoke. I don't remember whether it was he, or my mother, or I who made the first move to leave the warm room and the fire, but it was clear that something had been finished, some hand had been played out; there were no other cards left to any of us.

When we got into the room, my mother slammed the door and looked at me with fury. "I hope you're proud of yourself, wiggling your ass in his face like a common whore." And then it happened. I was covered over in rage. Some screen came down over my eyes, a screen of flame—or, not flame, a burning cityscape, buildings going up in flames before my eyes. I walked up to my mother, and I slapped her face. We were both terribly shocked. But she took control of the situation. "Remember this," she said, "remember this for the rest of your life. That you struck your mother."

And I heard an echo, an echo from my early childhood. My parents had been arguing, which they frequently did. They were standing beside their bed. My father, fed up, wheeled away from her to walk out of the room. In the process, he somehow knocked my mother down. She landed heavily on her behind, unhurt. But she saw her advantage. "Remember this," she said, "remember this all your life. That you knocked your wife onto the floor. That you threw me on the floor, a cripple."

I don't remember what my father did, but I know I burst into hysterical tears. In all my life, before or since, I have never known such remorse. My mother was right: I would remember it always, as I'm sure my father had. We had assaulted the afflicted body. There was no sense that this was, in any way, a permissible thing to do. That he, a man, had knocked a woman to the ground, that I had slapped my mother, were bad enough; but that we had done these things to a cripple—that was what made it unforgivable. Unforgettable. And she knew it. She knew her power.

After we got home, I realized that the most important thing about the trip for my mother was not the trip itself but that she could tell people that she had gone, and that it had been her daughter's idea, and that her daughter had planned everything.

Our most successful trip to Europe was not to Ireland or Italy, countries where she had what were known in those days by everyone as "roots," but our trip to France. We traveled as a threesome: my mother and I, and the man I was living with, although my mother didn't know that. In order to keep it from her, I installed, in the house where my husband-to-be and I lived, a special phone, called the red phone, which only she had the number for. My husband-to-be was told that he was never to answer that phone, under pain of death. So, when my mother phoned, thinking she was getting the apartment where I lived alone, a mournful, regretful divorcée, only I answered.

Was the French trip better than the Italian and the Irish ones because I was happy, happy as I had not been as a single woman (Ireland) or an unhappily married woman (Italy)? My mother hated it when I was unhappy; my unhappiness made her punitive; when I was little, she would hit me if I came to her with a wound, an accident. So perhaps it was as simple as that, an ordinary mother-daughter story: she was happy because I was happy. Of all narrative possibilities, the one that includes my mother and me in any category of the ordinary is the one I always move towards last, when all the others seem impossible.

When I say I took my mother to France, what I mean is that I granted her wish for a trip to Lourdes. Lourdes: home state of the afflicted. Before Lourdes, though, we stopped in Paris: the site of the movies she and I had wept over and loved. Was it because she had so many images of it from movies that Paris didn't frighten her as Rome did? Or was it because we both felt safe with my husband-to-be, as we hadn't (rightly, it turns out) with my first husband? Did she see us as replicating the three Americans in *Funny Face*? Me in the Audrey Hepburn role: an intellectual with no common sense; my husband-to-be as the unflappable Fred

Astaire; and my mother playing the Kay Thompson part, the working woman, impatient, bad-tempered in her beautifully cut suits,
famously competent, snapping her fingers and making her inferi-
ors jump? There's a number in *Funny Face* in which Fred, Audrey,
and Kay separately visit the famous tourist sights (the Eiffel Tower,
the Arc de Triomphe, the Pont Neuf), all pretending they are above
it all, too tired, and run into each other, laughingly falling into one
another's arms. We did take my mother to the Eiffel Tower, and
our luxurious hotel, the Hôtel Raphael, was right near the Arc de
Triomphe. It was a hotel that could have come out of a movie—
opulent, luxurious in the old, high way, obviously expensive—a
splurge I hoped she'd love. She didn't disappoint me; she was
thrilled by the thick towels warmed by steam-heated racks, the bro-
cade spreads and wall coverings, the croissants brought to her
room.

She loved everything in Paris, and everything went well. We
took a cab to Notre-Dame, got there in time for Mass, and when we
left the church to find it was pouring rain, we discovered that the
cab driver had waited for us.

At Chartres Cathedral, my husband asked my mother for my
hand in marriage. She agreed, weeping. Was she weeping for
sheer joy, for the sheer pleasure, the sheer relief of being, finally,
allowed to assume a role that placed her in the space of the conventional? Is that something I failed to understand: her desire to
be conventional, her gratitude to me that I allowed for something
she seemed to have been denied because of her affliction, because,
given the shape of her body, she could never look the part?

Before the asking for the hand, I had brought bread, cheese,
fruit, and wine for a picnic. My mother was being wheeled in a
wheelchair that looked like a large baby carriage. Did she like it for
that reason—because it looked like a joke, or because what she
really wanted was to be my baby, my baby and the baby of my
man?

When I opened the bag with the picnic provisions, I realized
that I had failed to provide a corkscrew. Then a miracle happened,

a miracle entirely unconnected to my nature. I had a mechanical brainstorm: I, who am famous for my mechanical ineptitude. I remembered that if you strike, very gently and at just the right pacing and pressure, the butt of a bottle of wine against the bark of a tree, the cork will pop out. The French people surrounding us watched me, mouths agape. When the cork popped out, I held the bottle over my head and all the French people applauded. And my new fiancé took the picture: triumphant, happy, with my mother, who is happy because I am chosen and she is being pushed (by me) in something that looks like a baby carriage, and because, in a great cathedral, a man whom she admires has just asked for my hand.

After this, when I went into a café to use the bathroom, I found something that shocked me so deeply that, nearly thirty years later, I can call to mind, with equal ease, both the image and the shock. Against the white porcelain floor of the urinal was a long, snakelike single turd. It was, in its way, perfect against the white porcelain, and I shuddered and closed the door and ran out. It was worse that I had found this in Chartres, under the eyes of the structure that seemed to stand for everything high and noble about human aspirations, the human will to greatness, to transcendence: the impulse to rise above.

That night, my mother gave my fiancé fifty dollars and told him to take me someplace special for dinner; she'd be happy just to eat bread and cheese in her bed.

To get to Lourdes, we flew in a small plane from Paris. I think, to my mother's mind, everything was a preparation for the real thing, marginal, however enjoyable. I hated the idea of Lourdes: the locus of a kind of literal-minded piety that gave me the creeps. Lourdes was the place where the Virgin Mary appeared to the peasant girl Bernadette, told her to dig her finger in the dirt, and—behold—a spring was found, whose miraculous waters would cure the sick. All over the world, false grottoes, made of plastic or cardboard or painted wooden rocks, were meant to represent the place where Mary had appeared.

We drove through the town, encrusted with pilgrim/tourist shops and cafés. When we got to the grotto itself, I asked where we could get a wheelchair so that my mother could participate in the candlelight procession. I imagined that one place there would be no trouble gaining access to a wheelchair was Lourdes. I was told to go to the infirmary and ask for the nun in charge. When I passed by a corridor chock-a-block full of empty wheelchairs, I was reassured.

I asked the nun if I could have one for my mother.

"Have you reserved a wheelchair?" the nun asked.

"No," I answered, trying to smile ingratiatingly, trying to imagine what an ingratiating smile might look like to a French nun.

"Because the hour for giving out wheelchairs has passed," she said, tapping the face of her watch.

"But I can just take one of these, can't I?" I asked, pointing to the rows of empty wheelchairs. "My mother is an old woman. She's traveled all the way from New York to be in the candle-light procession; she won't have another chance. We're leaving tomorrow."

The nun looked at her watch again. "The time for giving out wheelchairs is over at three. It's three-thirty."

I began to sputter. "There must be someone else I can talk to about this," I said.

She did the thing that nuns had, in my history, always done when they perceived a child was testing the bounds of their authority in a way that they couldn't control. "Speak to Father," she said. I waited for a moment. A very elegant man in a black turtle-neck sweater and tweed jacket (no Roman collar; no slapping cassock and soutane) asked what the trouble was. I told him that Sister would not let me have one of the wheelchairs. I pointed to the empty rows of them.

"What did Sister say?" he asked.

"She said the hour was up."

"Well, then, Sister is in charge. I can't go over her head," he said.

I began to get furiously angry. "Look," I said, "this is a place that is supposed to be the home of the afflicted, and I have an afflicted woman who's waited for this her whole life. Why can't you let me take one of these wheelchairs?"

Urbane, suave, unflappable, he said what any ignorant Irish priest might have said: "It's up to Sister." I began to shout. He did what every man does when a woman begins to shout. He talked to the man. Now, my fiancé had, and has, approximately one-third as much French as I. Speaking man to man, the elegant priest said: "Take her up to the top of the hill, where you can watch the procession; you'll get a very good view from there." I fumed; but I perceived that I had lost.

We drove up to the top of the hill and parked the car. Not far from the car, I saw a public toilet. Outside the public toilet was a wheelchair. We waited half an hour for the candlelight procession to begin, but the sun set slowly, and it would clearly be some time before the procession began. I noticed that, in half an hour, no one had come out of the toilet. I began to be alarmed. I knocked on the door. There was no answer. The door was unlocked. There was no one inside. I looked around: there was no one in the vicinity. I told my fiancé to open the trunk of the car, quick. I took the wheelchair, shoved it into the trunk, and told him to step on it—as if we were robbers needing to make a quick getaway. My mother put her hands in front of her eyes and said, "I don't want to know where you got that wheelchair from."

The three of us marched in the procession. In the dark, their faces illumined by candles, it was possible to love everyone: the sick, the caretakers, the merely curious and pious. And to love my mother when, after dinner (served by someone who could have been cast by Bresson), my mother opened her pocketbook, took out a plastic rain hat, and wrapped her leftover sausages in it. "For tomorrow," she said, "in case we want a snack on the road."

Was my mother kept from her rightful place in the great world? Because of class, gender, disability? Did she not become what she might have become, what she wanted to become? In one case this is true.

She had wanted to be a teacher. She had applied to the normal school in New Paltz, New York (a town where she later lived, where I was living, where I bought a house for her two blocks away from mine, where I believed she would be happy, but where she was horribly unhappy). They accepted her, not knowing that she was disabled.

When she arrived at the school, they took a look at her and told her she had to go home. She fought them. They told her she would be a danger to her potential students; if there was a fire, she would be unable to lead them in safety from the burning building. She told them they were wrong, she would be perfectly capable of something like that. All right, they said, we'll give you a physical exam. In the office of whoever was in charge—dean or headmaster or principal, whatever she or he was called—she was ordered to do squat thrusts. Which, of course, she could never have done.

I don't know whether she tried and failed, whether she got down on the ground and had to pick herself up in ignominy, or whether she walked out the door, her physical dignity intact. She spoke about it only when she was drunk, when she was resentful of the increased rights of the handicapped that hadn't happened until so many soldiers came back disabled from the Second World War.

Would she have liked being a teacher better than she liked being a secretary? She would have been a marvelous teacher; she was brilliant with young children, imaginative and funny and full of surprising comprehensions. But she loved her work as a secretary; I can't imagine another job that might have made her happier. If she'd become a teacher, what would her life have been like? Would she have traveled to Europe with other spinster teachers?

Would she have read different books, learned to look at pictures, understood the importance of museums and scenery? Would she have married my father?

It is possible that my mother found exactly the place in the world that suited her. That she didn't want any more access to the great world than she had. In fact, it rather frightened her. When she came to my graduation at Barnard, she gripped her chair in anxiety, and when my professors tried to speak to her, she went mute. Was her place in the great world at its door, opening the door for me, pointing the way so that I could be in a place she vaguely apprehended but didn't want really to approach?

Because, at the end of her life, she withdrew from the world entirely. Like her other sisters, she retreated to the fortress of her family memories—angry, alcoholic, finally demented, just as they were. In the end, she couldn't even remember the songs she had loved, or the movies she had seen. She didn't even remember my name.

But she had seen Europe. And no one else in her family could say that. No, not one.

My Mother's *Body*

My mother was one of the afflicted. She was stricken, at the age of three, with polio; I wonder if she had any bodily memory of running, of walking without labor, without anxiety—of movement as a joy. There is a picture of her, dressed to the nines in a white lace Edwardian outfit. I think she is around seven years old. She is trying to hide her crutch behind her body; if you didn't notice it, you might think at first she was normal. Until you saw the left leg—thinner than the other—and the left shoe—built higher than its mate.

Two of her eight siblings were stricken in subsequent polio epidemics. The merciful wing of history has brushed over our fearful memory: the terror, each summer, that one would be struck down. No more a commonplace: children in leg braces. Absent from the lexicon, the words so easily to hand, so dreadful: iron lung. Polio is no longer real to the generation of my children, although carelessness or suspicion about vaccines has caused its continuance as a plague in parts of the developing world. My mother insisted that I be among the first to be vaccinated; she woke me at dawn so I would be at the head of the line for the first dosages of what she saw as the sacrament of Dr. Salk.

One of her legs, the left one, was six inches shorter than the other. She walked with a pronounced limp; she couldn't, for all the years I knew her, walk more than a block at a time. She wore one built-up shoe, really a boot, and she couldn't take a step unless she was wearing that shoe. Stairs were a difficulty. A fall was a disaster. Her body was misshapen, asymmetrical. A body that was a problem, always. Never a gift.

Affliction: something suffered, something done to someone from which he or she has no recourse, no defense. I like it much better than other words that can be used to describe what happened to my mother—"crippled," "handicapped," "disabled"—because the accent falls not on the body itself but upon its fate.

Of course, some aspects of my mother's body were free of her affliction: her beautiful hands and arms, dappled with freckles like the skin of a young apple; her beautiful hair; her large gray-green eyes and high cheekbones; her clear, smooth skin without wrinkles almost to the end, never once in my memory marked by a single blemish, no, not one. Her enviable skin. It was called her "complexion." Yes, it was envied. People said, to and of my mother, "I envy your complexion."

And there were other desirable things whose source was her body, almost features, like high breasts or long legs. In my mother's case, her voice, charming, lively, robust, jocular, persuasive, sure; her laughter, a laugh you could identify in a dark movie house, a laugh that made everyone want to laugh. Women who didn't like my mother criticized her laugh, called it unseemly, something that drew improper or undue attention to itself, as if she had worn a dress that was too tight or too low cut, revealing something a proper woman knows well how to cover up.

How is it possible to speak of a mother's body?

Possible, that is, without betrayal.

And if it is possible, is it permissible?

To speak of it as if it were not a body but something that could be turned into a work of art?

The body of the afflicted mother. The body of the work of art. The impossible desire for shapeliness, for an intact form. For harmony, radiance, wholeness. My mother's body was unharmonious. But isn't it possible to bypass harmony, bypass proportion, in the search for, if not wholeness, then radiance? The daughter, born of the mother's body, looks at it for information, curses, clues. How can a daughter talk about her mother's body? Especially when she is a writer?

I know there are a number of ways I don't want to talk. A number of ways I don't want to write. I don't want to pity myself for being a child born of a body such as my mother's. And I don't want to describe my mother's body. Not any more. Not now. I did it once. But she was living then. Now she is dead.

In the last years of her life, she was, in her wretchedness, my tormentor. Her body tortured me: the sight of it, its smell. Living, she was a torturer, and now, among the dead, she is entirely innocent.

There was nothing I could do to stop the torment while she lived, while I was in charge of her—in the eleven years when I visited her in the nursing home once a week—while I had to supervise her care, her presence was unbearable. The sight of her blackening teeth, now only stumps; her hair, scraped down almost to her scalp; above all the smell of her made me panic, made me want to cover my face with my hands and cry out, "I can't, I can't, I can't do this." I wanted to run in some cold wind, some scourging rain, until I fell, exhausted, and I could lose the sight of her, the smell of her. Too tired to think. To remember that the body I once loved was now the source of hatred. Except when I loved her for her helplessness. Then I loved her to the point of weeping unstoppable, wrenching tears. Now that she is no longer among the living, I can miss her but the tears come lightly, they do not rip me apart. There is only missing. No desire to escape. No punishment, given or received.

Is it only because it no longer torments me that I no longer feel the need to describe my mother's body? Was my need to describe her body only a need for punishment? Now I feel a real aversion for the prospect. Now that she is dead, the prospect of describing her body makes me feel like Ham, the son of Noah, the betraying son.

This is my understanding of the story of Noah and his sons.

After his long labor, towards the end of the time on the Ark, Noah drank. Drank himself unto drunkenness. What was that like? What did he look like before he fell asleep? What was he wearing before his nakedness? Did he stagger, did he slur his words, did he curse the fates, the Flood, his nagging wife, his disappointing children? Did he pity himself for his responsibility, for being born a just man in the time of the Flood? Is this what enraged Ham—the admired father, chosen by God, all along a fraud? Not really a just man, merely someone waiting to turn into a drunk. All along a beast without the dignity of the pairs taken aboard. *I, Father, will expose your nakedness. I will look at what you have been all along, what you have always really been. If I don't look, there will be no one to witness this truth. Isn't truth-telling a kind of love?*

He knows that it is not. He knows that it is hatred. Hatred and perhaps desire—the desire of the eyes—is it somehow connected to sex? It could be, but it doesn't need to be.

He sees what he sees.

He tells his brothers.

His brothers will not look. They enter the chamber backwards, a cloak thrown over their shoulders, covering their heads. Not looking, they fling the cloak onto the naked body of their father.

The good sons.

They have not seen.

They have done the work of not seeing.

Someone had to do that work.

As someone had to do the work of seeing.

But suppose Ham had been an only child. Which work would he have chosen? The work of seeing, or the work of not seeing, of refusing to see?

He would have had to choose.

And then he would have had to make another choice: to speak or to be silent.

For the writer, this choice is also possible. Although we tell ourselves that it is impossible, a betrayal of our vocation.

But silence is a perfectly honorable choice. More honorable because no one knows about it.

The most dishonorable choice: to speak and then to confess one's own (superior) knowledge of the dishonor of speaking.

I know that this is what I am doing now.

I seem unable to give up the impulse to say some things about my mother that seem to me true. And in order to do that, I must describe her body. Because only if I describe her body, as something in space, as something that moved through space (awkwardly, uneasily), as something that was seen in space (misshapen, unpleasing), can the nature, the effect of her affliction be understood. But for whom is such an understanding necessary? The answer, of course, is only myself.

For a little while, I convinced myself that I would speak about my mother's body for the good of others, particularly for the good of other children of the afflicted. This new (false) conviction began when a friend of mine told me that her husband's father was the child of a polio victim and that his sense of his body, like mine, was greatly affected by this. She said that it would be an important thing to write about, that no one had written about it.

I will do it, I said, donning my heroic cloak. I had forgotten that I had already done it—written about my mother's body. That my friend hadn't read what I had written is another matter. I simply could have directed her to the book I had already written, the book in which I wrote about my mother's afflicted body, about being the child of such a mother. I wrote about my mother's body eleven years ago, when I was writing about my father. So I was writing about my father's wife, my father's widow. A living woman. When I wrote about her then, I said: "My mother is eighty-six and something has broken or hardened and worn out. When she hasn't combed her hair, when she has lost a tooth she won't have attended to, when she won't cut or file her nails or change her clothes she is distressing to look at."

When I wrote about my mother's body I used the word "rot." Many readers found that shocking. I told myself I used it because it was the truth. Her body was rotting. She had allowed it to rot; she wanted it to. She forced me to deal with her rotting body because she hadn't taken off her high-laced boots for three months. I found this out when I took her to the doctor's for a checkup and he told her to take her shoes off. She told him at once she hadn't taken them off, and he made her leave the office. He said the smell was not one he could allow in a professional office. In his office, he said, there could not be the smell of rot.

When we got home, I had to take her shoes off; she refused to do it herself. I knelt at her bedside as if I were saying my night prayers, unlaced her shoes, and took them off. The smell was overwhelming. I had to hold my breath so as not to take it in. And the look of them: the leprous flesh I had dreamed of martyring myself to as a pious girl. I told her I had to fill a basin of water, and while the water was running, I vomited into the toilet. I came back, bathed and dried her feet. Then I phoned an agency to hire a nurse to tend to her feet every day. I could do it once, but I couldn't endure the possibility of having to do it again and again. The possibility of that made the idea of life unbearable. Made me literally long for death. The idea of death was preferable to the task of continually tending my mother's rotting feet.

Rot is one of the works of death. My mother had made it happen. She had made it happen by not taking off her shoes. She couldn't explain why she didn't take off her shoes. She said it was too much trouble.

What kind of daughter uses the word "rot" in relation to her mother? What is the line between truth-telling and punishment? How could I want to punish my mother for something that was so clearly a sign of dementia? Was it simply the victim's impulse to take any turn that might occur to punish the one who had tortured? For whatever reason, at whatever time.

Now my mother is a skeleton, or ash. All those sites of attention, rage, despair, gone now. Where did they go? Were they vaporized into the air? Absorbed into the earth? The details of the bodies of the dead turn abstract once they are no longer in the world. Abstract, therefore no longer a cause of rage. Sorrow, rather, or regret. The burning rash of rage turning to the dull tumor of sorrow.

In the days when I had to think about her uncut nails, in the days when her life consisted of sitting with her head in her hands in a stupor, a stupor punctuated by periods of anxiety, I prayed for her death. But I must remind myself that my wanting her death, even praying for it, did not end her life. I wasn't even with her when her life ended. I do not now wish her alive. Not the mother who had become entirely wretched.

My last duty towards her was to choose the clothes she would be buried in. Her own good clothes had long since disappeared. I chose for her an outfit of my own, one that she would have looked good in. A black crepe blouse with a Fortuny collar, a black silk pleated skirt. Around her neck: a string of pearls. Dead, she looked beautiful. Dead, she had got back her elegance. I was glad of my part in giving it back to her.

I do not want the wretched mother back again in this life. But there is another one, desired, and desirable. A body I once yearned to be near. In the foreground of an Italian Renaissance painting I once saw was a cup with the inscription "Alas, I yearned exceedingly." There were times when I was a child when my entire body was a vessel of yearning for her. When she would leave me, sending me somewhere, for a day, a week's vacation, a summer with some member of her family who was meant to be doing us both a good turn by separating us. In the first years after my father's death, I felt separation from her body like a new wound on top of the old, mortal one of his death. But even before his death, I loved sitting on her lap; I loved putting my head on her firm, springy bosom; I was proud of her in her suits and hats when she left the house for work, unlike the mothers of my friends who slopped around at home all day in housedresses. Carelessly coiffed. Not a starched handkerchief among them, or a gold compact, or a purse with the clasp in the shape of a snake. This is the mother I want to meet again: the mother that I yearned for. I want to go back where I can meet that mother. Back past affliction, age, disease. This is the trick I want to pull: the trick of bringing the desirable mother back to life. The trick of Resurrection.

But I have no idea how I might go about it. Or if it is wrong to describe a miracle as a trick.

I travel to London to visit a friend whose lover of forty years has just died. In the Duty Free Shop on the way home, I spot a display advertising the perfume my mother always wore for "special occasions," Arpège by Lanvin. The young saleswoman is thin, in a short black skirt, black shirt, and black pumps with something called kitten heels. I ask if I can try a sample of Arpège. She sprays it on a little card and tells me to rub the card on my wrists. I do. I walk around with it. To see if I can bear wearing my mother's scent. To see if I can bear being my mother.

At first, the scent is sharper than I remember, less accommodating, less friendly, less sweet. And yet even as a child I valued it because as a scent it was mature, unapproachable. It was comprehensible, like the Hindu idea of God, only by what it was not: ungirlish, unfloral, unfruity, neither of the garden nor the woodland, an invented scent rather than a discovered one, composed deliberately rather than come upon (accidentally, fortuitously), an artifact, a product and a sign of city life, not worn in the daylight, or worn casually, but something hoarded, brought out for an occasion, the seriousness of which was marked by the very act of its having been brought out.

When my mother wanted to use Arpège, she would cover the opening of the bottle with her index finger, tip it back once, twice, then press her moistened finger first to her wrists, then behind her ears. Then she would hold a linen handkerchief against the bottle's opening and tip it back until a drop or two saturated the cloth. She would put the cloth into her special handbag—for evenings out—and the more vivid scent that the cloth had absorbed would be taken into the leather.

When she was away, at work or out at a meeting, I would go into her drawer, open her purse, and put my nose close, close against the leather, breathing it in, the animal leather smell an undercurrent still against the sophisticated scent that had become one with its essence, with its texture, the absorption transforming them both. So I would smell the leather, then the handkerchief, and then, in a fit of radical daring, open the bottle to smell the perfume itself. This led, once, to something terrible. I opened the bottle and knocked it over, and the perfume ate through the varnish of my mother's dresser, destroying its smoothness, leaving a pocked, scratched, fuzzy, denuded surface, instead of a varnished patina. The texture of the dresser top was the texture of the skin of an uncultivated peach. In all the years my mother had the dresser (thirty, perhaps, until she moved into a house that I bought for her and it was given away), nothing was ever done to make the dresser presentable once again. What could have been done? I always believed that nothing could be done. My horror when I saw the perfume eating away at the surface was the horror of despair. A despair at the inexorability of physical destruction. My conviction that nothing, nothing could be done to make it better, to repair it, was borne out. My mother's fury was negligible measured against my despair. Something in the world had ruined the beauty of something, as polio had ruined the beauty of my mother's body, and I was its minion, its agent, its stooge. From then on, the notion of the physical world's inexorability was mine.

But the accident of the perfume did not make me stop loving the perfume. Or believing that this was a sign of the best way of being female that was open to me—and worth a tremendous amount, although I had no idea what the currency might be, what might have to be given up.

But I don't want to be thinking about this, a memory of ruin, of sorrow. This is everything I'm trying to get away from: the sorrowful mother, the ruined mother. I want to get to the desirable mother, the mother who is the site of pleasure. I want an alternative to biography. To history. My own and hers. I want something larger, something outside the circle I have been traveling the circumference of, like a horse with blinders, the horse in Joyce's "The Dead" who keeps traveling around the statue of King William because he can't break his habits from being the workhorse at the mill.

I want to be outside myself, and her. Or outside myself but with her and her perfume. So I decide to learn about the perfume as a research project. That will take it out of the cramped domain of my own life. A person familiar with computers despite myself, I begin by Googling Arpège. "Google," a word my mother would never have heard of, that I hadn't heard of until after her death.

The first site I travel to is offering the perfume for sale. It tells me that Arpège was launched in 1927 as a soft floral fragrance for women. The site describes its scent as "powdery floral." It elaborates: "a luxurious, gentle, floral fragrance, combining honeysuckle, jasmine, roses and orange blossoms, accents of vanilla and sandalwood. It is recommended for romantic wear."

I see that I was wrong about its being unfloral. All those different flowers, hinting of hot climes—tropical, even—honeysuckle, jasmine, orange blossoms—but domesticated, familiarized by two of them, the vanilla and the rose. But what do they mean by "powdery"? "Powdery" implies a certain dryness, a certain enviable dryness. Absorptive. A civilizing element: it calms things down.

The business of the site, though, is selling the perfume. Whoever created the site must understand that Arpège has been absent from the larger imagination of fragrance for a number of years. They are too smart to try to sweep this under the rug; they make a charming tale of it; the passage of time, its erasures, become something that can be talked about: "This one your grandmother probably wore in her younger days. Naughty thing she is sometimes. Arpège is one of those classic fragrances that have made many a man go weak at the knees. Who says grandma should have all the fun?"

What is this, as a marketing strategy? To whom is it meant to appeal, and what might the appeal be? Obviously, to someone younger than I, someone more obviously in the sexual running. My mother wore Arpège. But they're trying to sell it to someone whose grandmother wore the scent. Someone my daughter's age. As is so frequently the case now, I see that I am too old to be the target audience.

And what glamour is being invoked? Naughty Granny—naughty in the twenties, the madcap thirties. White Art Deco bedrooms, Irene Dunne or Carole Lombard in lounging pajamas? Secrets kept from the naughty granny's daughter, the potential buyer's mother. (Me?) A drama of exclusion. A suggestion that respectability can be kept, that its price is not the price of pleasure. That a daring past is something that can be got away with. That the knees of the powerful man, the man who pays for your perfume, can turn to rubber. And no one will be worse off. You will make a good marriage—maybe not to the man with the rubbery knees, but at least you will have children, grandchildren.

In invoking the glamorous grandmother of the twenties and thirties, a historical gap is opened up as large—eighty years—as if I had, in the 1950s, evoked a glamorous image of the Belle Epoque. This seems wonderful to me, an encouragement to my plan for finding an alternative to history, to biographical fact.

A second Web site reminds me of the advertising slogan that went with the perfume, "Promise her anything but give her Arpège." What did the admen have in mind with this one? That the purchase of this scent would allow, encourage, validate false statements? That, as long as you gave this bottle to your honey, you could swear to marry her next month, leave your wife next year, give up men, or booze, or horses? Clearly, the message is pitched towards the man, because who would want to be deceived? What woman longs to be a dupe? In failing to understand this, am I failing to understand something important in the history of women? The acceptance of deception. The faked orgasm. The faked pregnancy. Perfume itself covering the animal truth. Does my inability to enroll myself in this ancient brigade mean that I have no right to wear the perfume? That I should count myself instead as part of the unglamorous sisterhood: bluestockings, do-gooders, unembellished, not a drop or particle of makeup on their natural skins, content with whatever God gave them, out to do God's work, to tell the truth, the whole truth, nothing but the truth? A life without glamour. I never wanted that. Even when I thought I would be a nun, I imagined myself glamorous in my habit. My mother, buying her suits, her face powder, her Arpège, insisted on being a part of the duplicitous world of female pleasure. As do I.

After a while I get it: it's not that I'm against deception. But I want the deception to come from me. I don't mind deceiving, but I don't want to be deceived. I don't want *anything* promised to me. It's not that I want *nothing*. I want *something*. *Many things*. But not *anything*. As if I had no choice. No scent, however desirable, is worth that. Especially when I could get the perfume for myself. Because of my mother, I always imagined myself a wage earner. Never dependent on a man for necessaries or for luxuries. No, never that.

Simultaneously proud and self-pitying, I buy the perfume for myself.

When I turn to the site called "Fascination Perfumery," I feel a shock. It tells me something I ought to have known but never knew, that the symbol on the bottle of Arpège is a symbol of mother and daughter.

I go to my own bottle. There it is—mother and daughter. The mother in an extravagant robe and turban, absolutely dwarfing the child, who kneels at her feet. Why did I never notice this? Perhaps because the images aren't an obvious mother and daughter: the mother so huge, so exotic, and the daughter so insignificant, not on her mother's lap, not in her arms, but at her feet. Overwhelmed.

I determine to track down the history of this image. Where did it come from? Whose idea was it? What was it meant to evoke, to represent? I turn once more to Google; I look up Jeanne Lanvin and find a French site, untranslated.

I am astonished to learn that her career as a couturière was derived from her life as a mother, from her adoration of her daughter, Marie-Blanche. I am told this even before I am told the details of her life, even before I learn that Jeanne Lanvin was born in 1867 (in America, the Civil War was only just over). She was the oldest of eleven children. Her father was an unsuccessful journalist. (So we have something in common, Jeanne Lanvin and I.) At thirteen, she became a milliner, but her career took off when her clients saw the extraordinary garments she had made for her beloved daughter, coveted them first for their daughters, then for themselves. It was by adapting the lavish details—*Broderie Anglaise,* exotic fabrics—that she had used for her daughter's clothes that she became one of the most successful couturières in Paris. It's almost as if she didn't mean it; she was just trying to express her love for her daughter. Almost incidentally, her marriage, brief, to Marie-Blanche's father, an Italian, is mentioned. As if everyone knows it didn't really count.

As a gift for her daughter's thirtieth birthday, she created the perfume Arpège, the name created by the daughter, a singer herself, who, upon smelling the perfume, said, *"On dirait un arpège"* (It's like an arpeggio). The site goes on to say that, despite her passionate but suffocating love, *"amour passioné mais étouffant,"* mother and daughter were, in the end, *"éloignées"*—estranged, distant, separated.

I am desperate to learn more about the Lanvins, but the well of the Internet has run dry. Or not quite: I go to Amazon and find that I can order from Paris a biography of Jeanne Lanvin.

I wait six weeks for the book to arrive. On the cover: Madame Lanvin herself, dolorous, forbidding, with huge, dark, Russian-looking eyes, her hair in a chignon, pendulous earrings, a choker of large pearls, not strung close together as would be customary, but separated from one another so the chain is visible between them, as if making a point about their size. Her massive head casts an imposing shadow on the wall behind her. On the back of the book I discover that its author, Jérôme Picon, is an art historian who has also written about Proust. In small black print the words "Grandes Biographies," then, in larger blood red, the name Jeanne Lanvin.

The précis of the book begins by saying that no good fairy hovered over the cradle at Jeanne's birth. No, it tells us, she made her own luck, she succeeded because of hard work, a sharp business sense, a genius for marketing, and also *"sa passion pour sa fille, son égérie et sa bien aimée, passion exclusive, égoiste, éperdue, douloureuse souvent"* (her passion for her daughter, her inspiration and great love, her passion: exclusive, egotistical, doomed, often sorrowful).

How did it happen that the mother and daughter ended up *éloignées?* On the same back cover, we are told, *"Le nom de Lanvin baptise un bleu mythique et orne l'image devenue célebrissime: de la mère et l'enfant, image que les flacons précieux d'arpège multiplient à l'infini."* A new shade of blue, baptized, the image of the mother and the child, gilded, multiplied into infinity. The infinite multiplication of maternal love. Sold then, by the daughter, who will flee from her mother, returning only after her death to head the corporation, the House of Lanvin.

But even before the estrangement, the daughter rejected the name her mother gave her, changing herself from Marie-Blanche to Marguerite. Marguerite makes a glamorous marriage into a noble family: she becomes the Comtesse de Polignac. The count takes his place in the history of impoverished noblemen supported by their wives' money, earned through commerce. Only this time it is the wife's mother, rather than her father, whose business sense turned straw to gold.

Marguerite's husband was not the first Polignac to trade his title for money; his uncle married the unattractive American heiress Winnaretta Singer (sewing-machine heiress: the machine Madame Lanvin started her career with), who was one of the models for Proust's Madame Verdurin. Marguerite had a minor career as a singer of Baroque opera; she was involved in bringing back into vogue the works of Monteverdi. But, most important, she was a patron of the arts, a generous friend to artists. Most especially Poulenc. And she commissioned her other good friend Edouard Vuillard to paint both her portrait and her mother's.

I see Vuillard's name and get a shock as unsettling as the one I got when I discovered that the symbol of Arpège was a mother and a daughter. For many years, Vuillard has been my favorite painter, the one I think of as mine. I have written about him; I have made pilgrimages to see his work. I chose one of his paintings to serve as the jacket art for a novel, *Men and Angels*. My legacy to my children: a Vuillard pastel, an extravagant expenditure made before I even had children, an expenditure that some people I knew considered foolish. My Vuillard, whose blues and whites are the sign for me, the map for me, of everything I want to accomplish in my work, this painter who appears in Proust—Proust, whom I begin each day's work by reading—how can it be that he is connected to Arpège, therefore to the body of my mother?

The web of accident, the web of association, a web spanning years, class, circumstance. Is it a web or a stream? Or a path that I have discovered—or have I just invented it? If there is a stream, or a path, in what direction does it lead? I think it is a stream, taking up whatever falls into it, whatever borders it. A stream with leaves, weeds; Proust's water lilies that approach the shore, stretch out, retract, return again. What is the source of this stream? Does it begin with the body of my mother, perfumed, with the artifacts (handbag, handkerchief, saturated with the scent) my mother carried into the world as she entered it on my father's arm?

Yes, it begins there, but where is the next step? Because I know what the last step is. A desire to be reading, writing, looking at (but not living in) the world suggested by the smell. The world of Vuillard, of Proust, of Poulenc. A world not quite ready to give up the nineteenth century: the complications, the embellishments, the difficult, elaborate forms. A world not quite ready to take up the modern world, the one perfumed by Chanel, Madame Lanvin's rival and nemesis.

My aunt Lil wore Chanel No. 5 on the occasions when my mother was wearing Arpège. She had a slim, boyish body, a modern body, small-bosomed, long-legged; she wore trousers and shorts, garments my mother never wore, not once. Even the bottles of the fragrances are radically different from one another: instead of the turbaned, voluminously robed mother as a symbol, simply the words in a black official-looking type: "Chanel N° 5." Jeanne Lanvin's biographer insists that, whereas Chanel dressed women in her image, Lanvin made her clothes for her daughter. The desirable woman as mother. The desirable woman as mother rather than sexual partner. A smell of tenderness rather than of danger. A world still faithful to the magic of the mother whose greatest love is the child, whose greatest happiness is the child on her knees. The mother dressed for the world, so that the child, mouth agape, relinquishes her. To the larger world. The world of men. The desired, desirable mother.

The first step, the love of my mother's perfume; the last, the desire for the world it suggested. But what about the second step out of my mother's arms, the one that allowed me to imagine that I could approach the world of Proust and Vuillard as a fellow cre-ator? The world of not just the apprehension of art but the creation of it? Because I am not the subject of the portrait but its creator.

Vuillard and I are joined here, here in this writing that I make, because of a connection forged by something that he made: por-traits of both Jeanne Lanvin and her daughter. He paints Jeanne Lanvin at her desk: an elderly worker (she is sixty-six). Her ledgers, her pencil holder, are given the same loving attention as the fabric of her dress, the jewels around her neck, the bust on her desk, the dog at her feet. He says that in this painting he wanted to get *les vérités, les sévérités* of green and gray. Verities, severities. Is a kind of harshness the only way to a kind of truth? The working woman's styptic refusal of romance. If someone wanted to paint a portrait of my mother, he would have been wise to paint her at her desk. Where she was happiest. Where she was most at home.

The portrait of the Comtesse is much less satisfactory, and Vuillard was much less satisfied with it. Marguerite is sitting on her daybed, idle, pampered, a figure in a drawing-room comedy, her face unformed, so unlike the face of her mother—the face of a tragic Roman emperor.

Vuillard was working on the painting of the Comtesse de Polignac when he got the news that his mother was dying. He put down the brush that was creating on canvas, the face of the daughter (whose body is on the bottle my mother tipped to fragrance her body), and ran to the deathbed of his mother. He described it in his journal:

> Begin sitting construction bed figure, telephone calling me back home; leave immediately, anguish, delay, confusion find Mama in her armchair . . . Ever more painful moments, "it's too much, it hurts too much, it's in my back"; soaked under her towel, let me lose consciousness, moans; long wait while Marie fetches Pantopon; drowsiness at last calms her; sit beside her hold her hand under the sheet; squeeze it from time to time; feel the pulse beating, then lose it, same state remainder of the day; cold sweats, wipe her forehead; eau de cologne; handkerchief on her head; asks me to put some scent on my beard; my good little mother; says I'm not good I'm wicked; convulsion, responds less and less to kisses; afraid to move . . . she's very bad; she's going to die; her back turned; I see her glassy gaze fixed sightlessly on the ceiling, the mouth twisted to one side; hand clenched once more over her stomach; end I hold her head still, my fingers near her eyes which I gently close after Parvu has raised a lid. Acceptance.

Vuillard said that his mother was his muse. He painted her over and over. She was the mother who made the boiled beef that the exhausted artists came to at the end of a hungry day. When he took photographs, he left her in charge of his negatives; they would sit stewing in a soup bowl, and she, vigilant, would turn them (as she turned her marinating beef?) at the proper time.

Dying, she wants perfume. On her son's beard. The fragrant body: not the mother's but the son's. Many people believe that after she died he considered his life over.

In the last show of Vuillard that I saw, there was a collection of his photographs. Not photographs in the exalted, artistic sense, but snapshots, taken with a Brownie. In the catalogue of the exhibit (an exhibit I traveled to see, taking the earliest train leaving New York to Washington, then returning home exhausted, elated, on the last train out of Union Station), I read about Vuillard taking pictures of his family:

> When the number 12 appeared on the little red window of the camera, Vuillard took it to his usual supplier . . . to have it reloaded. The printing of the film was then entrusted to his mother. Sitting by the window overlooking the square, doing some embroidery, she watched the frame exposed to the light and when it was time she proceeded to the "fixing," in a soup plate.

In my family, my mother was the photographer. There are only a few pictures of me and her; many more of me with my father, my grandmother. I remember the little red dot at the back of the Brownie; the excitement, the anxiety—don't open the camera, the film might be exposed. Exposed. To light: therefore ruin. At the end of her life, Vuillard's mother's degeneration was exposed by her son. Disturbing images. In the last photographs, she is toothless, bald. She is washing her feet, paring her toenails. Did he have the right to photograph her like that? Vuillard and I, the exposing children, Noah's bad sons: saying that art is an excuse for exposure.

Was Vuillard enraged at his mother as I was enraged at mine? But for what? It would seem she never failed him. How I envy Vuillard saying "My mother is my muse." How I envy Vuillard the mother who was always cooking the boiled beef so that his house was the one friends wanted to come to. How I envy Vuillard a mother who kept an eye on his negatives, turned his negatives in a soup bowl.

But Madame Vuillard—did she have wit that crackled, sparkled like champagne?

No, she was always an old woman.

Could she have made anyone go weak in the knees?

Not as her son painted her: the only mother we know.

But there is another mother, another life, the life of the woman not a mother, a woman who had a life before she was a mother, a life lived apart from the artist child. We have no knowledge of that life. Because the mother is known only through the artist child. And he or she sees only what he or she wants to see, tells only what he or she wants to tell.

I spray the perfume on my wrist. I put my nose to it: by "it" I mean both the scent and my own skin. It is always a shameful thing to be doing, at best a foolish thing: smelling yourself. Usually, you are checking to see that you don't smell bad. It's nothing you ever want to be seen doing. Yet I want to be doing it all the time. Walking down the street, in order to smell the flesh of my wrist, I pretend I am looking at my watch. But I am looking for my mother. For my desired mother, my desirable mother (the one who made my father go weak in the knees?). I can be with her again: the one with the beautiful skin and hands and arms. The mother I never want to leave. The one I can't bear to be separated from for one second. The one I yearn for when I'm not with her, the one whose proximity I weep for: at school, at the houses of my relatives. My beguiling mother.

With a good smell: there is the desire never to stop, but never the conviction that smelling something good is enough to be doing with one's life, one's day. But why? We think that looking at a beautiful painting or landscape, listening to beautiful music, the sound of the wind or the waves, is a fine thing to be doing with our time. But smelling? No, it doesn't seem to be a good enough thing to be doing with time.

Is it because smelling is too animal?

The worst thing you can say to someone: You smell bad. You stink.

The animal in paradise. Peaceful. Among good smells.

Paradise is peace. Is safety.

But with the added ingredient: stimulation. But a stimulation that isn't frustrated. Not satiation: rather, a stimulation that never loses the edge of its desire, its desire for more, though there is no fear of disappointment.

With a good smell: no disappointment.

A good smell is paradise.

A bad one is Hades.

Paradise: the desired place. Never to leave.

Hades: the compulsion to escape.

Always present in paradise: the fear of leaving, of being forced to leave, banishment, the angel with the flaming sword?

And what is the way back into the garden? It is necessary to believe that the banishment is final, even if the banishment was self-imposed.

Must it be the way of language, or the flesh? Can't it be some way that is beyond time, beyond words? The way of the beautiful smell.

I can do it. Whenever I want, I can open the perfume, I can put it on my own body. I can be with her in the smell. But what is a smell? Rousseau says it is the sense of the imagination. My imagination turns a smell into a place, a place where I can be with her.

But how can it be a place? There is no place to put your foot. Nowhere to step, nothing to step down on, nowhere to sit or to lie down. Nothing to swim through. To fly through. It could almost be a place of flight, a place of falling. But flying to where? Falling from what? To what? To the past? From the present to a future paradise, dreamt but ungratified. A smell is of the body, but if it is paradise it must go beyond the body. But to where? When you are in the place that is the smell, you don't believe that you will ever be anywhere else. Because to be in a smell is to be in an eternal present. Like the mind of God. Eternal desire, eternal horror. In the presence of my mother, or my mothers—the beguiling one, the repulsive one—I believed, fully, that time held no sway. I would be, always, where I was. Trapped. Eternally. Or in paradise . . .

At the end of her life, my mother's scent was a combination of a powder—called Shower to Shower—and the urine that she tried to cover up with the powder she sprinkled between her legs. From the elegant handkerchiefs and purse to the stained drawers. This was the trajectory of my mother's life, if you trace the trajectory of scent. The trajectory that moves from beguilement to recoil, from desire to horror.

In one of the more scientific studies of fragrance that I pursue, I am told that in perfumes the top notes are floral but the middle notes "are made from resinous materials which have odours not unlike those of sex steroids, while the base notes are mammalian sex attractants with a distinctly urinous or fecal odour." So is it really the same thing, the smell of urine, the smell of perfume, only we, unlike animals, are overrefined, unable to trace the common source? When I try to type the word "urinous," the computer automatically changes it to "ruinous." It is true: when my mother's dominant scent was urinous, it was ruinous of my love for her.

I want to go back, beyond that. Through the sense of the imagination. To that old place. The garden.

The paradise of *with*. Of a yearning that is satisfied and yet never used up: there will always be more, more yearning, more scent, and you will never go hungry, or be disappointed, sent away empty. Never enough—how could there be enough of this happiness? This is the paradise of the good smell. But the words— "smell," "nose"—are comic. And the comic is the sign of falling short of the ideal. Paradise does not fall short. You fall into the good smell, you fall and fall, and the fall is wonderful, there is no end to it, you fall, but you are carried, together. When I was a child, there was no desire for me to be apart from my mother. In her last years, I could barely bring myself to be with her for half an hour a week. The smell in the nursing home—*urinous, ruinous*.

I put my nose to my wrist. Arpège. The music: the arpeggio. I can follow the scent, like music, beyond the body, beyond words. I don't need to be in the ruinous place. I can be in the paradise with the mother I desire.

Mother, I want to be in the place where I was with you and you smelled so beautifully of the large world, of glittering cities, of furs and laces, of drinks in sparkling glasses, of candlelight, mirrors where women with piled hair are reflected from the funnel-shaped darkness of formal rooms.
  Where are we, Mother?

I can ask that question, but of course I will hear only silence. My mother has no voice. No words. The words must be mine. I must do the talking. I must say where we are.

235

· · ·

We are in a room. We enter it, leaning on each other's arms.

My mother is not limping. Or her limping doesn't matter.

Is that applause? Are we greeted with applause by the people sitting at the glittering tables? Are they saying, *At last, you are with us, you have always been one of us, we have been waiting. You are the most glamorous, the most shimmering, the most radiant of us all?*

In our ears, at our throats, jewels sparkle. We are dressed for the ball.

Beautiful mother.
   Beautiful girl.
   Where are we, Mother?

Or is there no need to name?
   But why not name it? There is nothing to be afraid of here.
   Here where we are.
   Paradise.
   Europe.
   Paris.
   Home.
   Where we belong.

If I had been able to speak like this to my mother, words rooted in the body but beyond the degraded and degrading flesh, would it have changed anything? Prevented anything? Rage, humiliation, stupor, degradation, or despair? It doesn't matter; I was never able to speak to her like that. With that kind of love. As it was, the love I had for her, love mixed with hate, the words I could speak to her, words of love and hate, were attached to the body that degraded rather than evaporated, like the scent of her perfume. And so nothing was prevented by my love. My impure love. I couldn't prevent her fate, or ours, any more than I could have prevented the perfume from eating the varnish of her dresser. Something was eaten, eaten away. There was nothing I could do about it. My love prevented nothing. Not one thing.

But, if I speak of her, if I write about her, it is possible that I can prevent her disappearance. She will not evaporate, like a scent that is absorbed in air, into a nullity. My mother will not be nothing.

But, no, it isn't words that will perform the miracle I need. There are no words that I can use to call her.

I put my nose to my wrist. And she is risen from the dead. She is risen indeed.

Bonnard and My Mother's Death

The artist's eyes add human values to objects and reproduce them as seen through human eyes. Moreover this visual image is mobile. Moreover, this visual image is variable. I am standing in a corner of the room near a table bathed in sunlight. Distant masses look almost linear, without volume or depth. Close objects, however, rise up towards my eyes. The sides run straight. This vanishing is sometimes linear (in the distance) and sometimes curved (in the foreground). The distance looks flat. It is the foreground that gives us our concept of the world as seen through human eyes, of a world of undulations, or of convexities and concavities.

—PIERRE BONNARD

I. FOREGROUND: WRITING THE DEAD

I am writing about my mother, who is dead. She has been dead three years. I do not mourn her death; I mourn her life. Soon after she died, people said to me, "Oh, it will hit you, it will hit you, just wait." But it didn't. Her life at the end was wretched; her death was, to me, only a relief. What it was to her I cannot know.

I write about her because I am a writer and it's the only way that I can mourn her. Perhaps, for a writer, there is no such thing as simple mourning. What we have we use.

The task has exhausted me. It is time to end it now. I think that I must end where I began. And so I make a visit to the paintings of Bonnard, who, through an accident, and most improbably, I connect with my mother. Because the first great exhibit of Bonnard I saw was interrupted by my having to run in and out to make plans for my mother's ninetieth birthday. And the contrast between Bonnard's paintings and my mother's life created in me an urge to write. So that they are linked forever in my mind—my mother and Bonnard. The link is made by the stuff of my own mind, a filament spun of words, tough, tensile, connecting like and unlike.

I am in the Metropolitan Museum of Art. One of my places of refuge, of contemplation, a sacred space. I come here as my mother would have gone to a church. "Just making a visit," she'd say, crossing herself, putting on a hat, or a little circlet of lace called a "chapel veil," which she would have kept in her purse for the occasion, or, in an emergency, pinning a tissue to her head with a bobby pin. She would have been visiting what she would have called "the Blessed Sacrament." She would have come to pray. In the Catholic catechism of my childhood, the purposes of prayer were four: Adoration, Contrition, Thanksgiving, Supplication. We children were given an acronym to remember this: The purpose of prayer, we recited, is ACTS.

My mother would have called it sacrilegious: to say that to come to a museum is a kind of prayer. But I want to tell her: Do you see that what I am doing is a kind of prayer? Adoration, contrition, thanksgiving, supplication. I am writing about you to witness to the mystery of an impossible love. I am sorry for the exposure that this entails. I am full of gratitude for what you gave me. I am, as artists are, a suppliant—but to whom? Saying to someone, faceless, in the air: Help me set down what I see.

. . .

When I first wrote about my mother and Bonnard, I didn't know that he and I shared the fate of living beside the physically afflicted. I had assumed that his wife's illness was psychological. Only now I learned that she had a skin disease. She suffered from tubercular laryngitis. But because she was a hypochondriac, it is difficult to track her illness accurately; in any case, for many years she lived the life of an invalid. She became reclusive; she had a strange, harsh voice. She didn't want her husband seeing other people. Bonnard lied to get away from Marthe; he would say he was taking the dog for a walk and meet friends in a café. When I was a teenager, my mother disliked all my friends; I had to lie to go to parties and dances; I would say I was taking the dog for a walk and meet friends (boys) in a candy store.

A not unpleasant combination: the shock that I have not entirely invented a connection between Bonnard and me, followed by the relief (a slightly smug one) that what I had intuited has some basis in fact.

Neither Bonnard nor I was able to bring happiness to the afflicted ones we lived beside. Our turning them into art did nothing for them. Perhaps because neither of them was really interested in art: they were interested in us; what we did for a living was an accident. We might have done anything; we might have done many things that would have made them happier, prouder. In his case, he might have made more money; in mine, I might have brought my mother to live with my family, to die among her own.

In Bonnard's images of Marthe, her skin disease is not represented as disfiguring. The colors yellow, purple, mauve, which in the paintings make an envelope of delight, could have rendered her complexion in life grotesque. *"Il faut mentir,"* Bonnard said: but he was not lying. For a painter, the requirements of truth are internal; for a writer, if she is claiming to speak of someone who really lived, some kinds of beautification are in fact a lie. There are lies and lies. The painter's and the writer's lies are of a different order. "Exaggerate what is essential," van Gogh said. The other side of this: the essential cannot be left out. So, to be truthful, the writer places, replaces, illuminates some things, shadows others. But to present a ruined face as beautiful—this is not permitted. Unless, of course, the writer really believes it. I did not find my mother beautiful in her last years. I believe that she was wretched at the end. If Bonnard believed this about Marthe, he did not put it in his paintings.

To get to the Lehman Wing, where my favorite Bonnards are, I walk through the wing of medieval sculpture, which has about it the feeling of a cathedral. Of all the rooms in the museum, my mother would like this best. My tense is wrong: what I mean to say is that she *would have liked* it best. She would stop before the Sorrowful Mother, from fifteenth-century Spain; the fourteenth-century German polychrome Madonna with the Baby Jesus on her outthrust hip. For her, as for the cheerful young mothers, babies were a source of energy, delight. She would be particularly drawn to the silver Byzantine cross from the sixth century. She would be stopping, though, to pray, believing that what she saw was only the beginning of something, not in itself the important thing.

I know what would have pleased her, because, despite having next to no interest in the visual, she did pass on to me a taste for the severely formal. Despite herself, she had an aesthetic: she was proud of her taste in religious artifacts (she would have called them "religious articles"). She liked good lines, and a lack of ornamentation. These things were connected in her mind with the Irish as opposed to the Italian, the masculine as opposed to the feminine, the demanding as opposed to offers of easy comfort. She passed this on to me. Along with that, she gave me an appetite for the ideal. This is a rare legacy from mother to daughter. It more than makes up for the fact that she never once made me a birthday cake, that our abodes were domestic disasters, that I had to clean up after her for years. For neither of us was most importantly a domestic creature. We were women of the world. For both of us, a home was not something to be admired, but a place where people were fed and entertained. A place to read. She would never have said: a place where art is made. She did not believe in art. She had no idea that it was important. But she believed in the idea of perfection of the form. So, even though she had no real regard for what I am known for doing in the world, she gave me the idea that something like it, something she wouldn't have used the terms of faith for, was of the greatest, the highest possible importance.

The Lehman Collection is closed for repair, so the only Bonnards I can see are in the Lila Acheson Wallace Wing. To get there, I must walk through the eighteenth-century rooms, past lolling alabaster goddesses, lounging aristocratic nudes. My mother believed that the nude in art was only an excuse for pornographic display. When she walked into my graduate-school apartment, her first words, upon seeing a print of a Picasso girl bare-breasted among flowers, were: "Tits in my eye. I didn't drive six hours for tits in my eye."

If she would dislike the rococo maidens, she would be even less sympathetic to the African gallery, which I must also pass to get to the Bonnards. She would have been censorious of wooden sculptures of women whose breasts are inverted triangles. She once told me that an African missionary priest described his topless parishioners as "looking like they had quart beer bottles attached to their chests." She found this hilarious; it was the kind of thing that made me cover my ears and run out of the room.

So how can I be looking for her here, in the Lila Acheson Wallace Wing? I was the recipient of a Lila Acheson Wallace award, which allowed me to take a year off from teaching to write a book about my father. Lila Acheson Wallace's fortune was made by the *Reader's Digest*. My mother liked the *Reader's Digest*, particularly the humor feature "Life in These United States." My mother would be much more comfortable reading Lila Acheson Wallace's magazine than looking at her paintings.

Nevertheless, she is with me here. She is my mother, and she is dead. She is at my mercy.

II. BACKGROUND: THE NURSING HOME, THE PHILLIPS COLLECTION

Shortly before my mother dies, I travel to Washington, D.C., to see an exhibit of Bonnard's paintings at The Phillips Collection. The day before my trip to Washington, I make another kind of trip: across the boundaries of class and taste. I go into a store at Broadway and 96th Street that is about to go out of business. I am there to buy my mother clothes.

What prompted me to go there was the aide who cared for her telling me she needed new clothes. The aide laughed. "She's always messing her clothes. Top and bottom. Going in and going out. Like a baby." Her laugh scared me, shamed me. "She is always saying she is cold," the aide continued. "Winter, summer, doesn't matter. Always cold." When she said this, my mother had been in the nursing home for eleven years. She was ninety-four years old. For quite a while, I believed it was possible that she would never die.

For at least five years, her days were spent in a stupor. For at least five years, she no longer recognized me. Once, in a deluded, foolish, possibly self-destructive moment, I asked her if she knew my name. She looked at the label on the pink lemonade I'd brought her and said, "Snapple." At first, I laughed. "That's right, Mom," I said, "but you can call me Snap for short." For a while, I couldn't stop laughing. I lay down on her bed—she was beside the bed in her wheelchair—and laughed. Then I began weeping. I could not stop weeping. She stared at the label on the pink lemonade. "Snapple," she said. Over and over again. "Snapple, Snapple."

When I touched her on the shoulder or the forehead, she often didn't respond. Sometimes she said, "Why are you doing that?" When I asked her to look at me, she would say, "What have I done wrong?" When I told her I loved her, she was silent.

"She needs new clothes," the aide said. "She needs them soon, soon." This is a command, and I cannot ignore it. Food, clothing, shelter. The nursing home provides the first and third. The second is up to me. The aide was right to press me; she had told me before that my mother needed new clothes. Why did I leave it so long, till there is nearly a crisis? Because I do not want to do it, one more thing, one more unpleasurable thing: buying ugly clothes for my mother, who needs many clothes because she is a soiler. I am happy to buy her flowers and cake: she will respond to them; they will give her a second of pleasure. But she doesn't care what she wears, and I don't either. And I have no choice but to buy her ugly clothes. The important thing about the clothes my mother wears is that they be tough, easily washable, able to survive in the punishing machines of the nursing-home laundry. Artificial fibers only.

There is no sense in spending much money. I know exactly where I'll go. I'll do it quickly, this shopping expedition. I allocate only a certain amount of time, the time I allocate each week, an hour, to see my mother, and this shopping expedition will put a strain on the rest of my day.

The store's name is Fowad. It is at 96th Street and Broadway, a stop on the IRT, express and local, the 1, the 9, the 2, the 3 all stop at 96th, and so it is a place where the gentry of West End Avenue and the poor of Amsterdam Avenue must meet. But Fowad is a store of the poor. On the sidewalk, clothing racks proclaim their bargains: in summer, sundresses; in winter, sweaters.

Fowad is closing; what was once greatly reduced in price is now almost incredibly reduced. It is raining lightly, a gray November rain that makes the air taste of metal. The clothes for sale by Fowad are no longer hung on racks; they are piled, shoved, into cardboard boxes covered with heavy sheets of plastic because of the rain. I lift the plastic on the box marked "Sweaters: $5.99." From the pile I select three: they must be cardigans, my mother doesn't like things being put over her head. I choose one rose-colored, a charcoal gray, one brown and white with a print of horses, because she did like horses, once.

I walk into the store looking for polyester shirts—lightweight, so they can go under her sweaters, and buttoning down the front.

There is very little room to walk between the racks of clothes, the tables of clothes, all marked down. "Drastically, Drastically" the sign says twice. There *is* something drastic about this place: the dead air, the false fabrics, the unloving treatment of the unlovely clothes. The gray carpet is ripped; the holes are covered over with the yellow tape that the police use to indicate the scene of a crime. Four large fire extinguishers are bolted to columns. From other columns, other objects hang: money belts in camouflage patterns, bow ties with a sign above them saying "Bow ties, 10 cents." Dusty fedoras and a sign above them: "Hats 50 cents." Shirts on racks saying "Shirts 99 cents."

I buy my mother four striped shirts. Seven items in all, including the three sweaters. I walk up to the cashier. The woman in front of me has put her gloves on the counter; the salesman, who is Arab, picks up her gloves and says, "Ninety-nine cents." "Those are *my* gloves," the woman says, outraged. What is the source of her outrage? That she would be charged for something she already owns? That he would think she would own something that this store would sell? That it would be worth only ninety-nine cents?

I go back to the nursing home with my trove of clothes. I give them to the aide. She takes the clothes out of the bag, carries them to the place where they will be marked with my mother's name. She comes back with one of the sweaters. She holds it up. The back of it is completely missing. It is not a hole, just a deliberately missing part. I cannot understand this. "They took you good," she laughs. "I'm not going anywhere near that store. Rip-off. No way." She points to my mother's laundry basket. "But it's good you got her more clothes." She holds up a light-blue sweater deeply stained with something brown. "You see what I mean? You see what I am telling you, why she needs so many clothes? She is always dirtying."

This was the business of my mother's life. Eating and dirtying. Sleeping—perhaps she was happy in her dreams. I couldn't know what was in her dreams, because she had lost not only language but range of expression. She neither smiled nor wept. She sat with her head in her hands. All day. Sometimes, there were bruises on her face. I thought, once, that she had fallen or been abused. I called in a friend of mine, a doctor, to examine her. She had not fallen; she had not been abused. The pressure of her hands on her face—she refused to sit in any other way—had made deep-purple patches on her face, below her eyes.

When I asked her if she was sad, she said no. When I asked her if she was happy, she said no. After a while, I no longer knew what to ask her.

The trip to Washington to see the Bonnards is a way of giving myself a holiday after a difficult autumn. Among the things I most need a holiday or a relief from is visiting my mother.

As I grow older, I crave more and more quiet. The train is not quiet. The train, which used to be a haven, a place I could read and write, has been taken over by cell phones. People making deals, people talking nonsense. Can't they be quiet? After an hour and a half, all the way to Philadelphia, I discover that there is on this train something called a "quiet car." I ask the conductor if I can move. She says I can if there is room. There is room. I move into the quiet car. It is a blessing, an oasis. A place I need because, before I look at the paintings of Bonnard, I must try to understand how once again to speak of my mother in the same voice I use to speak of a great painter, whose vision is above, beyond, decay, who loved many women, who was praised, honored, who believed in light.

The first painting in the exhibit that I focus on is called *The Red Checkered Tablecloth or the Dog's Lunch*. The dog is an intense apostrophe of darkness against the white wall, against the red-and-white checked tablecloth, the white coffeepot and cream pitcher and napkins. There is a ragged ellipse of white between the dog and his mistress, her blouse as blond as her blond coiffure, the red checks on the tablecloth matching the delicious ruby of her pouty lips. And I think of how much my mother enjoyed her coffee— because she did have her pleasures, my mother, and she treasured them. When I was small, she made her coffee in a drip pot, glass; then in a percolator on the stove; then an electric coffeepot. And then she reduced herself to instant: Taster's Choice, with Coffee-mate instead of milk.

And I think of how much she enjoyed her dogs. The ill-behaved one, named Jersey, I found for her when I went away to graduate school. Jersey, unkempt and cantankerous, would bite her when she combed him—then she would hit him, and he would bite her, and she would hit him again. But he slept in her bed, and when I slept in the room above her I could hear her talking to him in the middle of the night. When he died, I got a retired guide dog for her, and he cared for her like a husband. She respected his masculinity, his strength, his reserve, although she was not as good to him as his goodness warranted. One morning, she complained of not having slept well. "I had to hold his paw all night. He was scratching and scratching. I couldn't let him get away with it. I didn't get a wink of sleep." She never spoke of him when she had to leave him to go into the nursing home. As she did everything else, she gave him up.

When I look at a painting called *The Sewing Lesson*, I think of my mother and her mother, a master seamstress. In this painting there are two figures. The sewer, the teacher, eyes down, head down: we do not see her eyes. She is absorbed in her work. She does not look at the little girl, who is perpendicular to her, looking at nothing. Not, certainly, at what is being held or sewn. They stand or sit—in any case, they are separated by a pattern of great hopeful color: yellow and purple flowers and green stripes.

Postures of refusal, postures of absorption. And in the background, in the curtains, blue, pink, yellow, and on the floor, the yellow, red, and purple rug: the possibility of joy. My mother did not sew, nor did any of her sisters. The explanation for this was that their mother sewed too well.

My grandmother: monumental, resolutely against charm. Revered. The force that left her children, all of them, with the quick rage of starvelings, though they would never have admitted it. Not one of the nine of them would have admitted they were starved.

My implacable grandmother. Her starved children. My mother, starving, insisting to her death she was well fed.

There is a wall devoted to the posters that Bonnard designed for money. I think of my mother when I look at the one for *France—Champagne*. A giggly, seductive-looking girl with a cleavage made of two lines that come together like a child's drawing of a bird is up to her breasts in bubbles. In her right hand she holds a closed fan.

My mother was a drunk. An alcoholic. All the dark things I have to say about her, except for the ones about her being a cripple, are about her being a drunk. Cripple. Drunk. Cruel words. Now we are not supposed to say them. Alcoholic. Disabled. Differently abled.

When my mother was drunk, she referred to herself as a gimp. I hated that.

What was she after, in her drunkenness, what was she after that I can understand? I think that it was exaltation and oblivion.

Bonnard's Champagne Girl is giggly; tiddly, but she is in no danger. A good-time girl. Is she paid for it, for giggling, for giving men a good time? What kind of good time? The kind of good time men have when they are drinking champagne with a pretty girl? Or the kind of good time that makes good on the hint of the bird-wing cleavage: that begins with showing lovely breasts? Champagne, the drink of happiness, not the drink of drunks—or only upper-class ones.

My mother was not a happy drunk, and her being drunk was particularly dangerous to her because of the danger of her falling. If she fell, she would not be able to get herself up. For a long time, I believed this meant that I could never leave her.

Fear of falling. Fear of my mother's falling. They have marked my life. How to convey the fear of what would follow if my mother fell? What was I afraid of? That she would never, ever get up again: that she would fall and then die. Be dead. Or that she would smash like a china doll—that, as with Humpty Dumpty, all the king's horses and all the king's men would not be able to put my mother together again. And I was not a king; I was a child. I had no horses and no men.

I try to understand how my mother became what she became. The laughing girl, who made people happy, now sitting with her head in her hands, turning her face a blotched purple because she will not change her posture. How did she become the woman who, when I ask her if she is happy, says, "I don't know"?

And I don't know what happened to the laughing girl in Bonnard's poster.

What happens to laughter?

Where does happiness go?

I walk down a staircase—plain, unlike the formal great staircase with its prosperous mahogany banister, its marble steps—to a room devoted to Bonnard's pictures of his wife, Marthe. I think of the things I know about Marthe. Not one of them is happy.

Very little is known about Maria Boursin, who renamed herself Marthe Bonnard. Bonnard saw her first when she was getting off a streetcar; he picked her up. She changed her name. She concealed her background. She cut herself off from her family. Bonnard was a member of the middle class, the son of a civil servant, but she was not a member of the middle class; she was a working girl. Her job was sewing pearls onto funeral wreaths. Was there really enough of that work to make up a full job? Did she do other things to earn money? She was not respectable; she lived with Bonnard for years without marriage.

Upstairs, walking among the paintings, writing in a notebook things that I plan later to shape into something, I am in control. But when I look at the photographs of Marthe, I feel control slipping away.

I see my mother's face in her face. I know that this is crazy, and it frightens me, so I walk away from the photographs. But then I walk back, look again, walk away, and look back, and I know that I am not wrong. There is a formal similarity between my mother's face and Marthe's: the high cheekbones; the light, wide-apart, almost staring eyes. There is a photograph of Marthe standing with Bonnard, a photograph taken in the twenties. She is wearing a cloche hat, a close-fitting coat. I have a picture of my mother wearing the same kind of hat, the same kind of coat. The same hat, the same coat, the same cheekbones, the same wide-apart, large eyes. They were alive at the same time. I have not entirely invented the connection. They were together, at one time, in the world.

I move to the nude photographs of Marthe; her face is only partially visible, sometimes in shadow. I replace the featureless shadowed face of Marthe with the face, beloved and familiar, of my mother. My young mother. Charming. Happy. Full of life.

In the photographs, Marthe becomes my mother. At last, I have accomplished what I have always wanted: I have given my mother a beautiful body. And I have taken Marthe out of the shadows to which Bonnard so often relegated her. I have given Marthe my mother's face.

Her husband immortalized her, turned her affliction to riotous color: for as long as people look at his paintings, she is remembered as a beautiful woman. But he was unable to provide her with stories. I am telling stories about my mother; I am trying to remember her happiness, her charm: I am trying to tell, in order to get past the eclipse of her affliction, some stories that have in them something of lightness. Light and color: what Bonnard used to make of his unhappy wife a work of art.

Is there a place where Marthe and my mother speak? Where they are saying to each other, "We were not like that. We were not like that at all"?

I make myself walk upstairs, away from the photographs and their shadows, and the impulses that the shadows allow. Back to the color, the sanity of the paintings.

I arrive at the Bathers, Bonnard's most celebrated women. Their bathrooms are places not only of hygiene but of pleasure: a pleasure my mother was denied. The yellow, fuchsia, violet, aqua tiles, mirrored in the floor tiles, are a blooming knot of color. Everything blooms except the bather, who is faceless, like the dead.

In *Nude in Bathtub* (1941–46), the bather's neck is bent at an angle so that it looks uncomfortable—broken, even—the head propped awkwardly against the rim of what looks as much like a coffin as a tub. On the other hand, the dog, lying on the pink bath mat, an island of peace among the crazed diamonds of the linoleum, seems perfectly comfortable, alert, far more alive than his mistress, who could be, rather than a bather, a corpse.

I don't linger in front of this picture, because the bather reminds me that my mother will soon be in a coffin, will be faceless forever, unable to see the knot of color that is the world. I pass by because I don't like who I am when I think of it, because when I think of it I always hope that it will happen soon.

III. LAST LIGHT

While I was writing about my mother and Bonnard, my mother died. This makes it sound as if she died when I was writing; in fact, when she died I was asleep.

When the nursing home called to say that my mother had died, I screamed. I screamed and screamed and I heard myself screaming as if I were hearing someone else. I had no words. My daughter picked up the phone. She said, "Thank you, we'll be right there."

My husband and my children went to the nursing home with me to see my mother, dead. Her eyes were opened. Her mouth was opened. Because most of her teeth were nearly gone and those left of them were black stumps, she looked as if she had been dead a long time. I closed her eyes with my thumbs. They stayed closed for a while, then slowly they slid open, like a shade with a non-working cord. I thought of putting pennies on her eyes to weigh down the lids, but I couldn't. It seemed to be turning her into a thing; it seemed to suggest that she had become an object more like pennies than like flesh. Like me.

It was obvious that those eyes were seeing nothing. But what was their last sight?

I wasn't with my mother when she died, because I didn't live with her. I didn't live with her because I could not. Because she was, to me, unbearable.

My mother died alone.

I don't know what her last moments were. Her last thoughts. Her last words. Her last vision of the world.

Bonnard made a lithograph called *Last Light*. Strange, to use the form of a lithograph to express ideas of light. Light without color. Light as shadow.

It is a landscape: clouds, mountains, and pines.

What was my mother's last light?

Was it also drained of color?

I don't want it to have been drained of color. I don't want it to have been the work of shadows.

What light is she in now? What light will be her last?

My mother died with only a vexed and garbled connection to words.

Was she able to say, "This is my last light"?

Did she mean that, when it was over, she knew there would be no more?

No more. Does that mean that after the end of light there is darkness? But what if there is no end of light? What if she is still in the light that came to her last? By "last," meaning: there is none to follow it. But because none follows it, it does not mean that it will end.

Last light.

Everlasting light.

The two need not be contradictions.

What color was her last light? What color do I want it to be? Silvery, golden, the blue-gray of twilight, the rose pink of dawn, the hot yellow of high noon, the red-purple of sunset, the black of storms, the stippled dark of starlight? I want her to have, to have had, to be having all these lights at once. I want her not to have to choose. I want for her that abundance. This is possible because, wherever she is, she is outside time.

It was not possible, this abundant simultaneity, for Bonnard when he was painting. He could only paint in time. He could freeze only one moment at a time. He was the body's painter, not the mind's, therefore subject to time. Yet his picture called *Last Light,* without color, is therefore without specificity. It could be many things. But not all. For my mother now, all things are possible. Except one. To be alive.

For the artist, there is always the choice that will exclude others.

For the dead, no exclusions are necessary. Or perhaps it is better to say there is nothing that they need exclude, having been irrevocably excluded.

My mother has been excluded.

I will include her now.

I will include my mother.

She is among the dead. She is closer to Bonnard and Marthe than she is to me.

She has become my words.

Or dust.

Both.

How is it possible to comprehend this?

My mother has become incomprehensible.

I can no longer recognize her.

I want to recognize my mother. Re-cognize. To know again.

When Bonnard spoke about the artist's granting human value to objects, he spoke of distance; he spoke of vanishing.

I will try to keep my mother from vanishing. I will try to understand distance, but to understand that I will also have to understand closeness. I must enter a world of undulations. A world where everything is moving, nothing is forever still.

My mother is dead. Movement was difficult for her; now she has no need of movement.

But my idea of her cannot be still. My love.

I am trying to speak of my love for my mother. Of her charm.

Bonnard said: "Speaking when you have something to say is like looking. But who looks? It is because people have no idea how to look that they hardly ever understand."

I am trying to see my mother. I must begin now to learn how to look.

At the end of his life, Bonnard said, "I am only now beginning to understand. I should start all over."

A NOTE ABOUT THE AUTHOR

Mary Gordon is the author of the novels *Spending*, *The Company of Women*, *The Rest of Life*, *Final Payments*, *The Other Side*, and *Pearl*; the short-story collections *Temporary Shelter* and *The Stories of Mary Gordon*; and the memoir *The Shadow Man*. She has received a Lila Wallace–Reader's Digest Award, a Guggenheim Fellowship, and the 1997 O. Henry Award for best story. She teaches at Barnard College and lives in New York City.

A NOTE ON THE TYPE

This book was set in Scala, a typeface designed by the Dutch designer Martin Majoor (b. 1960) in 1988 and released by the FontFont foundry in 1990. While designed as a fully modern family of fonts containing both a serif and a sans serif alphabet, Scala retains many refinements normally associated with traditional fonts.

Composed by Stratford Publishing Services, Brattleboro, Vermont
Printed and bound by R. R. Donnelley, Harrisonburg, Virginia
Designed by Soonyoung Kwon